The Augustinian Imperative

MODERNITY AND POLITICAL THOUGHT

Series Editor: Morton Schoolman
State University of New York at Albany

This unique collection of original studies of the great figures in the history of political and social thought critically examines their contributions to our understanding of modernity, its constitution, and the promise and problems latent within it. These works are written by some of the finest theorists of our time for scholars and students of the social sciences and humanities.

The following titles are available as New Editions from Rowman & Littlefield Publishers, Inc.

The Augustinian Imperative

A Reflection on the Politics of Morality

New Edition

WILLIAM E. CONNOLLY

Modernity and Political Thought Series

ROWMAN & LITTLEFIELD PUBLISHERS, INC.
Lanham • Boulder • New York • Oxford

ROWMAN & LITTLEFIELD PUBLISHERS, INC.

Published in the United States of America
by Rowman & Littlefield Publishers, Inc.
A Member of the Rowman & Littlefield Publishing Group
4720 Boston Way, Lanham, Maryland 20706
www.rowmanlittlefield.com

12 Hid's Copse Road
Cumnor Hill, Oxford OX2 9JJ, England

Originally published in 1993 by Sage Publications, Inc.
Reprinted in 2000 by AltaMira Press
New Preface and Introduction Copyright © 2002 by
Rowman & Littlefield Publishers, Inc.

British Library Cataloguing in Publication Information Available

The Library of Congress has cataloged the previous edition as follows:

Connolly, William E.
 The Augustinian imperative : A reflection on the politics of morality / William E. Connolly.
  p. cm.—(Modernity and political thought : vol. 1)
 Includes index.
 1. Augustine, Saint, Bishop of Hippo—Ethics. 2. Augustine, Saint, Bishop of Hippo—Political and social views. 3. Ethics. 4. Political Science— Philosophy. 5. Nietzsche, Friedrich Wilhelm, 1844–1900—Political and social views. I. Title. II. Series.
BR1720.A9C65   1993
171—dc20   92-43392

ISBN 0-7425-2146-X (cloth : alk. paper)
ISBN 0-7425-2147-8 (paper : alk. paper)

Printed in the United States of America

♾™ The paper used in this publication meets the minimum requirements of American National Standard for Information Sciences—Permanence of Paper for Printed Library Materials, ANSI/NISO Z39.48-1992.

Contents

Series Editor's Introduction

Theodore W. Adorno has argued that whenever intellectual formulations are confined to the past, as though their teachings can be related to no other time but their own, the development of contemporary thought is thwarted. Adorno's concern animates this series. An assumption informing **Modernity and Political Thought** is that thinking flourishes when ideas are free to enter into confrontation and contestation with one another regardless of their time or place of origin. Contention encourages new perspectives on, and thus creates the possibility for changes in, established understandings, values, beliefs, and practices. By seeing things differently we may do things differently, want to do things differently, or perhaps at least learn that things could be other than they are.

What the authors of studies in this series seek to see differently is our own time, the time of modernity, a time that may be, as it has been referred to by some, late modernity, a period perhaps passing away, in transition to another era still difficult to define. To this end they have cultivated a variety of approaches governed by a common interest. The task is to inquire into the thought of figures in the history of political philosophy in light of their possible contributions to our understanding of modernity, the way in which it is constituted, the problems and promises that remain latent within it. Whereas, traditionally, work in the history of political thought has often adopted the view that a great work or thinker can be understood best in relation to the historical context in which the work appeared, strict adherence to such a perspective would limit modernity to a self-evaluation with only its own norms as the standards it brings to bear. It would be to view modernity from its mirror image. Our approach has little in common with that genre. To the contrary, although we also seek to reconcile the demands of interpretation with historical fidelity, the point here is to illuminate the contemporary significance of the history of political thought. And to examine past thinking as though it were present is to interrogate thinkers with respect to how their thought, too, is *implicated* formatively in what we have become.

Contributors to this series are cognizant, of course, that their examinations of figures in the history of political thought are shaped by our object of inquiry—modernity. After all, modernity is the ground upon which we stand. It is our interpretive standpoint. We can hope to disclose the extent to which our thought is shaped by modernity; we cannot hope to escape its authority, at least not entirely. Yet, by struggling reflexively with this issue of whether past perspectives provide us with the distance to view modernity from the "outside," we may already glimpse one of modernity's cardinal features—its tendency to universality, that there appear to be no thresholds beyond which modernity cannot pass. As the attempt is made to draw figures from the past into dialogue with modernity, we will still hear our own voices speaking. But perhaps we will hear them more clearly and respond to them more reflexively.

This approach to the history of political thought coheres closely with the way that political theory is taught at nearly every college and university in North America and Europe. To improve their understanding of the modern world, of its problems and prospects for change and development, college teachers invariably turn to the history of political thought, and for good reason. The authoritative list of books that comprise the canon of political theory, from Plato's *Republic* to the writings of contemporaries such as Hannah Arendt, is commonly believed to contain the richest tradition of political insight possessed by the Western world. Year after year the works of Plato, Aristotle, Thomas Aquinas, St. Augustine, Niccolo Machiavelli, Thomas Hobbes, John Locke, Jean-Jacques Rousseau, Edmund Burke, Adam Smith, G. W. F. Hegel, Karl Marx, Ralph Waldo Emerson, Walt Whitman, Henry David Thoreau, Alexis De Tocqueville, John Stuart Mill, Friedrich Nietzsche, John Dewey, Hannah Arendt, John Rawls, Juergen Habermas, and Michel Foucault, among many others, are assigned in the hope that they will enable students to think deeply and critically about a range of questions pressing upon them daily: What is the nature of justice and the common good? What are the best forms of government? Do democratic institutions possess the capacity to promote justice? Can democracy be sustained in capitalist and socialist regimes? Will citizenship flourish in modern democratic societies? Can the modern state retain legitimacy and the allegiance of its citizenry? What is the nature and role of "the political" today? Given the increasingly complex ways in which power is insinuated into our everyday lives, does it make any sense today to continue to use the language of liberalism—the language of rights, sovereignty, autonomy, citizenship, and self-realization? In the wake of the (reputed) "death of God" and the transcendental foundation this god once provided for a society's principles, must political leaders tell lies to their publics to ensure that they remain orderly?

Each study in **Modernity and Political Thought** explores such questions through an examination of the writings of a major figure in the history of theory. Authors of series volumes were asked to write on a figure whose ideas have entered into their own thinking, perhaps over the span of their intellectual lives, in order to assist them in reasoning through the theoretical problems about which they write. The figures of choice are those intellectual benefactors to whom contributors are often indebted for insight or against whom they struggle in developing their own thoughts. Each is a contributor's "familiar," the ever-present company who instructs, inspires, and advises when our thinking falters; who criticizes, provokes, and generally irritates when our ideas come to rest settled among carefully though prematurely arranged arguments; or who may finally emerge as the hidden architect of all we find fascinating and threatening. Each figure chosen, perhaps because of the intimacy and agonistic stress of their intellectual relationship, is not one about whom the contributor would necessarily be inclined to write. Consequently, each of the texts in the series has been conceived and written especially for it.

The mission of the series is to pursue a twofold analysis of figures in the history of political thought—to explore the questions we believe to be crucial to our understanding of modernity, and to articulate a more coherent picture of the meaning of modernity through the assembly of interpretive studies of thinkers as diverse as those we have selected. Among the questions to be examined by the contributions to **Modernity and Political Thought,** the relationship of liberalism to modernity is a recurring theme. This is no less true in those studies where it is approached indirectly—such as *The Augustinian Imperative: A Reflection on the Politics of Morality*—as in those where it provides an explicit focus. The versatility of the series can be illustrated by briefly considering a few of the dimensions of this relationship and, afterward, the manner in which William Connolly penetrates its inner recesses.

During the past two decades the debate about the nature, development, meaning, and fate of modernity has been joined by all disciplines, philosophical views, and ideological and political persuasions. The complexities of this debate are fascinating, but equally so is the simpler fact that the entry into the fray of so many positions forbids its definitive resolution. It may be that the concept of modernity has created a forum for a discursive struggle that makes possible an agonistic self-understanding. Modernity may be an interminable drama, through which we are constrained to learn about ourselves by recurrently risking the loss of what we believe is stable, fixed, certain, and true.

To infer that modernity is the agent and not simply the object of controversy is to suggest that posing questions about it is made possible by the spirit of modernity itself. It is not that modernity is controversial because it is the age in which we live. Rather, modernity may be uniquely and essentially self-referential. To raise the question, "What is modernity?" is, at the same time, to provide part of the answer. Modernity may *be the* standpoint that problematizes its own identity. Its nature may be to turn back on itself. If so, the essence of modernity is its reflexivity. If modernity is the historical form that calls itself into question, then no answer to the question "What is modernity?" can be asserted without a *doubt.* Where reflection is the aim of questioning, certainty silences questioning and betrays the very nature of modernity.

Thus, although there are myriad ways in which modernity is and is not like any other time, its singular feature appears to be its relationship to truth. No longer can religious, cosmological, or metaphysical systems unproblematically ground a concept of truth. Modernity is the age in which particular truths are reflexively examined, ruthlessly criticized, and often discarded. And in which, as a result, a society of critics develops an ever more tentative relation to the possibility of making truth claims at all.

Yet, despite the punishment it suffers the pursuit of truth never resigns. Does its perseverance call into question the view that modernity is intrinsically reflexive? Perhaps the resilience of the pursuit of truth along with the equally resilient attacks on truth force us to consider whether a metadrama is being played out behind the melodramas of the primacy of epistemology and its endless critiques. Not the problematic nature of the concept of truth, but that throughout its trials and tribulations the unavoidability of the pursuit of truth is forever sustained alongside its impossibility. Accordingly, there can be no thought that modernity's character is expressed in the determination to bring to final resolution the question of whether or not there are truths, and thus truth. Such a determination is only modernity's "good faith" disguise. The paradox of modernity may be that truth is affirmed in order to invite its denial and is denied in order to propel its affirmation. Such a paradox may express the essentially reflexive nature of modernity.

This paradox of modernity is expressed in social relations and is instantiated by social relations. Socially, the paradox is articulated as the production of new forms of life—new understandings, concepts, beliefs, and attitudes, and their embodiment in practices and institutions, cultures, subcultures, and lifestyles. This production unfolds, at least partially, through critique. Critique begins with attacks on particular "truths," particular forms of life, and the individual and collective identities they define, and graduates to the critique of truth as such and the hegemonic assertion of a particular culture. No matter how powerful, though, critique does not end with the abolition of truth. Rather, the concept of truth evolves one more of its endlessly protean forms.

In democratic societies, the paradox of modernity and its social expressions are underwritten by a logic propelled by liberalism. Liberalism protects both the pursuit of truth and its critique. It declares some truths to be self-evident, though it tolerates truths that are incommensurable and even incompatible with its fundamental faith in truth. Liberalism nurtures the belief in truth and in the possibility and necessity of its transcendental grounding, while it also relativizes truth and thereby problematizes its own epistemological foundations.

But liberalism rarely, if ever, carries its "spirit of critique" to the heart of truth itself—to the identities that truth and its vicissitudes engender. In this respect liberalism impedes its finest tendencies. For at this late stage of modernity, not simply this or that identity but identity as such has become vulnerable to the suspicion that its boundaries are arbitrary and accidental. To the minds of liberalism's unforgiving neoconservative culture critics, in fact, in the proliferation of new and the revision of established identities liberal societies have borne rotten fruit and have proven liberal rationalism to be guilty of relativism and nihilism. In their estimation, the failure of established identities to withstand the challenges to their hegemony has "stretched the truth" to its breaking point. For, according to the neoconservative critics, liberalism lacks the spine (which they usually locate in the state) to suppress perverse doctrines and deviant cultural formations that breed rapidly and effortlessly in the soil of liberal neutrality. Certainly, if one were to judge by these critics, liberalism has performed admirably as the benefactor of a multiplicity of cultural formations that neither coheres with nor constitutes moral sovereignty. But in their nearsighted preoccupation with the rationality of liberalism's championing of new forms of life, liberalism and its critics are both blind to what William E. Connolly, in *Identity Difference: Democratic Negotiations of Political Paradox* (1991), refers to as the "ugly moments" in the political dynamic of constituting identity and in the demands for the affirmation of its truth.[1]

What is this political dynamic and its ugliness? Identity acquires definition only when it is distinguished from that which differs from it. Identity, to *be,* thus requires difference, even though this "difference" constitutes a threat to its self-assurance. To attain security and self-certainty, an identity must convert difference into otherness. To fix the truth of identity securely, a range of differences is finally conceived as *intrinsically* evil, abnormal, irrational, mad, sick, primitive, monstrous, dangerous, anarchical, inferior, ugly . . . qualities to be embodied by those targeted to represent otherness by the carriers of an identity. This dogmatism of identity works most effectively when its carriers forget the role that self-protection and self-aggrandizement have played in their very constitution of the other. The ugliness is the violence—and the covering up and concealment of the violence—

inherent in the cultural and social histories that allow individual and collective identities to speak in the first person-singular or plural. And in their mutual concern that identity be grounded on truth, both liberalism and its critics obscure, and by so doing contribute to, the violence societies inflict on themselves.

Among other concerns, *Identity Difference* shows how liberalism forgets the role politics plays in the very construction of identity and its conversion of difference into otherness. Connolly pinpoints how liberalism unconsciously devalues the differences created by the identities it nurtures, and how liberal individualism and liberal individuality obscure the politics of identity and difference and deflate efforts to infuse these relations with the spirit of "agonistic respect." A politics of agonistic respect appears when contending identities mutually sacrifice their demands for self-certainty, exercising forbearance on their ambiguous relations of interdependence and strife. Only such a politics of "critical pluralism," as Connolly calls it in this study, can avert the conversion of difference into otherness and the naturalization and normalization of fixed identities that this conversion helps to effect. Politics now becomes the vehicle through which we locate threats to diversity and difference in the state, civil society, and in the interior of the individual. A politics of critical pluralism becomes the medium through which we come to terms with the contingency of our own identities and the violences to others we produce by the effort to conceal this contingency. This is a politics through which difference can begin to flourish, or at least not be converted into otherness and victimized. Through such politics, liberalism would be reconstituted, drawing inspiration from an unlikely combination of liberal skepticism, Nietzschean agonisms, and Foucauldian care.

Why does it seem so difficult for liberalism to make this decisive move, especially when it is inspired, in part, by a spirit of critique that brings it within range of such a political ethic? Although not explicitly concerned with liberalism, *The Augustinian Imperative* casts light on this problematic as it challenges the ideal of "intrinsic moral order" still implicit in some versions of liberalism.

The Augustinian Imperative is an archeological investigation into the intellectual foundation of liberal societies. Connolly excavates and deciphers a complex of discourses that, because of the extent to which they have become insinuated into linguistic practices, possess inertia, not simply toward the determination, but toward the overdetermination of our identities. Augustinian in theory and practice, these discourses contribute to the formation of identity, to the sort of powers by which it is formed and the sort of power it becomes.

If we were to place *The Augustinian Imperative* side by side with *Identity Difference,* we would learn this: The Augustinian Imperative is a moral infrastructure exercising hegemony over our words and thoughts and deeds. It is the structure that pulls identity toward its self-validation and dogmatization. It is the particular structure that constitutes order as intrinsic and identity as integral to the true order of things. The Augustinian Imperative is the holy father of moral order. And this imperative that there be an "intrinsic moral order" is lodged in the subterranean levels of liberalism.

In its theoretical insights and rhetorical power, *The Augustinian Imperative* compares with Michel Foucault's *Discipline and Punish* and his earlier *Madness and Civilization,* although in its genealogical stance Connolly's study has more in common with the later text.[2] As does Foucault with madness and punishment, Connolly locates the points in Augustine's work where knowledge and power intersect, where they are imposed on the body to constitute an authoritative identity and moral order taken to be intrinsic. Through his examination of Augustine's discourses—on god's will and human will, faith, mystery, divination, confession, condemnation, conversion, healing, self-discipline, heresy—the moral imperative, the tactics for its definition, the cultural forms the imperative assumes and the mechanisms of its cultural reproduction, and the extent to which it can order and organize our lives unfold before us as a densely textured universe of concepts, arguments, and proofs. A densely textured universe of words, within which each of us becomes entangled because, as Connolly puts it, "the Augustinian Imperative assumes a larger variety of forms in modern doctrines that relax the demand for eternal life but relocate the spirit of eternity in the cultural identities they endorse and the conceptions of intrinsic moral order they represent."

So compelling is Connolly's image of the imperative that we come to recognize where Augustine's framework has impressed itself on our own cultural practices, where it is at work in contemporary philosophical and theoretical positions. Along the way we recognize, too, that Connolly himself is implicated in the confessional complex and moral imperative he exposes, perhaps all the more as he contests, combats, and attempts to lighten its influence, to extricate his own thinking from its identitarian web. That Connolly cannot escape being drawn into the Augustinian maelstrom offers ironic support for his thesis. It also illustrates the departure he represents in contemporary studies of Augustine. Whereas Charles Taylor, for example, argues in his *Sources of the Self: The Making of the Modern Identity,* that Augustine's design is to move our attention away from the sensible to the insensible order, Connolly reveals how focusing our attention on the insensible is instrumental to riveting our attention on the order of the sensible world.[3] If Connolly's expose of Augustine's hidden agenda spells its failure, then the paradox is that Augustine succeeds even where he fails.

*   *   *

William Connolly's *The Augustinian Imperative: A Reflection on the Politics of Morality,* is the first volume in the Rowman & Littlefield series **Modernity and Political Thought** to enter into a second edition, which includes a new preface by the author. Each of the remaining nine original volumes belonging to **Modernity and Political Thought,** studies of Thomas Hobbes, by Richard Flathman, G. W. F. Hegel, by Fred Dallmayr, Adam Smith, by Michael Shapiro, Edmund Burke, by Stephen White, Jean-Jacques Rousseau, by Tracy Strong, Henry David Thoreau, by Jane Bennett, Ralph Waldo Emerson, by George Kateb, Michel Foucault, by Thomas Dumm, and Hannah Arendt, by Seyla Benhabib, also are scheduled to appear in second editions during the fall of 2001.[4] In addition, new works for **Modernity and Political Thought** are underway and will focus on such diverse thinkers as Plato, Aristotle, Thomas Aquinas, Thomas More, Niccolo Machiavelli, John Locke, Karl Marx, Friedrich Nietzsche, and John Stuart Mill, as well as a selection of contemporary political thinkers. As those who are familiar with the previous works of series authors will expect, taken together their studies adopt a variety of approaches and pose importantly different questions. As contributors to **Modernity and Political Thought,** however, their efforts also are commonly devoted to effecting critical examinations of major political theorists who have shaped our understanding of modernity—its constitution, problems, promises, and dangers that are latent within it.

I am especially grateful to Steven Wrinn of Rowman & Littlefield for shepherding **Modernity and Political Thought** through the transitional stages to our new publisher and home, and for his thoughtfulness and professionalism that make it possible for editor and authors alike to produce their best work. Each of the authors of series volumes will earn rewards and punishments commensurate with his or her contribution, but as the hidden architects of the series each must also share credit with me for launching **Modernity and Political Thought.**

—Morton Schoolman
State University of New York at Albany

Notes

1. William E. Connolly, *Identity Difference: Democratic Negotiations of Political Paradox* (Ithaca, NY: Cornell University Press, 1991). My discussion of Connolly's book focuses on arguments in its third ("Liberalism and Difference") and sixth ("Democracy and Distance") chapters.
2. See Michel Foucault, *Madness and Civilization* (New York: Random House, 1965) and *Discipline and Punish* (New York: Vintage, 1979).
3. Charles Taylor, *Sources of the Self: The Making of the Modern Identity* (Cambridge, MA: Harvard University Press, 1989), 127–142.
4. **Modernity and Political Thought** was first published by Sage Publications, Newbury Park, California. Volume 1, William E. Connolly, *The Augustinian Imperative: A Reflection on the Politics of Morality* (1993); Volume 2, Richard E. Flathman, *Thomas Hobbes: Skepticism, Individuality, and Chastened Politics* (1993); Volume 3, Fred Dallmayr, *G.W.F. Hegel: Modernity and Politics* (1993); Volume 4, Michael Shapiro, *Reading "Adam Smith": The Politics of Desire* (1993); Volume 5, Stephen K. White, *Edmund Burke: Modernity, Politics, and Aesthetics* (1994); Volume 6, Tracy Strong, *Jean-Jacques Rousseau: The Politics of the Ordinary* (1994); Volume 7, Jane Bennett, *Thoreau's Nature: Ethics, Politics, and the Wild* (1994); Volume 8, George Kateb, *Emerson and Self-Reliance* (1994); Volume 9, Thomas Dumm, *Michel Foucault and the Politics of Freedom* (1996); Volume 10, Seyla Benhabib, *Hannah Arendt's Reluctant Modernism* (1996).

Preface to the New Edition

THE PLURALIZATION OF RELIGIOSITY

T hinking is most stimulated, perhaps, when you explore a deep, morally intense thinker who disrupts your most basic convictions. The convictions so challenged have typically been entrenched through a series of interchanges with parents, relatives, neighbors, churches, and schools as you passed through the tender years. Augustine was reared by a devout Christian mother and a tempestuous father who was "Pagan." Both influences, or so I argue in this book, leave traces on his thinking. These influences, in turn, were honed and refined through a series of engagements with Epicureanism, Stoicism, Plotinianism, Manicheanism and Paul. Augustine discovered relatively early in life that he had become a question to himself.

In a predominantly Christian society, such as the one most readers of this book inhabit, critical self-reflection often gets off the ground when you engage seriously a non-Christian philosopher. Not Augustine, Aquinas, Rousseau, Kant, Hegel, or Tocqueville, though each is full of surprises. But a thinker who challenges something in Christianity all the way down, such as the very idea of the will or the connection between morality and the idea of an intrinsic moral order. In my case the process worked a little differently. Raised by activist, working-class parents who had broken with Protestantism and Catholicism respectively in their teens, I absorbed Christianity indirectly and, for the most part, casually. I did not read Augustine, for instance, until the age of forty-five. By that time I had engaged nontheistic and polytheistic thinkers such as Sophocles, Epicurus, Nietzsche, Russell, Freud, and Foucault. Each affected something in my thinking. So my late engagement with Augustine proved to be highly stimulating. He became both adversary and stimulus. What moved me was not so much the specific conclusions Augustine reached—I found myself contesting many of these. But two other qualities. First, the abundant evidence of existential struggle in reaching these conclusions, and better, his absorption of struggle into the practice of faith; second, the ways in which such struggles still infuse the culture of predominantly Christian regimes. It soon became clear to me how Western secularism is as indebted to Augustine in some ways as it is at odds with him in others. And how the contest between these two modern options goes on within us as well as between us. To probe critically the actualities and possibilities of contemporary life is to come to terms with two forms of indebtedness to Augustine, that is, of indebtedness in its assenting and agonistic forms.

What are the Augustinian themes addressed in this book? Perhaps most basic is his praise of a God who is Author of the world and Source of an intrinsic moral order to which we can become attuned. Augustine pours impressive energy and creativity into this effort. It is complicated by the awareness on the part of this brilliant North African thinker of how the Manichean and Epicurean traditions must be surmounted if the goal is to be achieved. The Manichean tradition calls into question the idea of a coherent moral order; Epicureanism challenges the necessity of placing a moral God at the authoritative base of ethical life.

I respect the majesty of Augustine's enterprise while dissenting from it. It does inspire morality in many; and it presses others to practice a modicum of self-restraint in this life out of fear of punishment in the next. But it is also stalked by a temptation that is difficult to shake: the temptation to translate a series of alternative faiths that deviate from the intrinsic order you confess into instances of blasphemy, heresy, evil, infidelism, or nihilism. I call this the Augustinian Temptation. This demoralization of others is not only a response to threats they pose to your livelihood, your life, your freedom, or the honor *you* bestow upon your God. Those are dangers the faith of others can present to you. It is often enough manifested as the imperious desire to inhabit a world in which everyone confesses your faith. That is the danger your faith poses to others. One objective of this study is to plumb the existential sources of the demand for an intrinsic moral order; another is to reduce the intensity of universalizing that demand by showing how the ethical life can be sustained without it. The Augustinian Temptation is most likely to be curtailed in a world where multiple ethical sources achieve a modicum of public legitimacy in and across regimes. The idea is to work through Augustine to discern the sources of such a demand and the places it surfaces in his day and ours. Doing so to support a vision of deep pluralism that coincides neatly with neither theological universalism nor secular models of private diversity and public deliberation. For neither secularism nor theological universalism suffices today.[1]

I embrace nontheistic gratitude for the abundance of being as my highest existential faith. I do not think this faith can be proven, though impressive arguments can be given on its behalf. It is a profoundly contestable faith, as are those it contends with and against. The trust of those who embrace it is that we can draw upon it to build a measure of forbearance and presumptive generosity into our desires, interests, hopes, anxieties and negotiating stances. Given the contingencies of experience, however, such a faith is very unlikely to provide ethical sustenance for everyone. It is appropriate as a candidate to those a) who find that a personal God is not a live option for them; b) who nonetheless feel surges of religiosity from time to time; and c) who find the thin, intellectualist conceptions of public life advanced by secularists to be insufficient to both the density of culture and the inspirational element in ethics. While the first condition breaks with Augustine, the last two slide closer to him than, say, to the spirit of Bertrand Russell or John Rawls. Hence my relation of debt and affinity to Augustine. But the difference is critical too. For to embrace publicly a nontheistic source of ethical inspiration without claiming universality for it is to support pluralization of the legitimate range of ethical sources within public life. The idea is to attend to the indispensability of inspirational sources to ethical life while dramatizing the comparative contestability of every particular candidate. Such an approach does not seek to eliminate Augustinianism. That would contradict a public ethos of deep pluralism. Nor does it seek to shuffle theistic and nontheistic faiths into the private realm to allow secular reason to occupy the place vacated by Christianity. In my judgment, and in Augustine's too, no practice of public reason is sufficient to political life. Rather, during a time when distance is compressed by the acceleration of speed in many zones of life, the way to move is toward a generous ethos of engagement between a plurality of faiths in private and public life.

Such an agenda informs my readings of Augustine on monsters, confession, memory, conversion, paganism, heresy, gentle rule, the divided will, grace, *Genesis*, mystery, heaven and hell. As I engage him on these issues I often encounter a debt or an affinity, even as I criticize this or that theme. The debts are the most gratifying. For example, I profit from Augustine's reading of memory, even while modifying one of its dimensions; I learn from him how important the practice of confession can be to cultivation of an ethical sensibility while dissenting from the authoritative cast he gives to the Pauline confessional; I join him in valorizing the experience of mystery against the overweening pretensions of rationalism while resisting his insertion of an incomprehensible, authoritative God at precisely those junctures where mystery emerges; and I appreciate how his authoritative reading of *Genesis* brings out the critical role of myth in cultural life, even while revising his version of the story.

Several times in this preface and the study I speak of rendering more "contestable" parts of a faith or doctrine heretofore treated as authoritative or obligatory. Several objections have been brought against cultivating appreciation of the contestability of the faith you honor most. It might clarify what I mean by considering some. The first objection goes like this: "You can't treat everything as contestable because the attempt to do so would subtract from life the preconditions of thinking, judging and debating as such. So the idea is incoherent." Wittgenstein is often wheeled out to support such an objection, drawing upon his sensitivity to the role an implicit background of prior judgments plays in setting the context for reflection into a belief, judgment, or doubt. Heidegger, Nietzsche, and Augustine could also be adduced in support of this thesis. Nor do I deny it. Rather, I insist upon a version of it in *The Terms of Political Discourse*, a book I wrote under the influence of Wittgenstein.[2] In this book, for instance, I speak of how

Myth is to theory/philosophy as faith is to argument.
Every philosophical argument resides within a nest of cultural understandings not themselves up for consideration in that analysis . . . Those who give

primacy to arguments are the least likely to ponder the cultural unconscious that drives their thinking . . . A philosophical culture, for example, governed by the theme of the sufficiency of reason, could never establish the truth of this thesis by the only means it accepts for doing so.[3]

To work through such statements is to see that it is indeed impossible to make everything contestable at any time. It is also to see that some things are so pivotal to your thinking that they could not be put up for critical reflection now, even if you tried hard to do so. Even more, the dicey character of the relation between thinking and the un-thought-like materials it absorbs and translates into thinking may mean that there is always a floating substratum *of* thinking that resists translation without remainder *into* thinking.

What, then, does it mean to affirm the comparative contestability of the fundaments you honor most? It means, first, that you strive to come to terms, by comparison to other faiths and theories with which you have come into contact, with those junctures in your thinking that fade off into indefiniteness or uncertainty, the very junctures that might be subjected to different interpretations by others. The last sentence in the above paragraph, for instance, represents such a projection on my part. It moves closer to Epicurus than to Augustine. For Augustine confesses a God at precisely the points where the insufficiency of thinking to itself arises, while Epicurus projects an "insensible" level of being that enables and affects thinking without itself taking the form of thought. It means, second, that when you encounter things in another faith at odds with specific elements you confess, you acknowledge the active possibility that the difference may be unresolvable by reference to an incorrigible set of arguments, or even to an experience potentially available to all. Just as the experience of grace is not equally available to everyone according to the Augustinian faith, some dimensions of experience of the world are inflected differently by people in different settings according to mine. It means, third, that you fold modesty and hesitancy into arguments you make on behalf of your faith, even as you affirm it robustly as your faith. For it is not a necessary affront to its vibrancy to acknowledge how alien it might well feel to others. And it means, fourth, *that you come to terms with how the activity of respectful contestation extends beyond intellectual argument even while including it.* Here Augustine, Nietzsche, and William James provide more help than some contemporary philosophers. For the former understand that contestation between faiths invokes a mixture of words, gestures, and signs that might touch, move, jolt, or inspire you in surprising ways. To contest is to move and be moved below the level of explicit belief as well as in the medium of belief. To contest respectfully is to set limits to the methods you use. To affirm the comparative contestability of your faith is to keep a window ajar to the possibility of conversion to something new. When you recall how conversion to this or that faith occurred at an earlier point in your life you become aware that something akin to it might possibly happen again. Augustine's movement through Epicureanism, Platonism, Manicheanism and Paulinism involved a mix of argument and conversion each time. Who knows what he would do today in confronting, say, Buddha, Kierkegaard or Nietzsche.

To affirm the legitimate contestability of your existential faith in the eyes and hearts of others is not to pretend that everything could be put up for grabs at one time, nor to dishonor your faith, nor to act as if everything in it is now on the same level of availability for interrogation, nor to assert that argument is necessarily sufficient to faith, nor to pretend that life is rich (or even possible) in the absence of existential faith, nor even to insist that you must fold self-doubt into the faith you now embrace. Many may seek to do the latter; they seek to become more of a question to themselves. That, to me, is admirable but never entirely successful. And it is not necessary to the vision of pluralism I endorse. To acknowledge the comparative contestability of your faith is to see that others, with different experiences infused and burned into them, are apt to find elements in it difficult or impossible to embrace. To *affirm* this condition as a persistent condition of existence is to respond to it without deep resentment. It is to fold a modicum of modesty into the sensibility that informs your faith, even when it faces overt contestation from others. One admirable ideal, to move close to Augustine's words, is to become a question to oneself to a greater degree than heretofore. Perhaps most of us feel tremors of dissent in the faiths to which we give ourselves. But to affirm the contestability of the faith you honor, it suffices to remain receptive to the probability that elements in it will and must seem perplexing, strange, and unassimilable to others who have experienced life somewhat differently from you and your kind.

The value of keeping a window ajar for respectful contestation is that, when generalized, it creates the possibility for negotiation of a generous ethos of engagement between interdependent constituencies who honor different moral sources. For the most basic problem of ethics does not arise when people share the same moral God, transcendental arguments, or contracted procedures, while differing in the willingness to live up to them. That is one problem, of course; it emerges as the problem of weakness of will in Augustine and Kant. But the most fundamental problem arises in those recurrent situations where interdependent constituencies honor different moral sources and are unlikely to be moved by argument or inspiration to embrace the same source. When that is the case the attempt to solve the riddle of public morality by consolidating one theological or secular source becomes a recipe for gridlock, cultural war, authoritarianism, or civil war. A better approach is, first, to cultivate those elements in your faith that allow it to forge relations of presumptive generosity with others and, second, to come to terms affirmatively with how human it is for others to contest specific dimensions that feel like the bedrock to you. The difference between this vision and secular liberalism is that the latter calls upon you to leave your fundamental religious/existential faith in the private realm and then to confess faith in the sufficiency of reason, procedure, or deliberation in the public realm. In the alternative vision of pluralism you bring relevant chunks of your faith into the public realm—as we all do inevitably anyway—while carefully cultivating comparative modesty about it.

Given such a perspective, one dimension of Augustine's thought should have received more attention in this study: his idea of love or *caritas*. It may be that Augustinian *caritas* is both tied to a specific dogma of grace and not entirely exhausted by the terms of that faith. There may be a promising tension between the Augustinian affirmation of love and the doctrine through which it is adumbrated. Such a tension can surface at surprising moments. In the sixteenth century, for instance, when a priest from Spain, Bartoleme de las Casas, encountered a new world unexpectedly populated by "Pagans," after much struggle and reflection he finally invoked Christian love to challenge the ethical pertinence of the Augustinian quest for conversion he had brought with them to the new world.[4] Or, in the early twentieth century, when Hannah Arendt mined Augustinian love to rethink the question of ethics.[5] Or in the middle of that century when Paul Ricoeur made a painful reassessment of the relation between Augustinian Christianity and the tragic Greek tradition, proposing significant modifications in the former.[6] Or at the end of the twentieth century when Charles Taylor called for modifications in Catholic Christianity to come to terms with a pluralization of religious experience that continues apace.[7]

   William James, writing in the 1920s in the United States, is another generous thinker who draws something from Augustinian love while nudging the doctrine that housed it. James, a psychologist by trade who suffered through a long bout of melancholy, eventually found himself probing positive possibilities in mystical experience. He embraced mystical experience while loosening the authority any particular creed could legitimately exercise over that experience. That is, he sought to allow such experiences to be interpreted within a plurality of creeds and doctrines. He thereby activated the imagination of a culture in which existential pluralism runs deeper and ranges wider than heretofore. James strives to convert his readers—many of whom had already undergone at least one conversion experience as secularized Jews, born-again Christians, or born-again atheists—to three themes, each subject to uncertain qualification by the others. The words and the numbers are his:

> (1) Mystical states, when well developed, usually are, and have the right to be, absolutely authoritative over the individuals to whom they come.
> (2) No authority emanates from them which should make it a duty for those who stand outside of them to accept their revelations uncritically.
> (3) They break down the authority of the non-mystical or rationalistic consciousness, based upon the understanding and the senses alone. They show it to be only one kind of consciousness. They open out the possibility of other orders of truth, in which, so far as anything in us vitally responds to them, we may freely continue to have faith.[8]

   It would be easy to deconstruct these injunctions. The first, for instance, contains a qualifier, "usually," that could undercut the robust pluralism it suggests if pursued far; and yet if that qualifier were dropped obvious and immediate counter-instances could be brought against the formula. (Indeed, some scholars build their careers around enunciating such counterexamples.) The phrase "absolutely authoritative" also ignores multiple side-perceptions within the self that might eventually lead one to contest the authority invested in that experience, as well as third person studies that show how the experience can sometimes be induced artificially. There is also a tendency in James to separate the feelings he delineates too sharply from the specific interpretations through which they acquire shape as experiences. That tendency, however, can be corrected by reflecting upon the paradoxical character of such states: the sources from which the experiences emanate subsist below the threshold of pure representation; and yet they cannot be consolidated as experiences until invested with interpretation. Such experiences are paradoxical in ways that Augustine, a master of paradox, would appreciate.

With these adjustments I receive James's three maxims less as a fixed formula and more as an invitation to cultivate a specific *sensibility* within individuals and a generous *ethos* of engagement in public life, a sensibility in which the presumption in favor of deep pluralism becomes embodied in the subliminal field of most participants and a general ethos of appreciation for doctrinal pluralism in public life. James, on this reading, embraces Augustinian love while contesting the insistence of doctrinal universality within which Augustine locates it. He thereby underlines the relevance of Augustine to today and the persistence of the issues he addresses.

Notes

1. The case against the sufficiency of secularism and in favor of a generous public "ethos of engagement" between diverse constituencies is made in *Why I Am Not a Secularist* (Minneapolis: University of Minnesota Press, 1999).

2. See *The Terms of Political Discourse*, third edition (Princeton: Princeton University Press, 1983).

3. Ibid., 93–94.

4. I explore Las Casas in chapter 2 of *Identity Difference* (Ithaca: Cornell University Press, 1991).

5. Hannah Arendt, *Love and Saint Augustine*, eds. Joanna Vecchiarelli Scott and Judith Chelius Stark (Chicago: University of Chicago Press, 1997).

6. Paul Ricoeur, *The Symbolism of Evil*, trans. Emerson Buchanan (Boston: Beacon Press, 1969).

7. Charles Taylor, *A Catholic Modernity?* ed. James L. Heft (New York: Oxford University Press, 1999).

8. James, *The Varieties of Religious Experience* (New York: William Morrow and Co., 1902), 422–23. For a very thoughtful engagement between Catholic faith and Jamesian religiosity see Gerald Bruns, "Loose Talk about Religion from William James," in his *Tragic Thoughts at the End of Philosophy* (Evanston: Northwestern University Press, 1999).

Preface

This book is not about Augustine, the young student of pagan rhetoric, the youthful Manichean, the initially reluctant priest, the Bishop of Hippo, and the master philosopher of a Christianity in transit from minority sect to cultural hegemony in Europe.[1] It, rather, examines the Augustinian Imperative, the insistence that there is an intrinsic moral order susceptible to authoritative representation. This imperative, in turn, is linked to an obligatory pursuit: the quest to move closer to one's truest self by exploring its inner geography. Although neither the imperative nor the pursuit is susceptible to full realization, each provides an indispensable complement to the other in the Augustinian world.

Augustine is neither the first nor last bearer of the Augustinian Imperative. But his exemplary constitution of it is still imprinted on the culture of the West, particularly, perhaps, on the political culture of contemporary America. It is not merely that Augustine helps to shape and generalize this imperative in his time. An analysis of Augustinian texts uncovers tactics by which this creative innovator installed these themes in the heart and the larger culture during a time when the appropriate strategies of inculcation remained uncertain and when the moral authority of Augustinianism was actively resisted by groups of Christians and non-Christians. By attending to Augustinian tactics of moralization during a key moment in the consolidation of Christianity, we might become more alert to their less dramatic and more pervasive counterparts in contemporary culture. We might defamiliarize sensibilities installed within and around us by becoming more familiar with Augustinian practices of moralization of the self and demoralization of the other. We might also become more appreciative of the role tactics play in the consolidation of any ethic, including the ones you and I endorse. We might, thereby, place ourselves in a position to become more ethical with respect to the tactics of morality.

I approach Augustinian texts, then, not as an Augustinian, nor as one who reduces a text to its specific historical context, nor as one who reduces it to a pile of arguments available for critical examination. I approach Augustine from a critical distance, from a (post-) Nietzschean perspective that seeks to reassess and modify effects of the Augustinian legacy on the present. I do not write extensively or directly about the present in this book, however; I have done that elsewhere. Rather, here I examine Augustinian practices to sharpen recognition of corollary tactics installed in moralities of the present.

I seek to disturb Augustinianism from an ethical perspective that is both indebted to it and at odds with it. The opposition will perhaps be more obvious to some than the debt. Some committed to the Augustinian Imperative in one of its contemporary variations may even identify amorality, relativism, nihilism, anarchism, or irrationalism in this study. But these very responses, on my reading, re-enact Augustinian tactics of identity consolidation: they constitute their own moral identity through de-moralization of the other. To create distance between my reading and this litany of responses, I sketch a series of (post-) Nietzschean rejoinders and alternatives to Augustinian perspectives. I challenge two interdependent models of morality—morality as obedience to transcendental command, and morality as attunement to an intrinsic design of things—by enunciating an alternative ethico-political spirituality.

I suggest, without arguing this point in detail here, that contemporary orientations grounding morality on a categorical imperative or a veil of ignorance or the counterfactual presupposition of a rational consensus or a fictive contract or a utilitarian economy, are more deeply invested in one or both of these Augustinian models of morality than their proponents typically acknowledge. In this domain, it is not simply what you confess about the grounding and shape of the morality you endorse, but the tactics you apply in fending off disturbances of the moral economy in which you participate. Similarly, it is less pertinent what your official line on, say, individualism, community, pluralism, or tolerance is, and more pertinent whether and how you engage sedimented strategies of discipline and moralization (almost) always already installed in the present.[2]

Chapter 1 exemplifies how the Augustinian Imperative precedes and succeeds Augustine. It does so not by examining philosophical texts written before and after the high point of Augustinianism. It proceeds, rather, through a reflection on two exemplary stories, one composed several centuries before the high point of Augustinian Christianity, the other several centuries after. This chapter is indebted to both Augustine and Nietzsche. For both thinkers understand how the stories that circulate through a culture—even more, the myths that set unconscious models for rumor, gossip, humor, and legal decisions as well as newscasts, novels, and talk shows—present the unconscious of that culture in a condensed and concentrated form. Augustine rewrites the myth of Genesis because he understands its shape to be crucial to the moral culture it re-presents. And Nietzsche writes counter-myths to such stories as Genesis and Oedipus because he too comprehends how such abbreviations expose a cultural subtext upon which philosophical argument and moral judgment rest. My comparison of *Job* and *Herculine Barbin* in Chapter 1, then, follows the lead of these two mentors. The presentation shows how the Augustinian Imperative precedes and succeeds Augustine, while mining themes within each story capable of disturbing its moral self-confidence.

Chapter 2 examines the Augustinian confessional as a set of tactics through which a general morality becomes defined and imprinted. While exploring the voice of Augustine's deceased mother, Monica, speaking through his *Confessions*, it asks whether Augustine confesses to a moral god or constitutes his moral divinity through the potent strategy of confession.

Chapter 3 analyzes a series of Augustinian Epistles, official letters written by the Bishop of Hippo to diverse people standing in a variety of relations to his authority and faith. This chapter explores the institutionalization of confessional practice, asking what effects the obligation to confess exerts on the politics of good and evil, identity and difference, true faith and heretical deviation.

Chapter 4 returns to the domain of myth. Augustine's exemplary reading of Genesis is examined, this time by placing it alongside a series of readings that contest it in various ways. If core myths help both to consolidate the cultural unconscious and to hold it up as a mirror into which we observe ourselves, the biblical story of Genesis, a story of the very first "founding," may remain the most important story to read, reread, and work on in the West. Augustine certainly thought so.

Chapter 5 draws together critical strands in previous chapters, exploring how a moral temper of the Augustinian type tends either to suppress the experience of the uncanny or to invest it in a transcendental source that tightens the screws of moral order. This chapter is crucial to those that precede it. For some neo-Augustinians surely will say: "Augustine is more open, pluralistic, tolerant, secular, etc. than you credit him." There is a real issue in need of debate lodged in this reply: "Do the differences in our readings flow more from disputes over what the texts really say or from the application of contending standards to the same texts?" It is those most closely bound to the Augustinian legacy of a single god (or one of its numerous modern surrogates) who are most likely to presume a single, authoritative standard of judgment from which to assess every text. They thus quietly resolve, under the guise of "correct reading"—the conservative's version of "political correctness"—the central objects of dispute. This last chapter, then, delineates more actively the critical terms of comparison through which my reading of Augustine proceeds, rendering it more possible to determine the degree to which disagreements in Augustine interpretation reflect different levels of understanding of the texts or contending presumptions, ideals, and standards of interpretation brought to them.

The theme of the last chapter is roughly this: A perspective most effectively contests the Augustinian Imperative if it combines genealogical critiques of smooth moral economies with active cultivation of an alternative ethico-political sensibility. Both dimensions are crucial—the first applies tactics of the self to the other and the self, the second tactics of the self to the self and the other. The bearers of such an ethical sensibility do not forget limits or detach themselves from ethical constraints. Those who have been touched by Nietzschean themes of a "spiritualization of enmity" or "passing by" or "the pathos of distance" or the new nobility as "many nobilities" can testify to this readily enough. Rather, such a sensibility contests violent modes of aggressive conventionality that reassure themselves in what they are through transcendentalization of themselves and demonization of the other. The idea here is not to elaborate an alternative moral *theory*, but to cultivate a modified *sensibility* entering into the actions, judgments, and interpretations advanced. It is, similarly, not to evacuate the confessional tactics of moralization introduced by Augustine, but to replace them with corollary tactics of ethical cultivation thematized explicitly as tactics of the self applied to the self and the culture applied to the culture.

This last chapter draws on Nietzsche and Michel Foucault for sustenance, not trying to duplicate either but to draw elements from each appropriate to a critical ethical sensibility in the late modern time. I use Nietzsche to fill out Foucault and Foucault to fill out Nietzsche until I arrive at a perspective I endorse. This chapter also draws certain strands from Augustine's model of moral awakening. For the confession, as he practices and commends it, is above all a set of speech acts through which one's sensibility is elevated.

The perspective I endorse, then, subverts Augustinianism and neo-Augustinianisms, but it also remains close to Augustine in certain ways. Its peculiar debt to Augustine is most abundantly expressed through its appreciation of Nietzsche. Whereas Augustine draws attention to the moral significance of memory, forgetting, sensuality, mystery, paradox, the uncanny, reverence, and awakening, Nietzsche redefines and relocates these same modalities. By comparison to, say, the dead leaves of utilitarianism, proceduralism, or contractualism, Augustine and Nietzsche share a lot. At those points where they converge before sliding off in divergent directions, they mark oversights and superficialities in doctrines that pretend to dispense with these dimensions of ethical life.

The highest objective here is not to replace one scheme of universalization with another, but to place a contending perspective more actively on the field of contemporary debate. If your idealism celebrates "many gods," "agonistic respect," and "critical pluralism," it is not simply unsatisfying to liquidate adversaries through conversion or conquest. It is better that they remain alive and vibrant, becoming perhaps less hell-bent on universalization of the agendas through which they congratulate themselves and more willing to enter into selective alliances with you for particular purposes.

Perhaps another word should be said about the way these chapters are organized. A chapter is presented as if it might exhaust the topic under scrutiny. But then the issue just dispensed re-emerges a chapter or so later, where additional dimensions are explored in a different context. These chapters are folded into each other, then, rather than each succeeding one layered on top of those that precede it. Such an approach is necessary because the density of these issues does not admit of a single, sufficient presentation. Confession and the will, just to take two examples, always return to haunt you in this culture, *whatever* stance you take on them. Augustine surely found this to be true with respect to the will; it was at once a linchpin of his philosophy and one of its most problematical components. He never put it to rest while trying to consolidate it. Nor do I while trying to problematize it. Similarly, a writer who criticizes effects of the confessional mode cannot do so without reservation. For critical writing participates in the confessional mode it resists. So, the interfolding of these chapters textualizes the perspective they represent.

This project might have been organized differently. As these comments may indicate, my agenda could be pursued by treating Augustine as the key inspiration and Nietzsche as the principal adversary. One could stir Augustinian presentations of sensuality, the divided will, confession, mystery, memory, paradox, and awakening until sublime sparks and flashes in these coals glow more brightly. One might even suggest that were Augustine to re-appear in this time, he would stir them differently himself. Similarly, one could challenge Nietzsche at those points where the writer's delight in rhetorical cruelty exceeds the *Nietzschean* Imperative to be hard on existential resentment wherever it spawns its deniable violences.

It is easy to discern, at a formal level, how such a reversal between Augustine and Nietzsche might proceed. But I have not proceeded that way, partly because the dominant current of interpretive "charity" in this culture still flows strongly in the other direction, partly because I continue to pull up short before Augustinian presentations of divine omnipotence, moral hierarchy, obligatory confession, heresies, paganism, women, nature, and salvation, and partly because we live during a time when authoritarian elements in the Augustinian Imperative have acquired new energy. I commend such an approach to others, though.[3]

* * *

Chapter 1 appears in Jane Bennett and William Chaloupka, eds., *In the Nature of Things: Language, Politics and the Environment* (Minneapolis: University of Minnesota Press, 1993). A couple of sections from Chapter 5, in revised form, appear in *Political Theory* (May, 1993) as "Beyond Good and Evil: The Ethical Sensibility of Michel Foucault." I am grateful to each publisher for permission to print these materials here.

I would like to express my gratitude to Judith Butler, David Campbell, Bill Chaloupka, Rom Coles, Bill Corlett, Ben Corson, James Der Derian, Michael Dillon, Kathy Ferguson, Patrick Lee, Barbara Herrnstein Smith, Kirstie McClure, and Michael Shapiro for comments on earlier drafts of selected chapters. David Dexter and Astrid Virding served as very capable editors of this manuscript at Sage, and I appreciate the contribution they have made to the final result. My appreciation, too, to graduate students in two seminars at Johns Hopkins, one "Augustine and Nietzsche" in 1991 and the other "Modes of Interpretation" in 1992. These seminar discussions have had significant effects on the themes in this essay.

Special thanks are due to Tom Dumm, Dick Flathman, Bonnie Honig and Mort Schoolman, for reading several of these chapters and discussing the issues involved extensively with me. My greatest debt, though, is to Janet Bennet, who found it quite impossible to avoid my pleas to read and reread early drafts. Those who know Jane's work will recognize its imprint at several points in this study.

Notes

1. To consider the life of Augustine in relation to the development of his doctrine, one could do no better than consult Peter Brown, *Augustine of Hippo* (New York: Random House, 1988).
2. I have considered Hobbes, Rousseau, and Hegel from this perspective in *Political Theory and Modernity* (New York: Basil Blackwell, 1988) and Charles Taylor, John

Rawls, and Jean Paul Sartre in *Identity\Difference: Democratic Negotiations of Political Paradox* (Ithaca, NY: Cornell University Press, 1991). Bonnie Honig, in *Political Theory and Political Displacements* (Ithaca, NY: Cornell University, 1993), treats Kant, Sandel, and Rawls as "virtue theorists" in a way that has affinities with this presentation of the Augustinian Imperative. Jane Bennett, in *Unthinking Faith and Enlightenment* (New York: New York University Press, 1987), shows how what I (now) call the Augustinian Imperative operates in two types of contemporary environmental politics and in theories of the state elaborated by Jürgen Habermas, Theodore Lowi, and Charles Taylor. I find Stuart Hampshire in *Innocence and Experience* (Cambridge, MA: Harvard University Press, 1989) to parallel my perspective in some ways.

3. R. A. Markus, in *Saeculum: History and Society in the Theology of St. Augustine* (New York: Cambridge University Press, 1970), takes some steps in this direction, considering ways in which the Augustinian presentation of the secular opens doors to plurality. His pluralism and mine, however, draw their boundaries quite differently. Joan Cocks in "Augustine, Nietzsche and Contemporary Body Politics," *differences* (Spring, 1991), 144-156, pursues such an agenda with respect to sensuality and sexuality in Augustine and Nietzsche, respectively. This is a commendable essay, and I endorse most of what she says, without trying to say it that way myself in this book. Hannah Arendt, in *Between Past and Future* (New York: Penguin Books, 1958), 143-172, defines Augustine in a way that probably comes closest to my characterization. But she also plays up the way Augustine's characterization of Genesis treats humanity as a beginning from which surprises will come. She is impressed with this connection between new beginnings and freedom, but then asks, How did it emerge in Augustine's thought? "The only explanation that comes to mind is that Augustine was a Roman as well as a Christian" (166). Augustinian Christianity receives the greatest attention in this study, even though I try to mark off areas where Augustine's thought might provide an impetus for other possibilities.

1

Voices From the Whirlwind

Nature and Culture

What is the character of things "below" or "prior to" culture? We will never answer this question as posed, for every attempt to do so draws on the resources of culture. And yet . . . , the attempt to pose such a question is unlikely to disappear either. For every political interpretation projects presumptions about the primordial character of things into its presentation of actuality and possibility, identity and difference, good and evil. It does so even if it strives to go "beyond good and evil" and, though more ambiguously and problematically, even if it strives to call every "metaphysical" or "ontological" assumption into question.

In modern cultures the question of what precedes culture is often posed through the vocabulary of nature. Some political theorists invoke nature as a set of regularities potentially knowable and masterable by humans. Others treat it as a meaningful order in which humans participate through their own embodiment and to which embodied selves can become more closely attuned. These two options together set the table upon which contemporary debates over identity, ecology, moral sources, sexuality, tolerance, and community are placed.

But the familiar differences between these two alternatives do not exhaust the range of discernible possibilities, even within the history of the "West." The Latin *natura*, meaning "birth, constitution, character, course of things," suggests other options for exploration, as does the root term *nasci*, "to be born." The closest Greek term, *physis*, folds "genesis" or "coming into being" into the idea—yet it is not perfectly clear that this energy that propels a thing into being was always and everywhere bound close to the theme of an intrinsic purpose governing it.

I will explore a subterranean legacy in this region by considering the stories of Job and Alexina, respectively, the first being a biblical story of a probable pagan living seven or eight centuries before the common era, the second being the memoir of a teenager living in France in the 19th century. The stories of Job and Alexina disturb interwoven concepts of divinity, identity, nature, moral order, and suffering governing their respective communities. They do so particularly when each strives to locate h/er suffering within terms established by h/er community; for the suffering of each exceeds and challenges fundamental conceptions through which the community strives to redeem it.

Job

The *Book of Job* is the site of a struggle over the interpretation of human suffering. The book is organized into three parts: a prologue in which the Accuser tempts the Lord to test Job's fidelity and receives instructions from the Lord, a middle section in which Job's experience with unrelieved suffering is presented through a dialogue with friends culminating in the engagement with the Voice out of the whirlwind, and an epilogue in which Job is restored to well-being by the Lord while his erstwhile friends are punished. But some scholars believe the epilogue was added after the poem that makes up the core of the book. And most agree that the book was the object of numerous "interpolations" before it acquired the form in which we receive it. The long speech by Elihu inserted at the end of the middle section, for instance, is widely thought (on grounds of style and content) to be a later intervention by a pious priest. It seems designed to subdue scandalous possibilities of interpretation in the theophany immediately following it.

The *Book of Job*, probably composed around the seventh century before the common era, remains a site of textual struggle, as scholars in later centuries have contested its meaning through the politics of translation and interpretation. Job's struggle is not only with himself, his friends, and his god, but with later friends, scholars, and editors who wish to interpret that struggle in particular ways. The persistence of these struggles signifies the continuing power of the book to inform and disturb. *Job* compels both because its themes continue to flow through the cultural unconscious of the West and because its energies disturb that unconscious.

Because the text, as we receive it, is splintered by multifarious contestations and clouded by numerous additions, revisions, and interpretations over the centuries, it is an excellent mirror to hold up to ourselves. It reflects demands and ambivalences often concealed in other texts through stabilized traditions of interpretation. Its ambiguities render it a relatively open book through which each individual can try to come to terms with the sources and effects of suffering. The book speaks to us through the incredible power of its rhythms, metaphors, and images; it presses us to respond to its surprises, reversals, and intensifications; it remains open to a diversity of readings; and it resists easy or full assimilation by any single response. Is this power to confound the unanimity of a single reading one of its strengths? I think so. But that judgment already implicates me in a particular reading, with its own agenda, lessons, anxieties, and hopes.

Let us concentrate first on the poem that makes up the center of the book. Job, apparently a man of integrity who has enjoyed uncommon well-being, now suffers immensely. He has lost his sons and daughters, his property and his reputation, through violent, uncanny events. His body is covered with boils. His wife ridicules him for refusing to "curse God and die."[1] But he perdures in his faith, eventually receiving three friends who come to counsel and console him.

He soon learns—as many have after—that these two functions of friendship do not coincide. Were these visitors, in the earliest version

of the poem, defined as friends or as functionaries assigned to squeeze
a confession out of one who might otherwise disturb the faith of the
community? We will never know. At any rate, the friends, at first
diplomatically and then belligerently, interpret Job's suffering through
the optics of an intrinsic moral order governed by a god who bestows
justice on human life. A beneficent, providential god rules the world;
he rewards the virtuous and punishes the wicked. This being so, Job
must either admit wrongdoings he has not yet acknowledged or search
within himself to uncover wrongs heretofore overlooked. For his suffering signifies his vice.

But Job resists these instructions, protesting his innocence and virtue.
The "friends" insist more actively, even though they must realize they
intensify the misery of this miserable man in doing so. Why must they
be so insistent? Job thinks he knows:

> You too have turned against me;
>   my wretchedness fills you with fear.
> Have I ever asked you to help me
>   or begged you to pay ransom . . .
> Look me straight in the eye;
>   is this how a liar would face you?
> Can't I tell right from wrong?
>   If I sinned, wouldn't I know it? (22)

The friends cannot console Job because their investment in the vision
of a moral world order drives them to accuse him for suffering. For if
Job suffers without desert, the same bad luck might befall any of them.
And if their current well-being is not the result of their own merit, it
cannot be to their credit now and it might vanish later for no reason at
all. If these things were possible their moral world would spin out of
control. Contingency, luck, and blind fate would replace providence,
justice, and order in the cosmos; these blind forces would inhabit every
human project from the inside and challenge it from the outside, opening up frightening possibilities. The fate of Job makes them fear the
world may be more precarious, fragile, and unpredictable than they had
thought, and their reactions to him seek to restore this reassurance in
themselves regardless of the toll its restoration might impose on him.

Moreover, the impiety in Job's protestations of innocence is dangerous to those clinging to the comforts of an intrinsic moral order: It is a blasphemy against the divine spider thought to spin the moral web of the world. Even considering this thought—let alone endorsing it—might bring down upon them the wrath that has fallen upon Job. Job, with his festering boils, thus exists as an exemplar of the riskiness in these thoughts. This communal web of faith in an intrinsic moral order presided over by a jealous god possesses an impressive capacity to still doubts among the faithful once its strands have been woven through and around the members. Its impressive capacity for self-restoration is one of its attractions and one of its traps.

Job has become dangerous to the friends through his existential response to suffering. So they become increasingly more insistent in their counsel, progressively shedding the pretense to console him in his suffering. The form Job's suffering assumes drives them to take a punitive orientation to him. They turn the victim of bad luck—or perhaps worse, the target of earlier communal vengeance—into an adversary of the community. Job exposes boils festering in *their* souls when he says, "My wretchedness fills you with fear."

The misery of Job is now compounded: He suffers the pain and grief of his condition, the anxiety of doubts about cosmic justice aroused by the experience of these injuries, the blame imposed on him by friends for (allegedly) bringing suffering on himself, and the hostility they aim at him for refusing to reaffirm the justice of this god by acknowledging his own faults. "You are undermining religion and crippling faith in God," (41) asserts Eliphaz, one of the friends. Job, in turn, now begins to discern how this very conception of a moral divinity provides the impetus through which the sufferer is converted into a stranger and an adversary.

But Job himself is implicated in the web of moral order he protests against, even as he exposes the cruelties it fosters. For as the "dialogue" proceeds (the exchanges become too bitter to fit this term well) Job's estrangement from his friends becomes joined to a profound bitterness against his god.

> I loathe each day of my life;
>> I will take my complaint to God.
> I will say, Do you condemn me;
>> why are you so enraged?

Is it right for you to be vicious,
    To spoil what your own hands made . . . ?
Why did you let me be born?
    Why couldn't I have stayed
in the deep waters of the womb,
    rocked to sleep in the dark? (29,30)

Here, and elsewhere too, Job accuses his god because it does not live up to the ideal of justice he projects onto it. "Do you condemn me?" "Is it *right* for you to be *vicious*?" This extraordinary passage recognizes a god who presides over a moral order even while it poses the possibility that this same god is vicious, that is, immoral, that is, not a reliable source of moral order. What the hell is going on here? Does Job's suffering demand a transcendent moral agent capable of being blamed while the character of Job's fate also makes him doubt the truth of this attribution?

Job now doubts that this god is a moral god. His experience belies it. But, still, there ought to be a moral god so that it can serve as the object of blame for failure to live up to the demands of moral order in the world. In appealing to this plaintive "ought to be," Job reinstates at one level the principle he actively doubts at another. He ambiguates his god. This ambiguous god now becomes the source of Job's deepest bitterness. Indeed, without a semblance of faith in this god Job would have no transcendental source to appeal to, but with such a being he suffers the additional burden of rancor against a god who does not consistently enforce its own principles. Even while the dangerous thoughts of Job threaten the self-certainty of his friends, his own thoughts have moved only a short distance from those of the friends. Job's existential rage is subjected to the torture of an ambivalence that renders it possible.

The friends/enemies, then, are disparate voices inside Job as well as members of the community he challenges. And the moral god he denies is also the one he condemns. That is why the debate within *Job* is so intense and repetitious. Its torturous ambiguities cannot easily be stabilized. As long as Job retains this existential "ought" ("My god ought to be what I thought he was but now doubt him to be"), he can cling to a slender hope that his suffering reflects a divine mistake or momentary lapse into injustice. But, also, as long as he clings to that slim hope amidst this wretchedness, his relationship to divinity will be one of bitterness. He will rage against a god for injustice he doubts it could commit. He will protect a doubtful moral divinity to provide a dubious target against which to project rage. How many people—suffering, say, as invalids on the way to long, painful deaths—have twisted and turned in this same chamber of torture?

Job's "friends" grasp something of his ambivalence; hence, they keep trying to draw him back to their faith. This is the one response that might convert his bitterness into remorse while reassuring them. So they cling to their project tenaciously, while (a voice in) Job continues to outrage the will to belief they embody. Listen as Job speaks to them again:

> I made a pact with my eyes;
> > that I would not gaze at evil.
> But what good has virtue done me?
> > How has God rewarded me?
> Isn't disgrace for sinners
> > and misery for the wicked?
> Can't he tell right from wrong
> > or keep his accounts in order? (73)

The thought in the last two lines has surely occurred at some time to every believer and doubter. But the friends find it too much to take. Job has become a "rebel" against their god by accusing it belligerently of deficiency; this reprehensible conduct during his suffering reveals to them retroactively how richly Job deserves the fate that has befallen him. His rebellion renders him intolerable. No new deeds have been added to his existential offenses (he has, for instance, neither stolen property nor murdered a member of the community). But these words are deeds enough. His metaphysical rebellion renders him an outcast from the community.

The debate with the friends merely provides a prelude to the main event. The vitriolic debate finally stirs up the voice in the whirlwind. This unexpected effect of Job's existential rebellion is also ambiguous. True, the Unnameable does respond through a powerful whirlwind that sweeps over and above the ground upon which the puny Job stands. But, still, Job's well-aimed arrows do generate a divine response, and this divinity has not heretofore been moved to speak so directly to any number of believers and tormented doubters calling on it to do so. The poetry reaches its highest level of imagery, energy, and irony as the voice speaks to this courageous rebel, this bitter accuser, this ambivalent devotee. If the friends inhabit Job as well as speaking to him on behalf of the community, is the "whirlwind" yet another voice within Job?

The voice speaks but does not answer. It refuses the questions Job posed to it. Its words recall previous formulations by Job and his friends about the wonder of the world, but it lifts those themes to a level higher than they were able to reach. The voice says familiar things, but delivers a new message through its mode of saying. The poet who crafted these lines must have had an ambiguous relation to divinity,[2] celebrating its power through the lines invested in it but rebelling against the injunction to piety through the very willingness to invest these human words in divinity. Is this ambiguity reversed in the hesitations of later priests and scholars who have worked on this text? Is the theophany too compelling to repress but too dangerous to present to the faithful without cautious editing and interpretation?

Speaking out of a whirlwind, the voice recalls forces and energies in the world that exceed human capacities for understanding and control. A whirlwind—a tornado—is an immense, uncontrollable force, erupting as if out of nowhere, wreaking devastation on anything in its path; emitting a roar that terrifies; following an irregular path that reveals no rhyme or reason from the perspective of human notions of regularity, merit, and virtue:

> Where were you when I planned the earth?
> Tell me, if you are so wise.
> Do you know who took its dimensions?
> measuring its length with a cord?
> What were its pillars built on?
> who laid its cornerstone . . . ? (79)

The voice bellows questions Job cannot answer. Hence it crunches the standpoint from which Job's questions, pleas, and accusations have proceeded. Do its ironic questions suggest that it presides over a moral order beyond the full grasp of mere mortals? Or do these dismissive questions crush the self-serving, anthropomorphic demand for an intrinsic moral order itself?

As the interrogative voice proceeds it calls up images of energy, diversity, strangeness, and uncanniness in nature. On one register it invokes whirlwinds, thunderclouds, lightning, deserts, ocean depths, darkness, ice, wilderness, and the unfathomable stretch of time. On another it calls forth lions, antelopes, wild asses, oxen, the ostrich, the wild steed, the hawk, the hippopotamus, and the crocodile. These energies, forces, and beasts reflect the wonder of an earth more diverse, strange, vital, and vast than anything Job or his friends have been able to digest into their morally ordered cosmos. Consider the Beast, transcribed as "Behemoth" in most presentations and commonly thought to be the hippopotamus.

> Look now; the Beast that I made:
>   he eats grass like a bull.
> Look: the power in his thighs,
>   the pulsing sinews of his belly.
> His penis stiffens like a pine;
>   his testicles bulge with vigor.
> His ribs are bars of bronze,
>   his bones iron beams.
> He is the first of the works of God,
>   created to be my plaything.
> He lies under the lotus,
>   hidden by reeds and shadows.
> He is calm though the river rages,
>   though the torrent beats against his mouth.
> Who will take him by the eyes
>   or pierce his nose with a peg? (85)

There is wildness in the world that exceeds the wish of humanity either to moralize or to master it. This Beast was not created for us. It is god's "plaything," certainly not Job's or yours. Its penis does not stiffen according to rules you prescribe. Indeed, the stiffening of a man's penis or hardening of a woman's nipples does not follow such a code of propriety either. There is more wildness inside and outside than Job and his friends have heretofore imagined. More important, their responses to the strangeness they do discern is centered on themselves and their moral projections. They assume that things are ordered according to

an ultimate code of justice, or, at the very least, that they ought to be. The
only god they respect is one who is accountable to their needs and wishes
for justice in the last instance. Hence they are unable to experience the
wonder of a world of diverse energies and strange vitalities that whirls
around and through them. A world that is more than a moral order.

What about the crocodile (or "serpent")? "Will you pass a string
through his nose or crack his jaw with a pin? Will he plead with you for
mercy and timidly beg your pardon?" (86) Try to look a crocodile in
that eye hovering just above the water level of the swamp. Do you detect
recognition of your humanity there? You are a matter of indifference
to it when it is full, a prey to be devoured when it is hungry. The eye of
the crocodile is a Jobian metaphor for the world. Not the only one, but
one, perhaps, that deserves more attention from those who demand that
"god" or "nature" be designed for them and them alone.

This god is not the designer of a cosmic womb that envelops the little
circle of human categories, wishes, fears, and hopes in its care. It is the
instigator of a strange, vast world of internal energies and external
forces; they clash, collide, converge, and career through, over, and
against one another in multifarious ways. Their multiple lines of intersection often produce unexpected effects. The world invoked by this
voice speaks to a protean vitality of being, not to the provincial demand
that it embody the particular conceptions of merit and reward of the
animal who speaks and ponders its mortality.

It is not only that the world invoked by the theophany is not designed
for humans. Humans are not the only *actors* in it. The world flows over
with diverse "energies" and "forces" that impinge on human life in
multiple ways and that sometimes react to human impingements on
them in unpredictable and uncanny ways. If a human actor is one who
makes a difference in the world without quite knowing what it is doing,
then germs, volcanoes, crocodiles, and whirlwinds have some of the
characteristics of actors too; the term *actor* now gathers within it a plurality
of variable dimensions, blurring or ambiguating the familiar divisions of
nature/culture, humans/machines, will/cause, and creator/creature. Moreover, even within human life, "the will," "the soul," and "the subject" can
now be seen to be insufficient or uncertain sources of behavior: The self
contains pools of "energy" and "impulse" that flow through and over
these officially defined centers of agency. When one emphasizes the

metaphorical status of terms such as *energy* and *impulse* in characterizing "drives" within and without the human animal, the corollary metaphorical standing of will and subject begins to shine through more brightly. The Greek idea of *demon* is no more problematic than the Christian idea of *will*: It is just that the latter stands at the center of modern conceptions of intrinsic moral order and, therefore, needs to be problematized more actively today for ethical reasons.

The characterization of the world in the theophany is also anthropomorphic, of course. Since a poet placed these words in the mouth of a god, this is unavoidable. But, still, this poetry gestures beyond the provincial boundaries of moral discourse: It allows the categories through which it grasps the world to fade off into an indefinite set of differences that calls the sufficiency of the categories into question. Such a perspective has disturbing effects on doctrines that demand a close fit between human conceptions of regularity/morality and world formations. Conceptions of nature construing it to be filled with a harmonious moral purpose to which we can become attuned are contested by this theophany. So are those that construe nature to be a plastic substratum susceptible to human mastery and control once its forces and energies have been translated into a matrix of regular laws.

Nature as intrinsic purpose or nature as plastic matter to be used. These two conceptions have competed for hegemony in the history of the West, with the second eventually becoming the majority voice of the modern age and the first receding into the reactive voice of nostalgia for a time when the teleological imagination carried more credibility. The Jobian theophany upsets both of these voices and the respective conceptions of moral order associated with each. Each sounds too much like the other from its vantage point, since each embodies transcendental narcissism. Each demands that the world be *for us* in the last instance, either as a dispenser of rewards for virtue or as a pliable medium susceptible to human mastery. The first invokes a god as mysterious master subject; the second, humanity as technological master subject. The second conception prides itself on its ability to transcend the anthropomorphic moralism of the first. But it remains remarkably close to its favorite opponent. Both demand compensation, either from a god who installs providence into nature or from a plastic world that has lost this god. They demand either equivalence between virtue and reward in the last instance or that the earth be placed at the disposal of humanity. The first vision appears holy to itself; the second, realistic to itself in its refusal of teleological comfort. But both appear provincial, self-enclosed, and narcissistic from the perspective of the Jobian theophany. Its portrayal of whirlwinds within and without repeals the world as intrinsic purpose or plastic matter. The whirlwind is a better metaphor for the difference flowing below, through, and over the structures of cultural organization than either the plowed field or the glow of the sun setting. Or, at least, both of the latter must be experienced in relation to the first before the uncanniness and contingency of nature begins to sink into the presumptions of established practices. Taming and moralizing are necessary ingredients in human life, of course. But everything depends on what projections into being accompany and qualify these formations. The earth is a fireball at its center.

One element in Job's suffering is relieved by the theophany. Job need no longer be bitter about a god who does not dispense the justice expected. That expectation turns out to be a form of cosmic self-indulgence, and its erasure takes away the divine agent one could be bitter against. To subdue the voices within and around us that project such a moral world order is, first, to overcome the existential bitterness that arises when one's virtue is not matched by divine reward and, second, to relieve the demand to convert victims of chance, fate, or human malevolence into scapegoats responsible for the fate they endure or strangers who have lost their right to the comforts and care of the community. Both responses are now exposed as violent tactics of self-protection against victims of bad luck (or human injustice) whose fate would otherwise call transcendental narcissism into doubt. The pious violence of the friends stands out in sharper relief when the vision of intrinsic moral order they endorse is interrogated by the voice in the whirlwind.

My reading of *Job*, then, finds the moral picture of the world to be unethical, striving to pry a gap between "morality" and "ethics" that remains to be examined.[3] It is not, on this reading, that people are best construed as utterly devoid of responsibility for what they do to others or what happens to themselves; but that the regulation of others is likely to be intensified and the attributions of responsibility to them to be inflated by those whose response to unorthodox acts, deviant beings, and surprising events is governed by the imperative to defend the vision of an intrinsic moral order.

The theophany, of course, does not dictate the interpretation given to it here. It simply enables it as one possibility to consider in competition with others. Although the simple picture of a moral world order, entertained by the friends, seems confounded by the theophany, there is another version that might still be entertained. One might claim that Job and his friends had too simple, transparent a picture of moral order. They expected virtue (as they already understand it) to be matched by punishment and reward (as they already understand them). The theophany, though, might be construed to represent a more complex moral vision, one that appreciates how the god's design transcends the human will to comprehend it, even though human beings can profit immensely from dark signs of transcendent order inscribed in experience and scripture. Although the reading endorsed here readily becomes a vision in which faith in divinity, understood in its usual valences, merges into respect for the prodigiousness, strangeness, and grandeur of nature, the "complex" reading of moral order preserves a persistent place for a mysterious divinity whose order one communes with while confessing severe limitations in one's prospects for comprehending it. Augustinianism is one form such an alternative perspective might assume.

Robert Gordis, treating *Job* as a critique of the "simple" concept of a moral order, preserves it as a defense of a complex one. "Just as there is order and harmony in the natural world, though imperfectly grasped by man, so there is order and meaning in the moral sphere, though often incomprehensible to man."[4] This retreat to an incomprehensible order protects the idea from devaluation under the hammer of experience, but it also confounds its ability to do very much work except through the authoritative interpretations of an organized priesthood. I support the first reading, then, the one that refuses to treat the god as a moral god, partly because this alternative resists powerful pressures structured into Western culture (and others too) to solidify the moral view by defining as heretics, enemies, sick beings, and evil agents those whose conduct or experience might otherwise destabilize it, partly because my wariness of the authority of priests is ecumenical. Others endorse a complex picture of moral order, partly because they doubt that any viable conception of

collective identity and moral life can sustain itself unless it is attached
to an external source of authority.

Job himself may leave both possibilities open for debate as he
responds to the Voice from the whirlwind:

> I have spoken of the unspeakable
>   and tried to grasp the infinite . . .
> I had heard of you with my ears;
>   but now my eyes have seen you.
> Therefore I will be quiet,
>   comforted that I am dust. (88)

Is Job comforted amidst his suffering because he sees there is no point
to rail against a god for the cosmic injustice of his fate? If you think of
the theophany as a voice within him, it is possible to see how it teaches
us to bear up under the pressures of contingency and bad luck by
cultivating reverence for the beauty and energy of life flowing through
and around us. It commends a struggle against the drive to existential
resentment that so often haunts life. Does that mean that one must
become resigned as well to those actions by the community that contribute to one's suffering? The poem does not respond to this issue, either
by specifying closely which portion of Job's suffering flows from communal vindictiveness and which from bad luck, or by suggesting very strongly
how to sort out responses to his friends from those to his god.[5]

Nonetheless, a good case might be made in favor of a divided
response. I might strive to overcome those resentments against my fate
and my community that reflect existential resentment, while opposing
undeserved burdens and sacrifices the community imposes on others or
me, including those imposed for the conscious or unconscious purpose
of protecting the experience of correspondence between its particular
organization of life and an intrinsic order of things. But which is which?
The *Book of Job* does not settle that issue, whereas the multiple voices
within it do suggest the value of keeping *this* debate alive.

Still, is not the contemporary insight to be drawn from Job's experience limited because of the radically different context in which it is set?
Have "we" not outgrown (or "lost") the very concept of an intrinsic

moral order forming the object of debate in *Job*? I have my doubts. An example closer to home may be pertinent.

Alex/ina

Herculine Barbin: Being the Recently Discovered Memoirs of a Nineteenth Century French Hermaphrodite appeared around 26 centuries after *The Book of Job*.[6] It raises similar issues in a different setting. The autobiography, written around 1863, begins, "I am twenty-five years old, and, although I am still young, I am beyond any doubt approaching the hour of my death" (3). Alex/ina was born to a poor mother in France in 1838. She was soon sent to a convent. She spent most of her youthful years under the tutelage of nuns and in association with other young girls receiving a religious education.

This text, too, has a prologue, in which Michel Foucault, who unearthed it from dusty archives, poses the issue of the relation between sexuality and truth. It, too, contains an epilogue, consisting of journalistic reports, the opinions of judges, and the analyses of pathologists, designed to control the range of viable interpretations to be placed on the memoir. These three parts together (the prologue, the memoir, the epilogue) pose the issue of suffering by a modern who does not seem to fit either of the gender/sexual categories available to her.

Her? The first issue posed by this text is the appropriate terms of identification through which to characterize the struggle of Alex/ina. If that issue is not posed, the terms selected will resolve the interpretation before it is launched. For the text speaks to nameless sufferings of one who could not find a place of sexual residence in a culture that maps sexuality onto gender duality and gender duality onto nature. As the reader, responding to the pathos of the memoir, stumbles in deciding between the pronouns *he, she,* or *it* that exhaust the legitimate range of cultural alternatives, this stumbling itself encourages one to ponder the role that the genderization of language plays—particularly in the instances of names and "personal" pronouns, but not there alone—in constituting the genders and sexualities to which it refers. I am not referring simply to the (now familiar) concern over the universal *he* that gives implicit superiority to men over women while claiming to be generic. But the very cultural imperative to say "he" *or* "she" every time a particular human is designated invokes gender as the first and primary mark of identification through which a self is to be characterized. This grammar, first, treats gender as the primary mode of individualization and, second, determines that gender must be divided into two and two only. The position of Alex/ina as Other in the community to which "she" belongs is thus more radical than that of Job in his. Alex/ina's ambiguous position is inscribed in the grammar of the community that constitutes "the hermaphrodite."

Do these terms map a pre-existing terrain or do they provide the cultural key through which the terrain is mapped? Is the genderization of grammar part of the process by which gender is first divided and then invested with an intensity that helps to shape everything else in life? And is the naturalization of gender duality part of the process by which bodies and nature are discursively constituted when they are said to be represented? The encounter with Alex/ina suggests the affirmative possibility in each of these questions. I know of no way to respond to this possibility satisfactorily while remaining "true" to the grammar of genderization. So, I will use the name *Alex/ina* and the pronouns *s/he* and *h/er* in this section to characterize the author of this memoir, and others as well, hoping by doing so to flag for a time at least how often these little words recur in discourse and how this repetitive grammaratization of names and pronouns constitutes a subterranean politics of genderization and sexualization demanding problematization.[7] Only a deployment of language that intervenes in the established grammar can begin to loosen the knots it ties.

Why must the knots be loosened? Because the exclusions and divisions sanctioned by those modalities produce sexual strangers required to sustain them? Because the social stabilization of gender duality sustains its purity, first, by translating unsettled differences and ambiguities within the self into definitive differences between selves and, second, by translating those recalcitrant to assimilation into either category into strange, sick, or monstrous beings to be suppressed, treated as mistakes of nature, or surgically repaired until they "fit" one category or the other?

We return, then, to the connection between Job and Alex/ina across all those centuries. They both suffer. They both become adversaries or strangers to their communities. And the definition of each as an adversary to be blamed seems to be bound up with the quest by each community to protect the sanctity of its identity from disturbance. Job suffers the double misfortune of a fate that h/is community blames on him, and h/is suffering is compounded further when h/is engagement with the putative author of that fate offends the sensibilities of h/is friends. Alex/ina suffers the even more intrusive rigors of adjustment to a grammatico-cultural definition of gender/sexuality s/he confounds; h/er suffering is intensified by efforts of friends to silence h/er or to help h/im find h/is true self.

After several years in a convent for young g/irls, studying diligently and entering into fugitive relations of love and pleasure with another student, Alex/ina's experience of h/er own desires and bodily composition, as they relate to h/er cultural expectations, become increasingly strained and filled with shame. "I suffered enormously from this sort of communal living. . . . I would have preferred to be able to hide myself from the sight of my kind companions, not because I wanted to shun them—I liked them too much for that—but because I was instinctively ashamed of the enormous distance that separated me from them, physically speaking" (26). S/he does not fit. And s/he tries a variety of strategies to disguise this condition from others and h/erself.

H/er desires became problematic. At the age of nineteen s/he views h/erself as the only spectator at a bathing party in which everyone else, or so she assumed, was simply a participant. "Of course, they were far from suspecting what tumultuous feelings shook me as I watched their carefree behavior" (39). Alex/ina is becoming a stranger to herself. And she senses that this strangeness would become a scandal and a humiliation if it were to become publicized.

H/er intense relationship with Sara, h/er illicit lover, pulls h/er to the abyss:

My God! Was I guilty? And must I accuse myself here of a crime? No, no! . . . That fault was not mine; it was the fault of an unexampled fatality, which I could not resist!!! . . . What, in the natural order of things, ought to have separated us in the world had united us!!! Try to imagine, if that is possible, what our predicament was for us both. (51)

"The natural order of things." Alex/ina affirms as natural an order that would define h/er to be monstrous if s/he allows the thin veil protecting h/er (non)identity to slide off. And s/he affirms as a fatality of nature her inability to fit into this order. This natural order—this order of gender and sex inscribed in nature—seems through the very desires it produces to drive together two beings it is designed to separate. There is a fault in this predicament, alright, but the text cannot settle on its proper locus. That is part of the predicament. If it were a willful "fault" in the conduct of the two young g/irls, guilt would reside with them. If it were a "fault" in nature, the very conception of nature as a gendered moral order would become disturbed and shaken. Would guilt reside there? There is, then, a "predicament" here, one that exceeds available terms of specification, one that demands a place to locate fault but can only locate a series of faulty candidates for the assignment. Perhaps, then, the fault resides in the slash? That is, perhaps this new grammatical mark takes a step toward translating the mark (lack, division) culturally imposed on Alex/ina into a mark (lack, insufficiency) within the grammar through which we are constituted?

The predicament of Alex/ina resonates with the quandary of Job. She sometimes feels blameless, a pawn of fate, but the culture she (imperfectly) interiorizes demands that blame for this condition be found within her. S/he can only appeal to the cultural legacy of original sin to resolve this internal incoherence, appealing to "that feeling that is lodged in the heart of every son of Adam. Was I guilty, criminal, because a gross mistake had assigned me a place in the world that should not have been mine?" (54).

What or who made this "gross mistake"? The thought of a *mistake* in nature is the thought of a divine agent who makes it, or, at least, of an intrinsic design that occasionally lacks the capacity to realize this or that detail of its own architecture. But the thought of an agent powerful enough to make *this* mistake does not seem congruent with it actually being thoughtless or weak or cruel enough to do so. Alex/ina, like Job, is moved to existential bitterness by a predicament that confounds the terms of reference each had been taught to revere. H/er interrogative voice retains a place for a providential god while it scrambles its previous understandings of the divinity who fills this space. Multiple valences of "nature" pour out of the text, as Alex/ina tries to pose the right question through which to define this predicament. "Wasn't Nature being asked to make a heroic sacrifice, of which she was incapable?" (72)

As the pressures mount, Alex/ina is driven to relieve them through confession. The mandate to confess defines the predicament to be a fault or rift within Alex/ina h/erself, rather than, say, a *dissonance* between the cultural configuration of gender normality and culturally inscribed bodies/desires that do not mesh uniformly with this contingent configuration. This interiorization of fault, it seems, defines the politics of confession. Anyway, since no representatives of the culture come forward to confess arbitrary closure in its gender/sexual configuration, Alex/ina has little choice. A confession is offered under cultural duress (as most confessions are) in the hopes of relieving unbearable pressures within and without.

The first priest s/he selects to confess to is horrified by the predicament s/he reports. "It was not pity that I inspired in him; it was horror, a vindictive horror. . . . Instead of words of peace, he heaped scorn and insults upon me" (55). This priest recalls Job's friends, readily enough.

Perhaps the suffering of Job and the suffering of Alex/ina are the same even while the occasion, the site, and the grammar of each vary. Each suffers initially from an effect experienced as fate. Each is then blamed to protect the community's cosmic vision of moral order. Job is blamed to protect the community's conception of moral divinity. Alex/ina is blamed because h/er indefinite sexuality and undergendered status—as perceived by authoritative bearers of the culture—threaten to destabilize the experience of gender/sexuality of those who stumble across it. Each is made into a stranger within its own community to arrest the cultural destabilization it threatens.

Can you imagine a society in which gender practices are pluralized, say, according to undichotomized standards such as depth of voice, muscular proportions, and variations in percentages of selected hormones? In which the pronouns *he* and *she* are similarly pluralized? This alternative "genderization" of life would not function exactly as gender does now. Nor would it be a utopian condition. The point of gathering these criteria together under the rubric of *gender* might be to differentiate among members according to their probable capacity to engage in, say, arduous labor or military combat, and the cultural need for the old point of "gender" might recede through a series of shifts in technologies

of erotic pleasure, conception, and reproduction. The new gender distinctions would overlay the old ones; the old ones might become subordinate
voices within the new. There might even be a discernible history of
development here in which the new mode is recognizable as an evolution
of old practices, and in which the old practices persist as a subordinate
feature of the new. The result would be a shift in the practice of gender
rather than a replacement of gender by something else altogether. The
differences and connections between old and new gender practices would
be comparable, say, to those between poly-theism and mono-theism, only
in this case the *poly* would be the later development.

     It is unimportant at the moment whether you would prefer the hypo-
thetical practice to the existing one. Not liking arduous labor myself
and being resistant to military combat, I am not drawn to the social
priorities this alternative order would reflect. But if you can even
imagine such a *possibility*, it helps to expose the role of convention in
the construction of gender today and to suggest how sexual and gender
strangers are now produced to protect the mapping of gender primacy
and duality onto nature.[8] Even the thought of a new possibility, as
Nietzsche says, can shake and transform thought. Think, he says, of how
thought of the very possibility of eternal damnation transformed the
terms of thought for centuries, and, I will add, how it was illegitimate
for centuries to treat this revealed truth explicitly as a mere possibility
open to debate.

     With this thought-experiment before us, the vindictiveness and hor-
ror in the voice of the first priest can now be heard as a sign of anxiety,
an anxiety that will authorize any act of repression to ward off the
intensification of self-doubt about correspondence between the cultural
map of gender and its natural design. Other voices signify this anxiety
in their own way in turn. It is pertinent to note, though, that this priestly
horror is not simply self-serving in a narrow sense of that term. The first
priest understands that if Alex/ina publicizes this condition in any way
in the current cultural setting s/he will become an object of scandal and
censure. *If* the cultural practices of gender are untouchable, perhaps it
is best to press h/er to re-press the predicament and to live silently with
this dissonance. The first premise may remain unthought by the priest,
but once it is unconsciously assumed a modicum of concern for the fate
of Alex/ina is discernible in h/is hardness. He is caught in a bind too.

The next priest Alex/ina consults is kindly and solicitous. H/is counsel:

> You are here and now entitled to call yourself a man in society. Certainly you are, but how will you obtain the legal right to do so. At the price of great scandal, perhaps. . . . And so the advice I am giving you is this: withdraw from the world and become a nun; but be very careful not to repeat the confession that you have made to me, for a convent of women would not admit you. This is the only course that I propose to you, and believe me, accept it. (62)

The cultural code of gender primacy/duality is so powerful that Alex/ina *must* be defined as a man or a woman. Since s/he has experienced gender uncertainty as a woman, s/he must be treated as a man whose natural gender was misidentified at birth. This is the first "must." But the cultural line of division between genders is so precarious in its definiteness, so fragile in its fixity, that an inevitable scandal will follow if Alex/ina switches from one side to the other. Alex/ina, the kindly priest decides, must hide out in a nunnery, where those most devout in their worship of this author of moral order reside. This is the second "must."

Horror and kindness; the imperative of a gender switch and the counsel to conceal a previous misidentification; the fear of scandal and the necessity of bearing up under it—these contradictory pairs set the shifting combinations through which Alex/ina is treated by h/er best friends for the rest of h/is life. Each combination dissolves as a viable strategy as soon as its inner dissonances become apparent, but no response can be devised that escapes these terms within the existing cultural matrix. Sophocles might have a field day with this predicament. But Alex/ina is a Christian writer, and, besides, s/he is the one who must bear up under the effects s/he records.

This particular predicament continues, but the problematic role of culture in its definition becomes increasingly more audible. The theophany in *Job*—with its (possible) refusal to inscribe a moral design into nature or to treat it as a plastic field that human initiative can reorder at will—may prepare one to disturb the cultural code through which Alex/ina is constituted, treated, and reconstituted. Alex/ina is a real person living in the 19th century. But s/he is also a metaphor for a more general murmur of artifice in the cultural constitution of gender duality. The eye of the crocodile, the whirlwind, Alex/ina, the ambiguity of "nature," the insufficiency of grammar: These are metaphors through which subterranean, fugitive experiences of strangeness within cultural configurations might disturb those persistent economies of grammar, moral order, and self-identity.

Things move fast for Alexina after s/he confesses. Suspicions mount against h/er as h/e refuses to heed the kindly priest's advice. A doctor is called in when pain in the abdominal area becomes severe. No priestly stuff from this worldly professional. H/e examines the patient's genitals and promptly announces Alex/ina to be male. H/e then encourages Alex/ina's distraught mother by saying, "It's true that you've lost your daughter . . . , but you've found a son whom you were not expecting" (78).

Alex/ina becomes redefined through a medical examination. H/e becomes a man. The predicted scandal sets in. H/e is sent to Paris. And h/e soon prepares for suicide as h/e finds that the human relationships available to h/im on this side of the gender ledger do not mesh with interiorized expectations of emotional tonality, routines of friendship, intimate relations, and personal demeanor either. Alex/ina is thus subjected to a "terrible, nameless punishment" (93) in which the agents are faceless, the crimes unspecified, and the carriers of punishment often unwitting.

Alex/ina is driven to reject the simple concept of a moral world order through the suffering h/e endures. "The world that you invoke," h/e says to himself in the memoir, "was not made for you. You were not made for it. In this vast universe where every grief has its place, you shall search in vain for a corner. . . . It overturns all the laws of nature and humanity." (98-99) "Where every grief has its place . . . " In confessing the absence of fit between h/is constitution and the cultural definition of gender normality h/e retreats to a more complex conception of moral order, one that promises to deliver h/im from a grief that has no place in *this* world.

> Oh, death! Death will truly be the hour of deliverance for me! Another wandering Jew, I await it as the most frightful of all torments!!! But you remain to me, my God! You have willed that I belong to no one here below, through none of those earthly bonds that elevate man by perpetuating Your divine work! Though I am a sad disinherited creature, I can still lift up my eyes to You, for You at least will not reject me. (93)

Alex/ina officially dies by h/is ow/n hand, though many other hands participate in the preparation of this act. Unlike Job, h/e seeks refuge in the Christian theme of an afterlife in which the experience of natural injustice in this world might be rectified by a god whose providence surpasses the comprehension of those whose suffering seems to "overturn the laws of nature and humanity." No theophany for Alex/ina. No reflection on the diversity of nature and the role of cultural artifice in gender identity. No drive to politicize the naturalization of cultural artifacts. Faith in divine justice in the last instance is wheeled out to replace Jobian affirmation of a world in which no divine hand orders earthly life according to a moral recipe of justice, natural identity, reward and desert. Job remains pertinent to the life and death of Alex/ina, but unavailable to h/im. And does Alex/ina not remain pertinent to the experience of J/ob?

In the absence of a politics that might denaturalize the cultural map of gender and sexuality, suicide emerges as the only viable line of escape for Alex/ina.

Critical Pluralism

A political constellation informed by (contestable) Jobian presumptions might explore multiple possibilities for life, pleasure, affection, and social relations exceeding the cultural script already in place. It might acknowledge the indispensability of culture to life while affirming the imperative for political contestation of closures in particular cultural matrixes. The paradox of culture, it might suggest, demands a culture in which politicization of fixed maps of identity and nature is a recurrent cultural phenomenon. Such a response discerns strains of unethicality running through these moralities of natural order and gender normality. It observes how scandal is deployed to reassure a culture when its naturalized practices become disturbed by surprising beings, unexpected actions, and unpredicted events. It might contest these terms of self-reassurance by exposing the role that sacrifice plays in fixing the dogmatism of identity. But these sentences are utopian gestures.

I mean to say that these sentences are utopian in the context under review without discounting the role of politics in defining the suffering of both Job and Alex/ina. Each encounter is quietly marked by the politics of the community in which it occurs. We have discerned this already in the political responses of friends, priests, and doctors to the suffering of both. And this politics of communal self-protection continues after Job and Alex/ina die. For we continue to read these exemplary texts, seeking to learn from them; and the epilogues appended to them by authoritative priests continue to police the legitimate implications to be drawn from them. Fortunately, this editorial policing of exemplary texts is susceptible to counter-policing.

Who knows who penned the brief epilogue to *Job* or when it was written? But its relation to the poem preceding it seems clear. It is designed to domesticate the reading of the explosive text to which it is appended.

The epilogue, four paragraphs long, restores a moral conception of the world by means of a simple reversal: It preserves the divine calculus of reward and punishment by converting Job into its beneficiary and the friends into recipients of divine punishment. The Lord instructs the three friends "to take seven bulls and seven rams and go to my servant Job and offer a sacrifice of yourselves. My servant Job will pray for you, and for his sake I will overlook your sin." (91) By submitting to the total power of his god and recognizing the unfathomable morality of its justice, Job passes the test of loyalty and earns his reward. Or so the epilogue insists. It stills the politics of interpretation by appending an official ending to a disturbing story. The "Job" it inscribes is divinely rewarded for endorsing a complex view of moral order; alternative lessons are repressed or muted by the rewards it presents to Job in the name of its god.

The epilogue is the political statement of the dominant community of believers. It protects the conception of moral order that reassures them by justifying divine punishment for the very representatives of the community who brought the original message from the community to Job. It creates a new set of scapegoats to preserve its old faith by clarification. The poet, on my reading, would boil over in h/er grave as Job is divinely showered with sheep, camels, oxen, donkeys, new sons, the most beautiful daughters in "all the world," and a healthy life lasting

140 years. The epilogue depoliticizes the problem of evil by placing a moral calculator in the hands of an inscrutable agent of rewards and penalties. The moral god thus returns, this time as a less-fathomable rewarder and punisher, one that needs authoritative priests even more than before to draw the community into close proximity to its mysterious moral order.

Job ends with an epilogue that mutes (but does not silence) the most powerful voice it introduces onto the theological register, but *Herculine Barbin* closes with one in which secular journalists, a mayor, and pathologists join priests in *pronouncing* the gender of Alex/ina. Does this epilogue, consisting mostly of secular documents, contest the theological message enunciated by the priests and seconded by Alex/ina in the memoir? Many of the pronouncements exude sympathy for the victim; and while some commentators continue to foment scandal, others condemn or surpass it. But none tries to contest the map that plots sexuality upon gender duality and gender duality upon nature.

A report by E. Goujon included in the epilogue, published in a journal of human anatomy and physiology in France after the case of Alex/ina became a medical issue, typifies the scientific judgment of the case. Goujon begins by describing a "young man" employed in railroad administration who "committed suicide by asphyxiating himself with carbon dioxide in a wretched room located on the sixth floor of a house" (128). The sympathy with which h/is plight is characterized almost buries the definiteness with which h/is gender is eventually delineated. It is not as though the author doubts there is a "mixture" of some sort here. "In fact, it is difficult . . . to discover a more extreme mixture of the two sexes, as concerns everything relating to the external genital organs" (129).

The report delineates the relevant organs in precise language:

As we shall see later . . . this organ was a large clitoris rather than a penis; in fact, among women we sometimes see the clitoris attain the size of the index finger. As he tells us in his memoirs, it was possible for the erection to be accompanied by an ejaculation and voluptuous sensations. . . . A vagina ending in a cul de sac . . . allowed him to play the feminine role also in the act of coitus. To this vagina, which was located where it ordinarily is in a woman, were annexed two vulvovaginal glands that opened at the vulva, on either side, and each next to a little duct that served for the emission or ejaculation of sperm. (132)

A scientific description followed by an authoritative medical determination of gender and sexuality. The memoir of the human who lived, loved, suffered, and died with the genitals so described is noted, but only insofar as its characterization of those organs corresponded to the culturally received vocabulary governing the analysis. The specific conjunctions in Alex/ina's life (the years in the convent, the relationships s/he established and interiorized, the literary education s/he received, the contingent structure of desire and habit organized through these conjunctions) is not considered relevant. *Gender* is not a term thought to be open to revision through reconstituted cultural practices. Even more pertinently, the way the medical description of organs is drawn from the vocabulary of a culture in which gender duality is lodged firmly in the assumptions of vocabulary is not noted as an element in the analysis capable of disturbing or destabilizing the terms of physiological characterization. The imperative governing the scientific report is to characterize Alex/ina so as to retain confidence that (almost) everyone else corresponds nicely to a natural division between two genders. This division must be naturalized, so that culturally en-gendered terms of bodily inscription cannot be disrupted or shaken through the multiplication of possibilities that scramble them, so that people will not be pressed to interrogate the confident correspondence between the cultural organization that inhabits them and an intrinsic purpose in nature taken to precede it, so that no cultural space will be pried open to create opportunity for "others"—including perhaps the other within oneself—to define modes of life and affectional relations that scramble and pluralize established terms of heterosexual normality and gender duality. The epilogue is a series of exercises in metaphysical reassurance to prevailing cultural practices of sexuality and gender. It is an exercise in power all the more effective because it takes itself to be a neutral representation.

Where, in the domain of gender, does cultural determination end and "raw" nature begin? Nobody knows, and probably never will know.[9] But everybody often purports to know. Or, better, *everyone* often invokes a vocabulary inscribed with the mark of this confidence, and most people regularly invoke such a vocabulary with utmost confidence in its sufficiency. The authoritative accounts in the epilogue presuppose the possibility of separating culture and biology into component parts and drawing them back together into a definitive report, while the report itself reveals the impossibility of doing so. The typical political effect of this vocabulary/practice is to produce strangers and scapegoats sacrificed to the altar of an unexamined faith in an intrinsic moral order of gender and sex.

Is the horror Alex/ina encountered in the first priest still detectable within the detached description and kindly manner of the doctor's words? Listen to the faith of Goujon as he smooths over the disturbing fact that there are "numerous cases" of the sort represented by Alex/ina:

> It would be easy to multiply examples of this kind, and it would even be profitable to science if all the documents that it possesses on this question were brought together . . . , which would become a precious guide for doctors who are called upon to give their opinions and pronounce a judgment concerning people who have been stricken with this kind of anomaly. It would be readily apparent from this work . . . , that if it is sometimes difficult and even impossible to identify the true sex of an individual at the time of birth, it is not the same at a more advanced age, and especially at the approach of puberty. In fact, at this time, inclinations and habits of their true sex are revealed in people who have been victims of an error, and observing those traits would help considerably in marking out their place in society, if the state of the genital organs and their different functions were not sufficient for attaining this end. (138-139)

Goujon is concerned about the (all too?) numerous cases of people "stricken with this . . . anomaly," but not with the cultural definition of gender that treats these numerous "cases" as anomalies, that is, as mistakes in nature deviating from a design intrinsic to it. That is why surgery presents itself so readily to him as the sufficient response, once the "true sex" of each anomaly has been discerned. He does not ask whether surgery *could* be so precise and extensive, first, to bring innumerable culturally defined elements of bodily composition into alignment with this truth and, second, to draw these elements into consistent correspondence with the contingent development of desires, inclinations, social expectations, and affectional possibilities in particular individuals. He never asks, with Michel Foucault, "Must we *truly* have a *true* sex?" When Goujon writes, the scientist/doctor has begun to challenge the priest as the culture's guardian of metaphysical comfort, and he plays that new role very nicely.

Is it possible to translate Job and Alex/ina from the discourse of wrongdoers/victims/anomalies/mistakes/rebels deviating from an intrinsic god/nature/norm/virtue/piety into a discourse of signs/metaphors/examples/disturbances calling into question simultaneously the ethicality of conceptions of intrinsic moral order and nature as a plastic medium of human action? If the purposes and effects of the "friends" in such cases were interrogated more actively and impiously, might it be possible to nurture a politics in which the dynamic of cultural reassurance through the production and reproduction of strangers is contested? What if strangeness were treated by more people as indispensable to identity in a world without intrinsic moral design, and, hence, something to be prized as a precondition of identity and a source of possibilities for selective alliances and more generous negotiations with others? And what if more adherents of an intrinsic moral order were to acknowledge the deep and persistent contestability of this projection (along with those that oppose it) so as to allow this issue to become a more overt object of political negotiation and contestation?

A politics of generous negotiation/coalition/contestation with friends and strangers through cultivation of strangeness residing within our own identities. And a politics of generosity toward the strangeness in ourselves through attentiveness to whirlwinds within and without. Not a generosity growing out of the unchallengeable privilege of a superior social position and moral ontology, but one emerging from enhanced appreciation of dissonances within our own identities and of persistent implication in the differences through which we are consolidated. A refigured generosity.

Does this combination suggest a political pluralism? Perhaps, but not that flat pluralism in which diversity expands indefinitely without imprinting profound effects on the cultural experience of identity and difference. In critical pluralism, each constituency would acknowledge its own identity to be bound up with a variety of differences sustaining it. Each identity depends on the differences it constitutes, and each attempt to define identity through difference encounters disturbing responses by those who challenge the sufficiency or dignity of its definition of them. Each identity is fated, thereby, to contend—to various degrees and in multifarious ways—with others it depends on to enunciate itself. That's politics. The issue is not if but how.

In a politics of critical or agonistic pluralism, each individual, group, and collective identity acknowledges the case for self-restriction in the way it contests those disturbing differences it opposes and depends on. One aggregate effect of such engagements, collisions, and restrictions is the provision of new political spaces through which to engage strangeness in oneself and others. The aggregate effect of these relations of interdependence and strife, when enough of those engaged in them appreciate the case for self-restriction amidst conflict, may open new spaces for politics and freedom. For freedom resides in the spaces produced by such dissonant conjunctures. It is always fugitive and precarious.

Even fundamentalists—who treat the faith that guides them to be a universal truth and who protect their fundaments by defining every constituency that disturbs their self-confidence as deviant—can participate in such relations of complementary dissonance, to the extent, first, they acknowledge how their own faith appears contestable and offensive in some respects from other points of view, and to the degree, second, they affirm restrictions in the ways they press their demands in the light of this first awareness. Yet, it must be admitted, in the (highly utopian) world of critical pluralism fundamentalists would run the greatest risk of becoming radical strangers. And fundamentalist dispositions inhabit all of us: they are inscribed in the condensations of shared vocabularies, in the obduracy of habit, in the institutionalization of established assumptions, in valiant struggles against mortality, in drives to revenge against those who have jeopardized the self-confidence of your identity most recently, and in a variety of other political tactics through which we reassure ourselves in what we are. The voice of the friends and the priests, my friends, always circulates through and around us . . . , though it may be possible to soften, stretch, politicize, and disturb its insistences to a greater degree.

To say even this much is to admit considerable distance between contemporary democracies and the impossible world of critical pluralism. It is to affirm that such a critical perspective functions mostly as a launching pad from which genealogies of contemporary normality are developed, fixed presumptions about "nature" are disturbed, criticisms of established codes of diversity are pursued, and alternatives for political change are pressed. It does not delineate an ideal susceptible to full actualization.[10] For any particular form pluralism assumes is itself susceptible to critical strategies of disturbance and deconstruction, partly, as we shall see in Chapter 5, because its crucial components never fit together as a coherent set at any single time. Thus, at any moment there is always something to be done on behalf of critical pluralism.

Critical pluralism is best presented, then, as a valuable cultural impossibility always susceptible to new possibilities of political operationalization. It is not a sufficient political ideal, but an indispensable component in an admirable ethic of politics. It stands or falls as a critical principle through its ability to expose how advocates of the normal individual and the integrated community (among others) complement one another in concealing violence against the many Jobs and Alex/inas they produce. That is, it stands or falls through its ability to expose the immorality in dominant moral codes. The theophany in *Job* suggests possibilities in this regard, without pursuing them. Corollary possibilities are suggested by Michel Foucault in the prologue to *Herculine Barbin* and in the subtext of Alex/ina's memoir. When these disparate texts are read together in response to contemporary definitions of nature, identity, responsibility, gender, normality, community, sexuality, monotheism, and secularism—that is, in the context within which this reading has been set all along—subterranean voices become more audible on behalf of the politicization of cultural mechanisms through which strangers are produced and subjugated.

Notes

1. *The Book of Job*, translated and with an introduction by Stephen Mitchell (San Francisco: North Point Press, 1987), 6. I use this recent translation, partly because it is convenient for use in undergraduate classes, partly because this new translation is refreshing in certain places, partly because its very newness underlines the continuing process of translation and interpretation in this area. Future quotations from this text will be cited in the body of the chapter.

2. Do I project an author into the text? Yes, that is part of the interpretive strategy I am adopting. That is not to say that I know, from independent studies written about "the author," things about him, her, or them, but that my reading of the story includes a projection into the presumptions and moods of the storyteller(s) that may as well be stated rather than hidden. Can other interpretations avoid some such set of implicit or explicit projections? I doubt it.

3. I will not develop this part of the thesis further in this chapter. The theme is pursued in *Identity\Difference: Democratic Negotiations of Political Paradox* (Ithaca, NY: Cornell University Press, 1991), especially the Introduction and Chapters 5 and 6. It is developed most extensively in the last chapter of this book.

4. See Robert Gordis, *The Book of God and Man: A Study of Job* (Chicago: University of Chicago Press, 1965; trans. by Yvonne Freccero), 133. Gordis first emphasizes the repudiation of the "anthropomorphic" god in the theophany and then tries to recapture as much of it as possible. My reading is closer to that offered by John T. Wilcox, *The Bitterness of Job: A Philosophical Reading* (Ann Arbor: University of Michigan Press, 1989).

5. In *Job: The Victim of His People* (Stanford: Stanford University Press, 1987), René Girard argues that Job's suffering is created by the violence of the community against him because they resent/envy the authority, reputation, and well-being he has acquired. Their isolation and punishment of him is a precondition of their own community and of the closure of dangerous rivalry among them. I find some plausibility in Girard's interpretation, but I also find his symptomatic reading of the text to be too closed and dogmatic. He is certain that all alternative readings are further symptoms of the sacrificial mentality he opposes. To put the point too briefly, Girard places the "sacrificial crisis" in the (Lacanian) realm of the imaginary, making it too universal and inevitable; he ignores symbolic/discursive modes through which it can be challenged, modified, sublimated, and opposed. In this reading, I want to focus on the relation between political theology and the production of scapegoats, regardless of whether the initial experience of suffering is caused by the community or by bad luck. For a book that enunciates the general structure of the Girardian reading of myth see his *Violence and the Sacred*, trans. Patrick Gregory (Baltimore: The Johns Hopkins University Press, 1977). For an excellent critique of Girard's treatment of the Gospels as the definitive recognition and resolution of the logic of sacrifice see Lucien Scubla, "The Christianity of René Girard and the Nature of Religion" in Paul Dumochel ed., *Violence and Truth* (Stanford: Stanford University Press, 1988), 160-178.

6. Introduced by Michel Foucault and translated by Richard McDougall (New York: Pantheon Books, 1980).

7. Judith Butler, *Gender Trouble: Feminism and the Subversion of Identity* (New York: Routledge, 1990), presents the most compelling analysis of this text with which I am familiar. She introduces the *s/he* and *h/er* terms without commenting on their role in the discourse. Butler's reading of *Herculine Barbin* is exemplary and I am indebted to it. But I do not think that Butler's critique of Foucault is quite so compelling. For I do not read Foucault to attribute to Alex/ina a natural sexuality before the officials tried to reconstitute it. Rather, these "nameless" and "furtive" "pleasures" were socially constituted too; it is just that they were more satisfying for the being constituted by them than the later definitions in that they did not, for instance, suggest suicide as the only line of escape from an impossible life. The general problems posed by the question as to whether one presupposes a conception of "nature" one cannot know to be true are endless; the regresses it generates are infinite. Whatever one says, one appears to constitute a new nature/culture divide ("satisfying," "a being") on a terrain where any such discursive division is always problematical. For the new formulation always draws on the culture (and its grammar) one seeks to dig below. One might say, then: The division is both indispensable and problematical, and every formulation that invokes a specific version of it can be problematized through a subsequent gesture. I doubt very much, anyway, that

this ambiguity can simply be dispensed with. If not, this condition itself opens every text to the charge that it reinstates its version of the division unthinkingly while criticizing its formation by others. (Or that it installs a new version covertly while pretending to dispense with it.) I have earlier considered the role that the introduction of a text such as *Herculine Barbin* might play in genealogy as a mode of social critique in "Where the Word Breaks Off," *Politics and Ambiguity* (Madison, WI: University of Wisconsin Press, 1987), ch 10. The theme there might be summarized in this formulation: "We insist that bodies fit into the duality we impose upon them and act as if we report actuality inscribed in nature. We then treat bodies that differ from these impositions as deviations from the telos of nature" (156).

8. Why do I introduce a possibility I do not endorse to make the point about the constructed character of an identity that has become (always imperfectly) naturalized? Well, partly because I am not writing in this instance about a social position I myself inhabit in a paradigmatic way; I am, rather, striving to open up *responsiveness* to it from an experience containing its own murmurs of dissonance within itself. The "critical pluralism" I will (shortly) endorse as a critical principle is one in which new spaces are produced for alternatives to consolidate themselves and to contest established closures, rather than one in which those outside a particular constituency legislate in advance the form *its* empowerment must take. The point is to expand one's (our) possibilities of responsiveness in some cases while pressing one's (our) own agenda in others. Still, it may be whispered in some circles, "What are you, a 'white,' 'straight,' 'male' 'with tenure,' 'over fifty,' 'teaching at a quasi-elite eastern university,' doing on this terrain anyway?" The reply: "Well, Jack, your question reduces me to a set of prefixed categories, either to reassure you in your own dogmatism of identity or, alternatively, to elevate your radicalism to such a height that no one else can climb up there. If you are a conservative carrier of 'identity politics,' your characterization reduces me to a self-hating male, professor, etc.; if a radical identitarian, to an inauthentic ally. But, you see, these categories do not quite exhaust me, and hence the alternatives you present do not suffice. Either way, you remain too much of a fundamentalist for my taste, and your politics are too self-encased to be very promising. These categories you enunciate, though, do touch me. Since they enter (differentially along with others you 'forget') into my 'subject position,' as it is constituted in this society, they should be taken into account in the way my responsiveness is articulated." My life experience has encouraged me to move from an appreciation of Job to a certain sense of the social constitution of Alex/ina and thus of the social constitution of my own gender experience, whereas others might find this trajectory reversed. It is where these two paths *cross* that interesting political possibilities may reside, that distinctive alliances and coalitions might become constructible. One point of political reflection, as I see it, is to open up possibilities for alliance where primarily identity and difference were experienced before, to pluralize new points of intersection so that the old fixtures of politics become more open to modification. May everyone resist the subject position impressed upon them them by the conservative and radical carriers of identity politics.

9. Judith Butler puts this point succinctly. "Is there a 'physical' body prior to the perceptually perceived body? An impossible question to decide. Not only is the gathering of attributes under the category of sex suspect, but so is the very discrimination of the 'features' themselves." (*Gender Trouble*, 114). I merely add that the introduction of *any* positive political alternative inevitably invokes presumptions at this level. The appropriate response to this ambiguity, I think, is to make the best *comparative* interpretive case available for the Jobian (as in my case) reading of nature and to resist the persisting temptation to elevate that interpretation into an incontestable discovery of the natural condition itself. To keep *this* irony alive, I want to say, is to appreciate the paradoxical element in politics and to enact one precondition of critical pluralism.

10. I have discussed some of the issues posed in this paragraph more extensively in *Identity\Difference*. Others, most significantly the status of an ethic appropriate to these issues in a world where the thematic of a moral order is contested, will come up for discussion in later chapters of this study.

2

Confessing the Moral God

Morality and Monsters

The theme of an intrinsic moral order, as we have seen, precedes and succeeds Augustine. Job's friends were carriers of it; Job himself was ambivalent about this faith; the priests, doctors, and journalists who came into contact with Alex/ina were drawn to such a theme; and Alex/ina iterated a painful version of this doctrine while striving to find space to live within it.

What, more closely, is the idea of an intrinsic moral order? It consists of two broadly defined themes usually connected to each other in a relation of interdependence and tension. The two themes revolve around the word *order*. In the first version, order operates as a verb (to order). An ultimate command is treated as the basis of morality. The command may emanate from a god or a law of nature or a transcendental subject presupposed by every person who acts rationally. Augustine, Hobbes (on some interpretations), and Kant can be thought of as carriers of this first concept of moral order. They differ, of course, among themselves, but they converge in finding the highest basis of morality in a command, in an order emanating from an authoritative source that cannot be superseded.

But the word *order* also functions as a noun. Here it refers to a structure or design that places things in their appropriate place. This concept of intrinsic moral order is not (necessarily) grounded in a command, but in an inherently harmonious design to which things may be predisposed or toward which they tend when they are on the right track. Aristotle (on some readings), Augustine, and Hegel are significant carriers of this second conception of moral order.

Moral order as high command and moral order as intrinsic pattern. I will call a conception a *morality* if it corresponds to one or both of these types, an *ethic* if it strives to inform human conduct without drawing on either as so described. These two thematics of moral order have been dominant in Western history. They enter into relations of interdependence and contention with each other, often jostling one another within the frame of the same doctrine. Proponents of these two conceptions have tended to converge in the conviction that an ethic cannot succeed unless it is a morality in one or both of these senses. The debate between them often operates within the compass of one mind, as it does in Augustine. For Augustine treats his god both as a sovereign in the last instance whose word is to be obeyed because it is his word, and as the source of a design that surpasses human understanding of its highest perfection but is sufficiently available to devout humans to provide them with guidance. Both concepts of moral order interact within Augustine's thought, though when the chips are down the unfathomable god of command is given priority.

Charles Taylor, in his study *Sources of the Self: the Making of the Modern Identity*, delineates effectively a key juncture operating in both concepts of morality. A morality, says Taylor, must draw on "sources" that invest it with meaning, direction, and authoritativeness. Otherwise it stands as a set of arbitrary prescriptions that one can endorse or reject according to whim or preference. So, Taylor contends, every morality invokes or presupposes a fundamental "source" from which it draws. Some moralities are blind to their own deepest insights because they cast a veil of ignorance between the code endorsed and the source from which it draws sustenance. The problem is that every such source turns out to lack the transparency or lucidity many of those inspired by it demand. A moral source, on Taylor's reading, is both indispensable and opaque, operative as an authoritative influence and dark in its implications for conduct. Some neo-Kantians and utilitarians try to escape this ambiguity by denying their dependence on such a source, but, Taylor contends, they eventually either become drawn back into its orbit as they encounter the deepest questions of moral complexity or they remain blind to the sources they themselves draw on. Augustine concurs on these points.

Taylor characterizes a source as an ambiguous ground that precedes human articulation of it but is always moved or altered by the terms through which it is articulated. We can never get it exactly as it was before we articulate it. Our relation to sources is similar to the relation we establish to the practice of an alien culture when we interpret it: The reading that makes it available to us does so in relation to contrasts and distinctions in our culture inoperative in its life-world; hence, although it may change us, we never read it exactly as it was before we drew it into the network of meanings through which we can make sense of it. This combination of an indispensable ground and its unavoidable alteration through translation constitutes the fugitive character of a moral source. Taylor says, "We sense in the very experience of being moved by some higher good that we are moved by what is good in it rather than that it is valuable because of our reaction." But this "sense" is problematical and always susceptible to further debate. Why make the effort? "Moral sources empower. To come closer to them . . . is for those who recognize them to be moved to love or respect them. . . . And articulation can bring them closer. That is why words can empower; why words can at times have tremendous moral force."[1] Moral sources "empower," a word that may carry more ambiguous freight than Taylor intends, floating, as it does, between empowerment of one's deepest intuitions and empowerment of discursive formations drawn into one's identity through articulation.

Moral sources move you, then. But they are problematical because no articulation does or could delineate its source exactly as it was before articulation. Taylor responds to this ambiguity by commending a strategy for drawing closer to the source and further from social distortions of it. "The most reliable moral view is not one that would be grounded quite outside our intuitions but one that is grounded on our strongest intuitions, where these have successfully met the challenge of proposed transitions away from them."[2]

A responsible moral perspective, on this reading, is necessarily interpretive. It cannot encounter the source it draws on without mediation, that is, without taking the form of an interpretation of experience, but the interpretation that gives it specific direction always draws on intuitions that might be revised after an encounter with unexpected experience or new possibilities of interpretation. Taylor's faith is that those intuitions that withstand the give and take of interpretive contestation are the most reliable. These are "the strongest intuitions." I would modify or problematize this faith more radically than Taylor has done. The engagement with Job and Alex/ina provides the first step in that process. For in each case the considered intuitions of an entire community can be seen, from another perspective, to oppress these two members—and a much larger group consituted as moral or sexual strangers by the same cultural logic—in the process of securing and consolidating its considered intuitions. And the sources these dissidents might draw on to contest the hegemony of each community are themselves contestable in some fundamental way. But I would also endorse some dimensions in Taylor's presentation of moral sources. If he said to me, as he might, "Your very delineation of these two cases modifies our intuitions and thereby gives a new status to alternative intuitions," I would reply that these modified intuitions enter into contestation with counter-intuitions that exert a powerful hold over the culture, and they draw on a fugitive source that remains a mere whisper in this culture. We would probably concur on the probability of contestability in those judgments; and we would probably diverge (but to what degree?) in our confidence over the extent to which these divergencies can be settled definitively.

Perhaps the basis of the difference is this. Although Taylor eventually concedes that Nietzsche may have access to a "moral source" structurally similar to the one Taylor admires the most, he finds it to be even more problematic, fugitive, and paradoxical than the more familiar sources in Western history. He finds the sources Nietzsche draws on to exceed intuitions that have earned the highest admiration in "our" culture. Let us call Nietzsche's source *life*, a set of fugitive energies and possibilities that exceed any particular identity, an abundance of possibilities that is neither a being, a principle, nor a design and that is never exhausted by the terms of any identity or community. Nietzsche is a modern Jobian, as I read the theophany in *Job*. I want to contend that this putative "source" is neither more nor less paradoxical than those (more familiar) moral sources that take the form of a god, a transcendental command, or an intrinsic design. And, eventually, I will contend that interpretations drawing on this source are more ethical than those that rest upon traditional sources of command and design. To mark off this difference and territory of debate, I will call a *moral source* one that offers a (putative) command or design from which interpretation and judgment can proceed, and an *ethical source* one that draws its interpretive inspiration from a nontheistic, nonteleological source such as "will to power" or "life" or *"différance"* or "untruth." This latter tradition of ethical discourse operates as a counter both to the Kantian/ utilitarian traditions Taylor criticizes and to the Augustinian tradition Taylor himself modifies. Bearers of the ethical tradition (we might include Job, Montaigne, Henry Thoreau, William James, Michel Foucault, Nietzsche, Gilles Deleuze, Judith Butler, and myself in this encampment) tend to find the moral conception of the world to contain unethical tendencies and implications, while bearers of the moral tradition (we might include Aristotle, Augustine, Kant, Hegel, Alex/ina, Carol Gilligan, and Charles Taylor in this camp) tend to find such an ethic to be immoral. Matters are complicated here because, first, each of the prominent names on these lists (and the variations along this dimension are of course extremely sharp) is susceptible to multiple, contending interpretations, and because, second, there are subordinate voices in several of these thinkers that, according to my reading of them, cross the line I have just drawn. We have already seen, for instance, how Job might cross this line from one side and Alex/ina from the other. The line itself is too stark to sustain itself indefinitely in this form. But it may provide a basis from which to begin.

Augustine is an exemplary carrier of the theme of intrinsic moral order. He straddles both determinations of *order* (as command and design); he reads history and myth through the lens of this conception; he offers authoritative prescriptions on the basis of these readings, and he strives to maintain congruence between both dimensions within this conception of moral order. Augustine himself both inspires a conception of moral order still exerting a powerful influence over modern life and exemplifies the attractions and difficulties such a conception runs into. A Christian god is the single moral source for Augustine. This god is both a commander and a designer. We receive the god's *commands* through scripture. But since these words are clouded by translation from the god to humans and from humans in one culture to those in others, these commands have to be subjected to interpretation. We receive glimpses of its *design* through scripture and through a common experience of harmonies in the world (within the self and outside the self). But since the overall design is beyond human powers of comprehension, we are limited in our attempts to fathom its character. When these two re-sources are combined, however, Augustine is confident they suffice to give us excellent guidance how to think and behave on earth.

Let us introduce Augustine's conception of intrinsic moral order through his presentation of "monstrosities," for this is the territory that brings him into most direct contact with the experiences of Alex/ina and Job. Pagan history, Augustine says, records a series of monstrosities. Some of these monsters may be figments of fevered imaginations, but others are credible and have been observed by Christians as well.

> Some of those monsters are said to have only one eye, in the middle of their forehead; others have the soles of their feet turned backwards behind their legs; others have the characteristics of both sexes, the right breast being male and the left female, and in their intercourse they alternate between begetting and conceiving. Then there are men . . . whose height is only a cubit—the Greeks call them "Pygmies," from their word for a cubit.[3]

Augustine draws on both divine command and signs of the divine design of things to define and respond to monstrosities. First, it is a command of his god, recorded in scripture, to remember that every human is born of that first human. "But no faithful Christian should doubt that anyone who is born anywhere as a man—that is, a rational and mortal being—derives from that one first-created human being. And this is true, however extraordinary such a creature may appear to our senses."[4]

The first reason to construe monsters as human, then, is that the scripture says all of us are derived from the same human. But what makes the *hermaphrodite*, for instance, a *monstrous* human at all? Our common experience registers "the norm of nature in the majority"; and that necessarily constitutes deviants from the norm as monsters. But why would a good, omnipotent god allow monsters to appear? Here Augustine turns to the divine design of nature and the element of mystery in it.

> God is the creator of all, and he himself knows where and when any creature should be created. . . . He has the wisdom to weave the beauty of the whole design out of the constituent parts, in their likeness and diversity. The observer who cannot view the whole is offended by what seems the deformity of the part, since he does not know it fits in, or how it is related to the rest.[5]

The Augustinian conception of an intrinsic design to which we can become more closely attuned but that transcends our limited capacities for full understanding shines forth in these sentences. The theme of inscrutable purpose is invoked to deal with the difficulty monstrous humans pose to the idea of an intrinsic design, while the beauty and regularity of nature is otherwise invoked to illustrate the outlines of the design. These two themes are drawn together through the faith that even those monstrosities that appear to break the design are somehow pertinent to "the beauty of the whole design."

Augustine admits difficulty in classifying those humans whose sexual characteristics confound the dictates of gender duality. He comes down, though, on the side of "prevalent usage," which "has called them masculine, assigning them to the superior sex; for no one has ever used the feminine names, *androgynaecae* or *hermaphroditae*."[6] The rationale for going with "the superior sex" is that this judgment conforms to long and common usage (to "considered intuitions"). Those who impute an intrinsic order to the world generally operate with a presumption in favor of long tradition, for their very conception of an intrinsic order to which humans can become more closely attuned over time leads them to expect that the accumulation of time brings "the tried and the true" into more refined correspondence.

Augustine's concept of intrinsic morality leads him to treat the "hermaphrodite" with a semblance of kindness because it is a creature and because its apparent defectiveness plays an inscrutable role in a larger design. The hermaphrodite is somehow useful to this higher design, even if the culture must impose incredible cruelty on it while it serves its unfathomable cosmic function. But the theme of intrinsic morality also encourages Augustine to treat "the majority" type as the norm of nature and, thereby, to constitute "the exception" as monstrous. Augustine, then, is kindly to monsters. But not kindly enough to reconsider the cultural pressures through which they are constituted as monsters. Augustine's conception of intrinsic order does not encourage him to ponder the way the culture he celebrates may create a set of abnormalities to constitute another set of normalities. His imagination of other possible organizations of cultural life is not rich enough to include one in which a larger plurality of differences and rivalries in this domain makes it unnecessary to define one subset as monstrous. From within Augustine's perspective, this sounds like a morally sensitive way to respect the intrinsic design while dealing with the occasional appearance of those who appear to deviate from the intrinsic norm of nature. From outside Augustine's perspective, this appears as a compromise device to preserve the conception of divinity he endorses at the expense of those whose formation differs from his projection of order. The latter judgment is supported by the way Augustine, turning from a discussion of individual deviations to pagan reports of entire deviant races, closes the issue: "I must therefore finish the discussion of this question with my tentative and cautious answer. The accounts of these races may be completely worthless; but if such peoples exist, then either they are not human; or if human, they are descended from Adam."[7]

That closing sentence may appear to those moving within the orbit of Augustine's faith—even to those who share a more general conception of intrinsic moral order with him—to provide the indispensable means by which Augustine defends the idea of an intrinsic source upon which moral judgment is necessarily grounded. To those who contest the faith animating Augustinian morality, though, it appears that Augustine is governed more by a concern to protect the divine guarantee of his morality than with care for those whose lives are negated by the divine recipe. Augustine's concern to vindicate the moral god produces unethical results. He is cautious about whether "pagan" reports are reliable, but he is incautious about the conception of intrinsic morality within which his constitution/appraisal of deviations is set.

Both the supportive and critical readings of Augustinian morality flow from the same source. For it is because we have all descended from Adam that the Augustinian owes a modicum of respect to all humans, regardless of type. But it is also because the creator who en-gendered this descent filled the world with an intrinsic design that a set of humans are defined as monsters. Things get worse when you encounter those who make themselves monstrous through their own sins.

Why must the creator invest the world with an intrinsic design? Because it is both omnipotent and good. Why *must* it possess both of these latter attributes? We shall keep this question before us as we follow the royal road to moral illumination in the Augustinian universe: The road that takes us into the interior of the self by way of the confessional imperative.

At any rate, we now have a preliminary picture of how the two dimensions of order function in Augustinian morality. Augustine looks for a pattern, a design, a norm, a purpose written into experience. Once locating it in the norm of the majority, he considers deviations from it as signs of mystery in the intrinsic design. But how to respond to these deviations? Here he tends to give priority to the command side of the moral equation. For the human experience of the design of being is limited both by human finitude and the effects of previous human sinfulness on the world. "For in truth society itself, which must obtain between God and us, is violated when the nature of which he is the author is polluted by a perverted lust." This introduces a new element of division and disharmony into the unfathomable design, even if, somehow, Augustine's god will deploy these latter perversities as well for good purposes. But the human ability to read the harmonies is now doubly clouded. A more direct order (as verb) is needed to trump the implicit order (as noun) revealed through experience. So "when God commands something contrary to the customs of a people, it must be done, even if it has never been done before . . . —for if it is a general law of human society for men to obey their rulers—how much more must God, ruler of all creation, be obeyed without hesitation in what-ever he imposes upon it!"[8] God as commander operates within both of the dimensions of moral order. Traces of the verb form inhabit the noun form from the start. It is the divine design we *obey* when we discern it, and the command dimension becomes more blunt and "direct" when a divine order is issued to close the gap between human recognition of the design and its unfathomability. It is precisely this *excess*—this "unfathomability"—of the divine design over human capacities to recognize it that invests divine commands with unquestionable authority. In the Augustinian moral economy, as we shall see in greater detail later, invocations of divine mystery function, first, to protect the core elements of Augustinian theology from falsification and, second, to invest divinity with an authority that exceeds the human capacity to comprehend its rationale.

In the Augustinian conception, morality is grounded in an unstable relation between the order of god and orders issued by god. These two registers combine to place us in the best possible relation—that is, a limited, imperfect relation—to the order of being.

The Confessing Self

The royal road to morality is also the rocky road to salvation. The route takes you through the interior of the self to a closer relation to god, the fundamental source of creation, morality, and salvation. The vehicle capable of carrying you along this route is confession. Through confession you call on him by calling into yourself. Confession serves as a vehicle of purification and moralization.

Words, for Augustine, provide the fuel of confession. Words do not simply represent a world of determinate things. Nor do they simply create (or constitute) things according to the dictates of cultural convention. Neither of these conceptions of language suffices for Augustine. Words do move life and constitute identities. But they do so either in accord with the divine source from which they draw or in opposition to it. Words, strained through the soul of those who speak them and hear them, can be media of perversion or of conversion. The first sort draw you away from god, as when hearing or speaking erotically charged words in the company of another man's wife induces illicit sexual excitement. The second sort draw you toward divinity, as when you read scripture aloud in the spirit of devotion at the right time. Divine words inscribed in scripture, when they are confessed to the one true god, are the most powerful media of conversion, healing, and moralization available to humanity. They turn one in the right direction. These words are media through which a change of heart occurs.

So Augustine's confessions to his god are replete with quotations from scripture folded into the flow of confession. Allowing these words to move through him at the right time in the right way contributes to the conversion he seeks. *The Confessions* would be half as long if all the scriptural quotations were excised from it. They wouldn't support the conversion effect Augustine seeks either.

> Therefore . . . you procured for me certain books of the Platonists that had been translated out of Greek into Latin. In them I read, not indeed in these words but much the same thought . . . that "In the beginning was the Word, and the Word was with God. All things were made by him, and without him nothing was made. What was made, in him is life, and the life was the light of men. . . ."[9]

Augustine, ashamed of his previous pride for being the best student in a pagan course on rhetoric, remains mesmerized by the power of words to move the soul long after his conversion has been consummated. Words change you as they move through you, turning you in one direction or the other: They help you to turn to god (*convertere*) or to turn away from god (*pervertere*), though only god's grace can complete the turn to him. Words are the medium through which god creates and through which it moves humanity. They are, above all, the medium through which humans are repaired through confession, when they say back in the spirit of timely confession to the god what it previously said to them.

What is it to speak in the spirit of confession? It is to acknowledge your subordination to a higher source while admitting that you have not consistently done so in the past. It is to turn your future self in the right direction by humbly admitting defects in your previous self. It is to *give voice to* defects in the self because you admit that no finite, embodied being could be without them. It is to open yourself to conversion through admission. Confession is the medium of conversion; and conversion is the goal of life.

Does the persistent, devout practice of confession draw Augustine closer to the source he loves? Or does it produce the god he worships while engendering a self prepared to kneel before this production? The divine source as discovery or as projection. Both readings are compatible with the effectivity and ambiguity of words, that is, first, with the power of words to move one and, second, with the opacity that surrounds the relation between words and the fugitive sources they draw on. The first reading construes Augustine to serve a divinity that towers above him; the second construes him to project himself into a fictive divinity and then to represent the fiction as an 'order' he counsels himself and others to obey. The first presents Augustine as a humble servant; the second as a sly or self-deceptive master whose will to power over others is advanced through the illusion of subservience.

Listen to Augustine confess to the god he represents to us and represent to us the god to whom he confesses:

> What you take vengeance on is what men inflict on themselves, for even when they sin against you, they do evil to their own souls. Man's iniquity lies to itself, whether by corrupting and perverting their own nature, which you have made and set in order, or by immoderate use of things permitted to men, or . . . by a burning lust for that use which is contrary to nature. . . . Such things are done, when you are forsaken, O fountain of life, who are the sole and true creator and ruler of the universe. . . . Therefore by humble devotion return is made to you, and you cleanse us from evil ways, and are merciful to those who confess to you and graciously hear the groans of those shackled by sin, and you free them from the chains that we have made for ourselves.[10]

A set of imperatives humbly articulated within a confessional mode: "Man's iniquity lies to itself"; a nature "you have . . . set in order"; "a burning lust . . . contrary to nature"; "you cleanse us from evil ways"; you are "merciful to those who confess to you"; and so on. Augustine *defines* his god through confessing to it. The arrogance of the persistent drive to define is shielded by the humility with which blame for deviation from these definitions of divinity is attributed to humans. From within Augustine's faith this sounds like a contrite confession to god of its own power, sovereignty, goodness, and grace set within an appreciation of the role that contrite confession plays in drawing the faithful closer to this god. From a position outside Augustinian faith, these same words sound like the cultural production of a divinity by the persistent confession of the specific attributes it must have. On this latter reading the humble confessor emerges as the wily creator of the one fiction he is willing to bow before. "You must be what I iterate and reiterate you to be, my fountain of life, because this is what I demand. You must be omnipotent, beneficent, untouched by evil—above all, responsive to devout confessions made to you. You must be. For by humble devotion return is made to you, and you cleanse us from evil ways and are merciful to those who confess to you . . . " The will to command can be heard inside the groans of confession. And vice versa. The difference between insistent constitution through confession and loving devotion through confession now becomes slippery and controversial, unless you have a prior base from which to proceed in dividing them. But the very idea of a confessional faith is that such a basis remains insecure until a more intimate relation to the source has been achieved . . . through confession. The very structure of a confession—involving as it does these slippery relations between words, sources, and effects—engenders the ambiguity of its status while it diverts attention away from this ambiguity among those who pursue it most devoutly. Perhaps monsters hear this ambiguity?

In both of the above readings words produce effects on faith and identity. So, I reiterate (repetition is a favorite tactic of Augustine's): Does Augustine confess to a source with those attributes or confess these attributes into the source? Is Augustinian confession a practice of transcendental humility or transcendental narcissism? If this question is appropriate to Augustine, it is pertinent to every moral/ethical perspective, including those theistic and nontheistic alternatives you or I may endorse. And, I confess (or do I insist?), this thins out the ice upon which we slip and slide together.

The trajectory of Augustine's confessions proceeds from an adolescence of perversion to a dramatic moment of conversion. He advances by turning away from his earlier perversion and toward conversion. By confessing the perversity of his past Augustine prepares himself for conversion, and by continuing to confess after conversion he prepares himself to continue to receive grace from the divine source. For in Augustine's system you are either moving away from the source by the force of your own action or being drawn toward it through its grace. There is no neutral or indifferent space in which thought and action escapes divisibility into the pair perversion/conversion.

The paradigm act of perversity occurs when Augustine steals pears with a group of teenage friends. It must be confessed years later, for this act recapitulates the original sin of Adam. The fruit was not taken out of need. They were not starving. The young boys threw away most of the fruit after a bite or two while dancing along joyously amidst delight in their perversity. So what, Augustine asks his lord, was "in that theft to give me delight"? How, more pointedly, does this insignificant act disclose the essence of perversity? It was an act of pure rebellion against divinity, which by insisting on the right to do anything simply because of the pleasure in doing it, expressed a perverse drive to omnipotence. It parallels that first, fateful act of Adam's, in which *disobedience* to the divine will was so sinful because it was so easy to do otherwise.

> Thus the soul commits fornication when it is turned away from you and, apart from you, seeks such pure clean things as it does not find except when it returns to you. In a perverse way, all men imitate you who put themselves far from you and rise up in rebellion against you. . . . What therefore did I love in that theft of mine, in what manner did I perversely or viciously imitate my Lord? Did it please me that as a captive I should imitate a deformed liberty, by doing with impunity things illicit bearing a shadowy likeness of your omnipotence? . . . O rottenness! O monstrous life and deepest death! Could a thing give pleasure which could not be done lawfully, and which was done for no other reasons but because it was unlawful?[11]

"Turned away," "returns to you," "perverse way," "put themselves far from you," "against you," "perversely imitate"—these phrases sprinkle the logic of *pervertere* and *convertere* throughout the formulation. They are joined to the language of power: Power that is perverse, deformed, rebellious, imitative, and rotten when exercised by humans alone; power that is pure, clean, and omnipotent when exercised by Augustine's god. Why is there *nothing* of discernible value in this youthful burst of anarchic energy? One might suggest, for instance, that in testing the existing boundaries of the law it discloses something about the ambiguity of law, and that, once these transgressive energies are refined and tempered, they might help to generate more effective space for singularity, diversity, and spirited contestation in life. Subversive energies, it might be argued, are ambiguous goods in cultural life because powerful tendencies toward dogmatism of faith and identity need to be disturbed, disrupted, and contested to create space for singularity and diversity.

Convert/ pervert/ subvert/ invert/ divert. Augustine's *vertere* logic is bimodal just where it should be polymodal. Just where it should stretch the logic of good and evil.

The act, though, is defined by Augustine to be an imitation of omnipotence. And hence it is a pure act of impurity, that is, perversion, because it pretends that human beings can participate in this singular divine attribute. Only this god is omnipotent. Augustine subtracts omnipotence from humanity only to bestow it upon his god. *But why must omnipotence be located anywhere?* Is the insistence that omnipotence be located somewhere itself perverse? What relation to power does the creator of this god maintain in confessing it to have absolute power?

Augustine's official reason for investing his god with omnipotence is that it must be perfect, and perfection includes within it absolute power. But why must this god be perfect (there are plenty of faiths that forfeit this demand)? And why must perfection include omnipotence? I think there is another line of insistence operating inside the confession of divine omnipotence and the corollary confession of perversity as the pale imitation of omnipotence. The case on behalf of this perverse interpretation will be supported by showing how it makes sense of other imperatives within the Augustinian doctrine. I will introduce it here and pursue it later.

In *City of God*, while criticizing "pagan" conceptions of divinity, Augustine notes their most fundamental defect. "Are men such fools as to think in their hearts that the worship of these gods can be of advantage for eternal life?" And again: "In spite of their having no connection with the true God or with eternal life (which is the essential aim in religion), they might have allowed some kind of explanation relating to the natural order."[12] The key defect in the multiple, limited, disputing pagan gods is that they did not have enough power, separately or in combination, to hold out the realistic prospect of eternal salvation to humans, a prospect "which is the essential aim in religion." Augustine endows his god with omnipotence to enable it to deliver on the promise of salvation. He endows it with care for humanity to make it want to do so. When these three demands are combined (omnipotence, care, and salvation), you generate a god who must be the author of an intrinsic moral order and you have a moral order under powerful pressure to constitute itself restrictively and coercively.

Not only pagans are found wanting in this regard. An examination of the major heresies invented by Augustine and his friends within the rubric of Christian monotheism will show, I think, that the major defect in each flows from the way each inadvertently throws the very possibility of salvation into supreme doubt. Is the Augustinian confessional driven by a covert drive to human power, that is, by a drive to defeat the bird of death through the authoritative constitution of a salvational god? What are the earthly effects of this demand to invest omnipotence in the divinity one confesses into being? We will return to this question later.

As Augustine confesses his progress from perversion to conversion he also professes the mysteries of desire, will, memory, and time. These form compelling and enduring moments in the text, both for those who enter empathetically into the confessional quest for a true identity lurking within the interior of the self and for those who find such a quest to be destructive. These explorations unearth phenomenological material every modern theorist of subjectivity and morality must respond to somehow, some in the interests of reconsidering the Augustinian conception of will still exerting effects on modern life and others in the interests of shoring up this same conception. Let us consider, then, his confessions of memory and will, taking memory first to enable it to set a model for the more complex exploration of will.

Memory is both slippery and fundamental to human identity. Sometimes I will to remember something and the recollection appears readily. At other times I fail to remember despite my best efforts. But then someone else pronounces the name or recalls the event, and immediately I too recall it. Since I now recognize the name or event, rather than learning it for the first time, it must have been in my memory bank all along. The memory was lurking deep inside the chamber of memory, but it remained unresponsive to my will to recall it. At still other times a memory comes when I do not will it to do so. It appears as if of its own accord to delight or shame me, to fill me with joy or to strike me with a sharp sense of remorse. Without memory I would not be a unified self acting in time. "I" would be a series of disconnected passions and deeds, with no cumulative narrative drawing me into a unity with a past, present, and future. But as I contemplate this mysterious fund of remembrances "I" begin to sense how deep the recesses of my soul reach, how much of myself is opaque to me, how much of me stretches beyond the control of my self.

> Great is the power of memory, exceeding great is it, O God, an inner chamber, vast and unbounded! Who has penetrated to its bottom? Yet it is a power of my mind and belongs to my nature, and thus I do not comprehend all that I am. Is the mind, therefore, too limited to possess itself? Must we ask: "Where is this power belonging to it which it does not grasp? Is it outside it and not within it?" Great wonder arises within me. Men go forth to marvel at the mountain heights, at huge waves in the sea, at the broad expanse of flowing rivers, at the wide reach of the ocean, and at the circuits of the stars, but themselves they pass by.[13]

To the Jobian mystery of uncanny forces in nature and the Alex/inian mystery of dissonances within gender formations Augustine adds the mystery of the unbounded, inner chamber of memory. His exploration calls into question every theory based on the presumption of transparency and self-control of the self. Augustine treats this discovery of the unbounded self as a revelation of dependence of the self on a higher will. "Lord," confesses Augustine, "I truly labor at this task, and I labor upon myself. I have become for myself a soil to work and demanding much sweat. . . . Consider: the power of my own memory is not understood by me, and yet apart from it I cannot even name myself."[14]

Augustine confesses that he changes himself by laboring on himself, though he also confesses that the credit for those changes that draw him toward conversion must be given to his god, who is the author of *everything* good. He also converts this revelation of the dependence of memory on something beyond the will into a sign of the necessity of his god. This comes out in his exploration of the memory of happiness.

We seem to know something about pure happiness, but no humans after Adam have experienced it. Perhaps traces of the happiness of the first man are lodged deep in the recesses of memory. Adam possessed free will and happiness until he sinned. And we must remember that period of happiness even while we yearn to restore it. Otherwise it is difficult to understand how we could love something completely opaque to us. "Consider this knowledge. I am perplexed as to whether it is a memory, for if it is then all of us have already been happy at some period, either each of us individually, or all of us together in that man who first sinned, in whom we all died, and from whom we are all born in misery. Of this I do not now inquire, but I inquire whether the happy life is in the memory. . . . Unless we knew it we could not love it."[15]

Augustine proceeds through an exploration of memory to an appreciation of human dependence on forces not fully within their control, to the dim memory of happiness, to the claim that the memory of Adam's happiness lurks within each of us. This last move links us to Adam and to his first, original sin. Hence, the very mystery and dependence of memory links us precariously and imperfectly to Augustine's god. "Behold, how far within my memory I have travelled in search of you, Lord, and beyond it I have not found you."[16]

Why must the mystery of memory link you to Augustine's god? Because the god's omnipotence makes it the independent source of everything that is dependent. Why does labor on memory make you aware of dependence on a higher source while surrounding the source with mystery? Because the omnipotence of this god ensures that much about it will be mysterious to those whose powers are finite. Why must divine omnipotence be invoked so authoritatively when so much else about the god is mysterious? Why, then, such a highly selective deployment of mystery? These questions return us to the connection between the Augustinian attribution of divine omnipotence and the Augustinian quest for salvation. Is it possible to appreciate the mystery of memory without taking much of this appreciation and this mystery back through the insistent presumption of omnipotent divinity? Job seems to entertain this possibility. So does Nietzsche.

Augustine confidently confesses knowledge of a host of this god's attributes even while confessing its unfathomability. Listen to another confession of faith:

> Yet in none of those wavering thoughts [about the origin of evil] did you let me be carried away from the faith in which I believed both that [1] you exist, and that [2] your substance is unchangeable, and that [3] you have care over men and [4] pass judgment on them, and [5] that in Christ, your son, our Lord, and in [6] the Holy Scriptures, [7] which the authority of your Catholic church approves, [8] you have placed the way of man's salvation unto life which is to be after this death.[17]

These points of faith, plus a definite commitment to omnipotence (9) added later as he grapples with the problem of evil, form a fixed context of certainties within which the mysteries of Augustine's god are set. Note how these insistences are recorded in the passive voice, diverting the critical mind from interrogating the relation between confession and production.

These articles of faith are not presented as things Augustine projects hopefully and contestably, but as insights into the true character of divinity confirmed through confession: "In none of those wavering thoughts did you let me be carried away from the faith." Is mystery humbly invoked to confess the unfathomability of this god or strategically deployed to protect crucial elements of faith whenever relations among them become too contradictory or paradoxical? Does the selectivity of mystery and the passive mode of its invocation reflect a humble tactic of earthly power? Is Augustine so knowledgeable about this unfathomable god in the areas that count the most to him because he is in the best possible position to know the essence of the being he has created? However one responds to these questions, the Augustinian account of memory will remain important.

As Augustine confesses the sins of his past and the problem of evil he is moved to ponder the character of human will. The confession here parallels the confession of memory. Augustine finds that he has done things he did not will and has willed things he did not do. This leads him to suspect that the source of evil and human suffering resides deeply within the will itself, in the very structure of human will and desire.

Why should it be? Mind commands body, and it obeys forthwith. Mind gives orders to itself, and it is resisted. Mind gives orders for the hand to move, and so easy is it that command can scarcely be distinguished from execution. Yet mind is mind, while hand is body. Mind commands mind to will: there is no difference here, but it does not do so. Whence comes this monstrous state? Why should it be?[18]

Augustine is not worried about the mind/body problem that has perplexed Western thought at least since a mechanistic conception of nature became popular in the 17th century. This is not a Cartesian question about how the mind interacts with the body. For that relation is pretty reliable: "Mind gives orders for the hand to move, and . . . command can scarcely be distinguished from execution." Augustine is concerned about a mind/mind problem, about a perplexity or dissonance interior to the will itself. You will not to invite your attractive friend for a late drink, but the words crawl out of your mouth anyway. Augustine wills to be continent, but he is incontinent. He wills not to doubt his god but doubts flood forth in the questions he poses. His friend, Alypius, wills to forgo the violent blood of the circus, but under the prodding of friends he sinks into it again. The question is not whether those acts are okay despite the values of those who resist them, but why one does the thing one wills not to do once one has willed not to do it.

The answer, for Augustine, is not that the body overwhelms the will or that the will is in combat with dark forces that sometimes overmatch it. The first answer would take him too close to Platonic paganism and the second too close to the heresy of Manicheanism. The source of the conflict must therefore be a division *within* the will itself.

> It does not will it in its entirety: for this reason it does not give this command in its entirety. For it commands a thing only in so far as it wills it, and in so far as what it commands is not done, to that extent it does not will it. . . . But the complete will does not give the command and therefore what it commands is not in being.[19]

Note that although we have now moved to the interior structure of the will itself to respond to this issue, the Augustinian conception of the will is not well stated in the modern Kantian problematic of autonomy/heteronomy. In the latter problematic a heteronomic will is one dependent on an external force of whatever type, whereas an autonomous will is self-dependent.[20] Augustine confesses, however, that it is the very rebellious attempt by the willful will to be self-sufficient that fosters its internal divisions and dissonances. A free will is not an autonomous will, at least not a will without dependence on Augustine's god. A free will is one converted from internal dissonance, division, uncertainty, and self-contradiction to unity, consistency, harmony and healing.

A "complete will" cannot arise of its own accord. Thinking that it can forms part of the perverse human fantasy of self-omnipotence. A divided will is an incomplete will that strives to be self-sufficient. "Therefore it is no monstrous thing partly to will a thing and partly not to will it, but it is a sickness in the mind. . . . There are two wills, since one of them is not complete, and what is lacking in one of them is present in the other."[21] The unfree will is divided into two wills that struggle with each other in the same self.

Given the human formation of obstinate habits—those obdurate dispositions congealed out of one's previous history of willing—the open wound in the will can be healed only by the conjunction of confession that labors on the self and the receipt of god's grace. Grace is essential to a healed will. The will approaches freedom when it is healed by grace, partly because it now confesses that it is unable to unify itself by its own resources alone. "I was so foolish," before conversion, "that I did not know that, as it is written, no man can be continent unless you grant it to him."[22]

So the will is mine but I am not in control of it. Although it can will evil alone (as we shall see), it cannot will the good alone. My will is my own but it becomes healed only through confession of its dependence on a higher source and from the undeserved receipt of grace from that source. Once again, Augustine goes into himself through confession and then through himself to a closer awareness of his dependence on his god. He emerges with a doctrine in which the free will is the healed will and the healed will is the will infused with grace. A free will, that is, is an obedient will.

Even those who diverge from Augustine's response to the division he encounters may be touched by his account of the issue. It seems to me, for instance, that Hannah Arendt, René Girard, Friedrich Nietzsche, and Sigmund Freud all follow Augustine part way down this path, identifying persistent dissonances at approximately the juncture he demarcates as the "divided will." All of them find action to be infused by sources that extend beyond the scope of consciousness or intention. All, too, find modern conceptions of "free will" to be insufficient to experience. And all search for "supplements" through which to convert these dissonances into productive energies. But then each responds to this general issue in a distinctive way.

Nietzsche, for instance, locates the supplement needed not in obedience to the will of a god, but in a series of tactics the self applies to itself to make itself into a more singular and less vengeful piece of craftsmanship.[23] He appreciates the indispensable role habit plays in life and finds a certain "sickness" haunting the life of the human animal. Nietzsche's response to the condition he defines is sharply opposed to the Augustinian doctrines of divided will and grace. But Nietzsche remains sufficiently attentive to the power of Augustinianism over the cultural unconscious to recognize that some alternative supplement must be introduced into the cultural equation if the doctrines of will and grace, or their functional equivalents, are not to win by default. The Augustinian doctrines of divided will and grace provide an account of dissonance in the human condition that must be responded to actively by a perspective seeking to challenge a legacy of presumptions still operative in the culture. That is part of the value of Augustinian theory to its opponents. Even as adamant an adversary of Augustinian inwardness and divine dependence as Nietzsche, then, profits from Augustine's drive down the royal road of confession to the interior of the self.

The Monician Conversion

Once Augustine has confessed the division within his will, he has been turned toward his god sufficiently to open up the possibility of conversion. He now understands the imperative to receive another will into his own to heal it. Now he needs only to receive the gift if his god is indeed willing to offer it. A conversion event is needed. The conversion itself takes the form of a triangle marked at one corner by a dramatic engagement with "stains and sores" covering his soul, at another corner by a struggle to accept the demise of those pleasures of the flesh required to heal his will, and at the apex by the receipt of a fateful message delivered at just the right moment. While Augustine is weeping, "in a most bitter condition," he hears a voice "like that of a boy or girl, I know not which, chanting and repeating over and over 'Take up and read. Take up and read.' " He interprets this to be "a command given to me by God to open the book and read the first chapter I should come upon." And so Augustine rushes back to his open Bible, reading, " 'Not in rioting and drunkenness, not in chambering and impurities, not in strife and envying; but put you on the Lord Jesus Christ, and make not provision for the flesh in its concupiscences.' "[24]

That is enough. "Instantly, in truth, at the end of this sentence, as if before a peaceful light streaming into my heart, all the dark shadows of doubt fled away."[25] The magic of words, again: The receipt of the timely words of a child; the words of Scripture read at just the right moment; the effect of Augustine's words on Alypius, spoken inadvertently at just the right time; the power of Augustine's confessions to move the reader. Words, spoken and heard in a spirit of devotion, are the medium through which moral awakening occurs.

A moment later Alypius, his close friend, joins him, and they are converted together. Augustine's will is healed. He becomes more free through an act of grace that draws his will into a closer obedience to his god. Augustine's will is not completely healed, of course. It is healed sufficiently so that we hear little after the conversion about new sins of the flesh, only about new encounters with paradoxes and mysteries of time, eternity, the relation of form to matter, and the creation of the world. The confession of mysteries that show the converted Augustine to remain a finite, limited being in relation to the infinite god who has healed his most grievous wounds.

Every ethical perspective includes somewhere in its compass the theme of a conversion or an awakening or a change of heart or an advance in self-consciousness or a therapeutic advance or a heightened clarity of reason or a new sense of belonging to a community or an intensification of freedom or the dramatic enactment of one's true self. Every ethical perspective, then, invokes a conversion effect in which your perceptions, identity, faith, and judgment are elevated after this awakening. Consider a counter-perspective. Nietzsche's Zarathustra, in his early, naive stage, strives to "awaken" directly those within range of his voice. "Let your will say: the overman *shall be* the meaning of the earth! I beseech you, my brothers, *remain faithful to the earth*, and do not believe those who speak to you of otherworldly hopes! Poison mixers are they. . . . Despisers of life are they . . . , of whom the earth is weary: so let them go."[26] Here Zarathustra opposes identification with a Christian god and its heaven to identification with "the rich ambiguity of life" and "the earth." You turn away from the poisonous demands of eternal salvation and toward the abundance of life. An awakening or conversion is sought. Later, a chastened Zarathustra delivers his message less directly, but the theme of a new awakening never disappears from his prose.

The issue, then, is not whether but how a conversion is effected, what authority relations it inaugurates, what relations it establishes between its identity and the differences it constitutes to solidify itself, and what punishments it holds out to those who oppose or resist its advances.

Conversion is not in need of examination because its effectivity is doubtful, though "backsliding" is a common feature of every faith. It is to be examined because the experience, in one form or another, is so widespread, and because the conversion event is so readily susceptible, when the conditions are right, to colonization by many and diverse orientations to life.

The dilemma of conversion may be this: After the process through which you are converted, you now interpret your past and future through a new set of sensibilities; but you still lack an independent vantage point from which to appraise whether this new effect controls the perspective through which you experience or reflects a new truth opened by it.

We will consider the Augustinian conversion by considering how Augustine's relation to his mother Monica shapes his mode of confession after conversion. Monica is a crucial, if shadowy, figure throughout *The Confessions.* She suffers immensely as her young son wanders away from her Christian faith (his father, who is an equally significant absence in this text, is pagan). She prays for her son at strategic moments of crisis, and Augustine is confident that his providential god responds to these prayers even before his conversion. Monica is also crucial in dismissing the (unnamed) "concubine," with whom Augustine had a child, when her departure was essential to Monica's plans and he himself was unwilling to initiate it. Monica is pivotal in this conversion narrative because she links Augustine to his god even before his conversion; she remains shadowy because as one already converted to the true faith herself, her conduct is not filled with that radical division from which illuminating drama flows. In Monica's case as confessed by Augustine, her role as mother is definitive. Her place in the conversion drama is set by her attempts to mediate relations between Augustine and her god in preparation for her son's conversion, not by her own struggles with her own fate.

Immediately after their conversion, Augustine and Alypius rush to Monica.

She was filled with exultation and triumph, and she blessed you, "who are
able to do above that which we ask or think." She saw that through me
you had given her far more than she had long begged for by her piteous
tears and groans. For you had converted me to yourself, so that I would
seek neither wife nor ambition in this world . . . [27]

The relations among Augustine, Monica, and his god are intricate,
even delicate. What do they reveal about the complex structure of moral
authority and effectivity in Augustine's faith? Augustine accepts a
hierarchy of gender relations then current and now up for cultural contestation. God stands at the apex of the pyramid of moral authority; men,
women, children, and beasts follow in approximately that order. The
"masculine" symbolizes activity, authority, and power in Augustine's
world. The "feminine" receptivity, obedience, and docility. But these
formal "subject positions" do not exhaust the possibilities residing within
those who inhabit them.

Shortly after his conversion, Augustine and Monica experience a
brief glimpse of eternity together. Then she dies. After her death,
Monica continues to live within Augustine as a set of tactical dispositions through which to relate to the (masculine) god who stands above
him. Augustine internalizes the voice of Monica with respect to his god.
Specifically, I want to suggest, Augustine enacts the traditional code of
a devout woman with respect to this god and the traditional code of an
authoritative male with respect to human believers and nonbelievers
below him. We will consider the first Augustinian voice now and the
second in the next chapter.

In confessing to his god about the character of Monica, Augustine
emphasizes her modesty, sobriety, patience, and meekness. The mettle
of the recently deceased woman, he asserts, was tested by her husband,
the kindly, tempestuous, and violent pagan, Patricius. Monica always
accepted this man as "her lord," refusing to criticize him in public, to
rebuke him while he was in one of his rages, or to fly into a rage herself
after his infidelities. Still, the meekness and caution required by her
subject position did not render her ineffective as a servant of god,
according to Augustine. She made the most of possibilities available to
her in the patriarchal world she inhabited.

Monica devised a strategy that allowed her to avoid the beatings so
many wives in her situation faced while gradually and ineluctably

bringing this volatile pagan under her sway. She "learned to avoid resisting her husband when he was angry, not only by deeds but even by words. When she saw that he had curbed his anger and become calm . . . , then she explained what she had done, if he happened to be inadvertently disturbed."[28]

Monica was calm but persistent, gentle but effective. When asked by other suffering wives how she was so successful with such a tempestuous lord, she advised them to introduce a program of patient obedience and mild instruction into their own marriages. This, anyway, is how Augustine represents his mother while confessing her case to his god. He goes on to report how effective these tactics were in the most fundamental domain of all. "Finally, towards the end of his earthly life, she gained her husband for you."[29] This humble woman cultivated such potent tactics to woo those above her in the great chain of being that she saw her son's concubine pulled peacefully from his eager grasp, the conversion of her son to her own faith, the taming of her tempestuous husband, and the eventual conversion of her pagan husband himself to Christianity. She converted the subservience of her official position into a gentle strategy of obesiant influence, one that depended for its success on the willingness not to flaunt it too openly or pursue it too impatiently. Patience was a virtue with Monica because she had eternity on her side.

Upon Augustine's conversion and Monica's death, Monica re-emerges, this time as the dominant voice through which Augustine confesses to his god. She provides the model through which Augustine forms his relation to divinity—the model he imitates in confessing to this masculine, mysterious, powerful god. Augustine becomes an artful, traditional, subordinate woman with respect to this masculine god. He converts it, through cautiously reiterated imperatives and devoutly articulated celebrations, from the awesome, vital, tempestuous force encountered by Adam and Job to a providential source of morality, conversion, and salvation for those who receive its grace. Augustine never challenges this lord directly or commands it to change. Rather, modifying it cautiously by confessing devoutly to it, he gently folds benevolence into its omnipotence and grace into its willfulness. The Monician *Confessions* of Augustine tame divine omnipotence while preserving the formal subject position of divinity as unfettered power.

The Monician conversion, then, reconstitutes two figures, the identity of Augustine as a devout Christian and the identity of Augustine's god as a benevolent saviour. To what degree does the Monician voice within Augustine shape the character of "the lord" he bows before? To what degree does it enable him to unveil a divinity already there? The debate over this delicate issue may never end, but Augustine himself does not open it up as a topic of reflection and robust debate between rival onto-theo-political creeds.

The god you represent—the source you interpret or confess—is ambiguously a projection of yourself and an effect on what you become. The problem—and the relief—is that the terms of this ambiguity are susceptible to multiple readings. The source you represent is something of a Rorschach inkblot without a master therapist in charge of its interpretation. How you interpret it provides a blowup of what you expect others to be and how you would influence them to be those things. On my reading—a reading that projects my soul onto a larger cultural screen—Augustine's will to earthly power and a universal religion is channeled through the medium of contrite confession. He invests a god with gracious omnipotence to still anarchistic impulses in himself, to fulfill his dream of eternal peace, and to manufacture a basis from which to present himself as a servant while exercising moral dominion over others. Why, though, must omnipotence be located anywhere at all? Would a less perverse divinity not willingly forgo such a standing? What might an ethic be like that affirmed the need to set limits around human conduct but refused to ground itself upon *any* omnipotent, unquestionable source, godly or ungodly?

Augustine's confession of his conversion discloses an element of paradox within it. The very rubric of *confession* through which the conversion is enacted guarantees this to be the case. But the confessional mode itself does not come up for critical or detached scrutiny in this text. Rather, the questioning to which it is subjected is constantly folded back into the confessional mode itself, as each new doubt and mystery is subjected to confession in its turn. We are not asked to judge whether confession constructs the moral authority represented through it. Whether it draws you closer to your deepest self or folds a set of contestable moral imperatives more deeply into your soul.

To those who contend that Augustine's recurrent questions, doubts, and uncertainties do constitute an interrogation of the confessional mode itself, one might reply: Augustine knows that faith precedes "knowledge"; it establishes preconditions for its receipt. But he fails to consider actively enough whether the knowledge one attains through conversion is worthy of persistent social contestation *because* of the undecidable role faith and confession play in producing/uncovering it. We will have to examine the Augustinian conversion to confession further in the next chapter, then, this time considering the un-Monician voice speaking through Augustine when he engages those inside and outside his faith who have strayed too far off the true course.

Notes

1. Charles Taylor, *Sources of the Self: The Making of the Modern Identity* (Cambridge, MA: Harvard University Press, 1989), 74, 96.
2. Taylor, *Sources of the Self*, 75.
3. Augustine, *Concerning the City of God: Against the Pagans*, trans. Henry Bettenson (Middlesex, UK: Penguin, 1984), Bk. 16, chap. 8, 661.
4. *City of God*, Bk. 16, chap. 8, 662.
5. *City of God*, Bk. 16, chap. 8, 662.
6. *City of God*, Bk. 16, chap. 8, 663.
7. *City of God*, Bk. 16, chap. 8, 664.
8. *The Confessions of St. Augustine*, trans. John K. Ryan (New York: Image Books, 1960), both quotations from Bk. 3, chap. 8, 87-88.
9. *Confessions*, Bk. 7, chap. 8, 168.
10. *Confessions*, Bk. 3, chap. 8, 88-89.
11. *Confessions*, Bk. 2, chap. 7, 73.
12. *City of God*, Bk. 6, chap. 1, 228-29; Bk. 7, chap. 33, 294.
13. *Confessions*, Bk. 10, chap. 8, 238.
14. *Confessions*, Bk. 10, chap. 16, 245.
15. *Confessions*, Bk. 10, chap. 20, 249.
16. *Confessions*, Bk. 10, chap. 24, 253.
17. *Confessions*, Bk. 7, chap. 7, 166-67, numbering added.
18. *Confessions*, Bk. 8, chap. 9, 196-97.
19. *Confessions*, Bk. 8, chap. 9, 197.
20. For an account of the Kantian problematic that draws it right back into the Augustinian mold, see Gordon E. Michalson, *Fallen Freedom: Kant on Radical Evil and Moral Regeneration* (New York: Cambridge University Press, 1990). Michalson argues that Kant constantly falls back into a heteronomy his theory formally opposes and that,

finally, he covertly reinstates the grace his version of Christianity is officially out to bypass.

21. *Confessions*, Bk. 8, chap. 9, 197.

22. *Confessions*, Bk. 6, chap. 11, 150.

23. I have discussed this feature of Nietzsche's thought in *Political Theory and Modernity* (Oxford: Basil Blackwell, 1988), chap. 5.

24. *Confessions*, Bk. 8, chap. 12, 202.

25. *Confessions*, Bk. 8, chap. 12, 203.

26. Friedrich Nietzsche, *Thus Spoke Zarathustra: A Book for All and None*, trans. Walter Kaufmann (New York: Penguin, 1966), Bk. 1, 13.

27. *Confessions*, Bk. 8, chap. 12, 203.

28. *Confessions*, Bk. 9, chap. 9, 219.

29. *Confessions*, Bk. 9, chap. 9, 220.

3

Gentle Wars of Identity\Difference

The Paradox of Conversion

A healed will is filled with the will of Augustine's god. And this happens eventually to Augustine.

> But you, O Lord, are good and merciful, and your right hand has had regard for the depth of my death, and from the very bottom of my heart it has emptied out an abyss of corruption. This was the sum of it: not to will what I willed and to will what you willed.[1]

Freedom as obedience to a higher source. Augustine's will is not now perfectly free, of course. But we no longer receive long confessions of perverse thefts, or giving in to "lust's itchy sore," or self-serving lies, or a desire to delay giving up sinful desires. The preponderance of *The Confessions*, after the conversion of Augustine and the death of Monica, shifts from a confession of previous sins to a confession of current limitations of thought in coming to terms with the mysteries of memory,

time, eternity, and the being of his god. The drama *within* Augustine's
will is curtailed after conversion, after an abyss of corruption has been
emptied from his soul. His will has changed. Now it is more full of piety,
that is, humble obedience. It is governed by the code: "Not to will what
I willed and to will what you willed." But it can will what its lord wills
only to the extent it experiences the pull of the latter will on its will,
only after and if it receives grace.

The will that is filled with the will of the god to which its bearer
confesses is less corrupt than before. When the healed will exercises
authority over itself or others it does not do so to still its own uncertainty, to promote its own interests, to provide its own reassurances; it
does so to enact the will of the lord, which fills it. Of course there is
always a risk that it will slide away from this higher will. And it is never
fully at one with it on earth. Hence it must always be humble and
cautious. But, still, Augustine displays considerable confidence after
conversion that what he wills for others is good for them because his
will is filled with the will of his lord. What instills this confidence? The
experience of conversion. Before conversion you read your life in one
way; after conversion you read your past and present life in another. In
the light of conversion you are convinced that this new stance is more
true than your old one. All the old events, deeds, and thoughts feel
different now. You have a better perspective on them.

But what if it is humanly possible to undergo conversion in many
different directions? And what if, after conversion in several different
directions, each set of converts undergoes the same sort of changes
reported by Augustine? The will of each feels more coherent and each
reviews her past actions from a new, superior perspective. Perhaps there
is an element of paradox in the experience of conversion that can never
be stilled completely. Perhaps a significant change in your habits of
perception, judgment, and action flows from the experience of conversion, but you now inevitably draw on these very dimensions to judge
that the new stance is true or superior to the previous one. Perhaps
because the sources from which ethical life draws are more protean than
any particular articulation is able to capture, the conversion experience
is more uncertain and problematic than the convert tends to feel it to
be. And this would apply not only to the question of whether you have
really accepted conversion, but also whether the effect of a successful

conversion opens your soul to the truth or encloses you more completely in a circle of self-aggrandizing fictions. If that were the case you could not have confessed the experience of conversion very well until you had gone through at least two of them and had had a chance to review commonalities in the inward experience of both alongside differences in the directives of each. But even then, there might not be an untainted vantage point from which to review and assess these two experiences. You would already be inclined toward one or the other as an effect of your last conversion. And that paradox, too, might be elevated until it became an ingredient in ethical reflection, informing the *way* you support and advance the ethic you endorse.

Maybe it is ethically productive to cultivate a certain dissonance or skepticism amidst all the pressures to confirm a fixed faith or conform to a settled identity. Maybe the dissonances Augustine experiences prior to conversion can be not only a source of waywardness or corruption but also a gateway through which creativity in life and generosity in relations of conflict with others could enter.

The lord to whom Augustine confesses is designed to prevent this circle of conversion experiences from becoming a whirlpool. If the lord is omnipotent and caring, and if the directives in Scripture are fairly clear to faithful readers, then—and only then?—the paradox of conversion becomes less dramatic and more manageable. But *if* it still remains a question whether these two crucial elements of faith flow from a hope implicit in the conversion effect or a message received from the god who embodies them, the paradox re-emerges in another guise. Is this lord confessed because its truth is graciously received through conversion? Or is the conversion effect governed by an overweening imperative to still persistent uncertainty through confession? The issue arises with respect to every lived experience of faith, identity, cultural foundation, transcendental proof, or discovery of primordial truth. Augustine's version allows us to place the issue under a magnifying glass so that it can be reviewed more reflectively in these other cases as well.

Augustine himself repeatedly confesses how perplexities similar to those I have summarized enter his soul, but he also follows each of these confessions immediately with a second, supervenient confession that treats the first as another step on a spiral stairway drawing him closer to the fundamental truth. The piety through which the second move

receives consistent priority over the first creates space for us to interrogate critically the strategic role of piety in the politics of conversion.

> Lord before whose eyes the abyss of man's conscience lies naked, what
> thing within me could be hidden from you, even though I would not
> confess to you? I would be hiding from myself, not myself from you. But,
> since my groans bear witness that I am a thing displeasing to myself, you
> shine forth, and you are pleasing to me, and you are loved and longed for,
> so that I may feel shame for myself, and renounce myself, and choose you,
> and please neither you nor myself except because of you.[2]

Are the groans of piety a movement of self-purification and renunci-
ation or an artful concealment of transcendental egoism through which
your most stringent demands are converted into commands humbly
relayed to you from a higher source? Is piety a covert, deniable strategy
to still uncertainty in the fundaments of your faith while warning others
implicitly against blasphemy in interrogating these fundaments vigorously
and publicly? These questions become important politically whenever the
pious confess an *authoritative* and *universal* god (or identity or intrinsic
moral order, or sufficient code of rationality, or neutral method, etc.) and
insistently press its directives on others.

The Politics of Identity

I have examined how the intrinsic moral order is defined and determined through confession, but it remains to be seen how the confessional imperative is generalized. The politics of confession emerges in
the strategies by which the confessional culture is generalized.

After Augustine became the Bishop of Hippo he exercised direct
authority over his parish in North Africa and extensive indirect authority through the effects of his writings over a larger group of priests
scattered throughout the Roman Empire. In these circumstances it was
possible to institutionalize confession, that is, to institutionalize the
Augustinian lord through the generalization of confession. It is in
Augustine's official letters to authorities, members, converts, opponents, and heretics of his church that we can trace the confessional

politics of moral order most effectively. We shall consider first the political constitution of identity and second the constitution of difference, though, of course, each of these enterprises is incorrigibly bound up with the other.

The institutionalization of confession draws on a few preliminary dispositions of the self. First, the practitioners generally conceive themselves already to be sinful or divided selves who seek repair of this division. Second, they might think there is a higher being who cares for them (or a deep truth within the self that might be approachable by inward reflection). Third, they might think that they can move closer to this being, essence, or identity by piously admitting their most fundamental faults. Fourth, they might presume that the long road to elevation of the self involves coming to terms with new elements of murkiness and corruption within the self at each stage, preparing oneself in this way to be drawn closer to the source of being if it, in its infinite wisdom, decides to do draw them closer. Confession is thus a self-propelling and self-renewing practice that is never self-sufficient. To practice it faithfully is to hope that limitations in success are connected to some defect in previous confessions, and that this defect might possibly be reduced through further confession.

A stable culture of confession needs a set of supporting institutions. It functions best if there is an authoritative conception of divinity or identity that a company of sinners confesses together—if there are institutional authorities available to nudge the confessors in the right direction, to instruct them concerning the issues most likely to be in need of confession, and to suggest where they may have gone astray in previous rounds of confession. Augustine's own confessions are so creative and distinctive because he practices this art before its institutionalization is consolidated. After his own conversion he can now devote more energy to setting the context of authority through which others confess in turn. This constitutes the Augustinian politics of confessional identity.

A personal disposition needs a social context to be; and a particular social context requires a supporting set of personal dispositions to maintain itself. We can gain some sense of how disposition and context are interwoven in the politics of confession by examining a letter Augustine wrote to a group of sisters living in a convent in Hippo in 423. Their order had been torn by gossip, strife, and unhappiness centering on the rule of the mother superior. Augustine begins his letter by calling on the sisters to love and obey their superior, informing them that their grievances are the effect of pride and faultfinding emanating from themselves. If the fault of discord lies in the complaining self, the appropriate response is to examine one's interior dispositions more closely. But, also, if the issues revolve around disagreements over the interpretation of rules governing the order, the appropriate response is to state the rules more closely. Clarification of the rules and repair of the souls of those who dispute them might heal the discord that tears them apart.

The members have "chosen to dwell with one accord in fellowship under the same roof, to have 'one soul and one heart' unto God."[3] Augustine does not here suggest that the quest for such close accord itself spawns discord and strife. For he believes that this discipline itself, properly cultivated, accords with the moral order of being. This being so, the primary fault for strife must dwell within the rebellious hearts of the subordinates. "May God calm and compose your hearts! May the work of the devil not gain the upper hand in your hearts, but the peace of Christ rule in your hearts!"[4]

But the sisters cannot pinpoint the points of disturbance in their hearts precisely enough unless they are given a set of rules for proceeding. So Augustine lays down a more refined set of rules. Thus, for instance: No one is to call anything her own so that, sharing everything in common, they will be able to "dwell together in the house as single-minded sisters"; and each is to receive, not equal portions of food, clothing, and materials from the common stock, but "to each one according to as she has need."[5] Here, we can discern how refinement of the rules allows each member to pinpoint more precisely defects in her self. But the refinement of rules also creates new faults to be remedied. For now if anyone desires something for herself, this has become a fault to be corrected; if anyone thinks another has been given more from the common stock than she needs, a new instance of selfishness can be discerned. A detailed specification of virtues, a proliferation of defects in the self, and a dense practice of confession support one another. Each is a precondition and effect of the other two.

Augustine specifies a complex set of rules. Each specification opens up new possibilities for authoritative criticism and self-confession. And

because every rule is unavoidably vague at the boundaries, the proliferation of rules endows authorities with new opportunities to exercise
discretionary judgment if and when new infractions have occurred. A
new rule creates new occasions for conflict as it presents itself as the
solution to old conflicts. It is always possible to suggest that a sister did
not live up to the spirit of this or that rule. And if she replies that this
very slippage in the network of rules is being used as a lever of
discrimination against her, she, as a confessed sinner, very probably
discloses yet another sore in her rebellious heart in need of confession.

Augustine's delineation of rules continues. They include: inconspic-
uous dress; making sure your hair does "not fly loose through careless-
ness *or* be arranged with fastidiousness"; walking in procession so that
each can observe the others; not allowing the head to be too erect while
walking; letting your eyes cast over anyone, but be "fixed upon no one";
subduing your "flesh by fasting and abstinence from meat and drink";
meditating within your heart as you pray aloud with others; and so on.[6]

The rules simultaneously create a dense context of self-discipline and
multiply new occasions for confession. They produce the confessional
imperative to heal the self in a setting that necessarily opens up new
wounds in the self. The order that celebrates confession produces a
culture in which it is repeatedly imperative to renew confession.

The intimate relations between the shape of the social order, the order
of desire, and the practice of confession can be discerned in Augustine's
instructions on regulating desire. This order constitutes the very desires
it criticizes. Those, for instance, who must neither allow their hair to
fly loose nor be fastened too fastidiously have been ordered to avoid
close attention to their appearance by meticulously attending to it. Each
sister is thereby placed in a double bind. The first bind consists in the
command to do what she is ordered not to do. The second consists in
the implicit command not to call attention to the first bind but to
translate it into a fault in her will. How can she avoid self-absorption
while fastidiously attending to the imperative not to let her hair appear
too loose or too arranged? The rule generates a desire—the desire to
attend to one's appearance—in the way it orders the self to suppress the
desire to self-absorption. Such a set of binds is perfectly designed to
spawn faults to be confessed. They become drawn even more tightly:

> In walking, in standing, in deportment, in all your movements, let nothing
> be done that might attract the desire of anyone, but let everything be in
> keeping with your holy character . . . ; when you are in procession you
> are not forbidden to look upon men, but to desire to make approaches to
> them or to have them make approaches to you. It is not by touch only and
> by bearing that a woman solicits approaches or makes them, but by look
> as well. And do not say that you have chaste minds if you have unchaste
> eyes, because the unchaste eye is the messenger of an unchaste heart . . . [7]

Those governed by the imperative to purge illicit desires from their
souls work in a factory that manufactures those desires. A sister is
carefully informed how a man's attentions are solicited. The desire for
this attention is incited by description of the rich panoply of tactics
through which its presence is revealed and by oblique reference to
pleasures that must accompany attainment of a desire whose manifestations are so multiple and so difficult to circumscribe. Now there is
something definite to confess and correct. Floating sensuality becomes
fixed as particular desire through specification of its occasion, character, and signs. The rules of self-scrutiny through which the illicit is
disclosed also serve as the means by which it is produced. Does the
consolidation of desire precede authoritative determination of its signs?
How could anyone unsort this spiral of causes and effects? Once
consolidated there are surely secret ways to release illicit desire within
the convent. But enactment of these possibilities simply recirculates
occasions for exposure, guilt, confession, and penalty. We are treated
to a preview of the world of young Alex/ina by listening to the instructions of Augustine to the nuns.

What is going on here? New thoughts, desires, temptations, and acts
are being created through the authoritative practice of confession. Sin
is produced to enable confession; confession is pursued to disclose and
correct sin. Is the inward self being uncovered? Or is it being manufactured by a particular conjunction of rules, desires, and the confessional
imperative?

The institutionalization of confession in the convent requires the
extension and regularization of surveillance. Sisters who eat, sleep,
walk, and pray together are also in an excellent position to observe each
other. Augustine, the master politician of religious identity, pursues this
opportunity, admonishing the sisters to "keep mutual guard upon your

chastity." If, he says, you observe a sister with a "forward eye," admonish her privately at first. "But if, even after admonishment, you notice her doing the same things again on any other day, whoever has had the opportunity of noticing this should report her for treatment, as one afflicted with a sore, but not before she has been pointed out to a second or a third, so that she may be convicted from the mouth of two or three witnesses and be punished with becoming severity."[8] Note how the forward eye of one can only be observed through the forward eye of the other. It will not be surprising if those who pursue *this* task too actively must be brought under observation in turn. For some of them may be too forward in checking their sisters for a forward eye. An infinite regress of forward eyes.

If the offending sister goes to the point of receiving a gift from a man "let her be pardoned and prayer made for her, if she confesses it of her own accord; but if she is detected and it be proved against her, let more serious punishment be inflicted on her at the discretion of the priest-superior."[9]

A system of graded authority, the imperative to moral unity, a meticulous specification of rules, the production of sinful desires, the obligation to confess, a network of mutual surveillance among equals, a system of punishments, the manufacture of the inward self, the confession of a divine source hovering over the entire complex. These faiths, dispositions, rules, desires, and surveillances form the confessional complex. They constitute the authoritative network of confessional morality. Augustine is authorized to delineate rules and presumptions governing the complex because he confesses his will to be filled graciously with the divine will. Because he is a consummate *servant* of the lord he confesses he exercises *authority* over its flock. The confessional complex authoritatively recapitulates the structure of Augustine's own confessions. It distributes among selves the various roles Augustine played with respect to himself, while it calls on each member to re-enact that distribution within herself as well.

In this great chain of being the line of obedience runs up from the sisters through the mother superior, the priests, the Bishop of Hippo, to the lord the bishop confesses. The obligation to obey flows down from the one who confesses his god creatively to those who confess to this same god through a more extensive mediation of earthly rules and injunctions. The creative element in confession declines as you move down the hierarchy of being; the specification of standards, desires, identities, confessional imperatives, and penalties inclines as you approach the lower levels. The young girls are drawn into this world through the faith, hopes for salvation, and dissonances of will experienced before entry. They are then constituted as "sisters" by desires, standards, obligations, deceits, confessions, punishments, and hopes for salvation invested in them. Every secret pleasure, modest subterfuge, and petty opportunity for power now becomes possible material to be worked on through future confession. All this order in accord with the commands of a specific deity confessed into being by authorities whose wills obey its will.

It takes a lot of work to keep an intrinsic moral order intact. Everybody must develop an unchaste eye so that no unchaste eye becomes the messenger of an unchaste heart; and everybody must develop a forward eye so that no eye becomes too forward.

The Augustinian politics of identity is not restricted to the convent, though it does find its most elaborate expression there. Ecdicia, a member of his parish, complained to Augustine about her husband's failure to live up to the ideal of a chaste marriage—the highest form marriage can assume in the Augustinian world—and about his fits of rage and adultery following this attempt. Augustine chastises this loyal follower for insisting on enacting the ideal of chastity before her husband, the natural authority in the marriage, fully consented to it. Augustine is "greatly grieved" by her actions and attitudes, including her participation in charity for the poor without receiving her husband's prior permission. The guilt of the husband would have been severe enough had he returned to his own wife's body, but

> how much more deplorable it is now that he has plunged to deeper destruction, with such precipitate collapse into adultery, furious towards you, injurious towards himself. . . . This great mischief has come about because you failed to treat him with the moderation you ought, for although by agreement you are no longer coming together in carnal intercourse, yet in all other things you ought to have shown the subjection of a wife to your husband in compliance with the marriage bond. . . . Indeed, if you, a believer, had had a husband who was a non-believer, it would have been your duty to conduct yourself with submissiveness, as the Apostles enjoined, so to win him to the Lord.[10]

The Augustinian politics of responsibility. Neither the hierarchy of authority between men and women nor the possible seeds of discord sown by the ideal of marital chastity itself can become objects of critical scrutiny in the Augustinian politics of identity. They are insulated from critical reflection because they are inscribed in the intrinsic moral order. The fault for the collapse of this marriage, then, must be located elsewhere. In this case, the primary fault resides with the one lowest in the hierarchy of being. Monica understood this point of faith well enough. Thus: Ecdicia had pushed the ideal of chastity before her husband was adequately prepared; and she took other independent actions without consulting his authority. She therefore absorbs principal responsibility for his fall from chastity, his adultery, his rage, and the collapse of their marriage.

The church during this period may have exercised a greater hold over its women than its men, and this in turn may have been linked to the subordination of women in the natural order of things. Perhaps this fact made it tactically effective to load the heaviest responsibility for discord on those most accessible to the church's authority. But Augustine makes no reference to such tactical considerations. When the Augustinian code of moral order is combined with this operational code of effective influence, Ecdicia emerges as the leading candidate, first, to receive the heaviest burden of blame for errors of the past and, second, to initiate reparations. Augustine—the highest authority in this triad of bishop, husband, and wife, and the author of the ideal of marital chastity—escapes any trace of blame. The husband, given his natural authority, escapes extensive blame because his wife initiated certain actions without his authorization. God, the author of this moral order, is completely exempt from any responsibility for any discord arising in it. Yet, blame must be located somewhere in a moral order built around the priorities of will, blame, guilt, and responsibility. Given the natural order of things, then, it becomes the wife's obligation to initiate reparations contritely. Augustine writes this logic into his letter to Ecdicia without, however, laying bare its structure so blatantly.

I am grieved at what your husband has done as a result of your irregular and imprudent conduct. It is your duty most earnestly to think how he may be restored, if your wish to belong to the church is sincere. Put on therefore humility of mind, and . . . do not scorn your husband while he perishes. Pour forth for him devoted and constant prayers; offer the sacrifice of tears . . . , and write him an apology. . . . Promise for the future, with the help of the Lord, that, if he repents of his evil conduct and returns to the continence he had abandoned, you will be subject to him, as it is fitting you should be, in all things.[11]

Augustine is grieved by the conduct of his "daughter" (as church custom would have it) and the man's "wife." Her responsibilities are written into these two roles and these roles are written into the intrinsic moral order. Ecdicia is thus instructed to behave toward her husband as Monica, his own mother, did to Patricius before her. Augustine's instructions to her also correspond to his own conduct in confessing his heavenly father, if you interpret those confessions to be a set of tactics by which an unruly god is converted into the source of Augustinian moral order. Augustine, then, only calls on Ecdicia to behave to her husband as his mother did to her lord and as the highest authority confessed by Augustine commands her to do.

It is arduous and delicate work to maintain an intrinsic moral order. Things keep slip/sliding along. If something is not now sliding out of place, it is probably on the verge of doing so. Except the moral order itself, which remains intact. Everybody in the family (father, husband, son, sister, mother, wife, daughter) has a crucial role in promoting accord between cultural practice and the intrinsic moral pattern. Let's now consider the role of some who don't belong to this family.

The Politics of Difference

So far we have considered the confessional politics of hierarchalization within the folds of the Augustinian faith. But a cultural identity is consolidated not only by the norms and abnormalities it defines inside its circle, but also by types placed outside that circle and by the codes of conduct it develops toward outsiders.

Augustine has a complex relation to "paganism," the religion of his father and very recently the official religion of an Empire that had persecuted Christianity. He believes that torture and killing are unacceptable ways to respond to pagans because they too are creatures of the true god and because they might later become open to conversion. But he also develops tactics, first, to circumscribe the public role of pagan activities in Christian society and, second, to turn pagans away from the licentiousness of false gods and toward conversion to the *universal* god. To hold your god to be the single, universal saviour is to place the politics of conversion high on your agenda.

Augustine's eagerness to convert encourages him to warn pagans of the dismal fate awaiting them if they abjure the true faith. On receiving a letter from a group of pagans who apparently mocked his religion by pretending to honor his station within it, Augustine issues a reply. It warns of what is in store for them if they continue to delay conversion, "reminding" them of how the Holy Scripture has so far proven correct in its prophecies of what would happen to those who refuse this opportunity.

> You plainly see the Jewish people torn from their abode and dispersed and scattered throughout almost the whole world . . . everything has happened just as it was foretold. . . . You plainly see some of the temples of [pagan] idols fallen into ruin and not restored, some cast down, some closed, some converted to other uses . . . ; and you see how the powers of this world, who at one time for the sake of their idols persecuted the Christian people, are vanquished and subdued by Christians who did not take up arms but laid down their lives . . . ; and you see the most eminent dignitary of this noble Empire lay aside his crown and bow in supplication before the tomb of his fisherman Peter.[12]

Augustine here recalls the friends of Job, who also presume that those who suffer thus signify their desert in the divine order of things. Such a floating presumption, capable of being wheeled out on some occasions and wheeled in on others, may be the most dangerous danger in providential theologies and histories. At any rate, Augustine warns these pagans of the historical fate awaiting them, couching this fate as a continuation of divine interventions previously foretold and now accomplished. The divine tide of history flows against them, as it did against the Jewish people previously. Moreover, because the world is now populated everywhere with Christians no pagan can safely defer conversion by pleading ignorance. "Yea, verily, just as they all came about, so it too will come. Nor will there be any man of our times who at that judgment will be able to put forward any defense for being an

unbeliever, when the name of Christ is on every man's lips . . . "[13]
Augustine prays for these insolent pagans as he condemns their paganism, for he trusts in the potential convertibility of every human to the true
faith.

In 408, Augustine is not mocked but appealed to by a pagan, Nectarius,
who complains in a letter about official punishments meted out to those
who celebrated a pagan holiday against the edict of the Christian emperor.
Nectarius requests leniency for those swept away by a series of unexpected
events. Augustine refuses the appeal for leniency, "reminding" Nectarius
of the offense in carefully selected terms.

> In defiance of quite recent legislation a sacrilegious celebration was held
> on the first of June, a pagan feast-day . . . , with such insolent effrontery
> that an impudent crowd of dancers actually passed along the same street
> in front of the church-goers. . . . When the church attempted to stop this
> most illegal and insulting procedure, the church was stoned. . . . When [a
> week later] our people wanted to lodge a complaint in court . . . their
> rights were denied [by a shower of stones]. . . . One servant of God who
> was wandering about they put to death. No attempt at repression, no
> attempt at rescue was made by any of those who could have exercised
> some weight of authority.[14]

Defiance, sacrilege, insolent effrontery, impudent dancers, illegal
acts, insulting procedure. These moral denunciations are contrasted to
legislation, our people, church-goers, rights denied, and a servant of the
god killed. The terms within which the reminder is couched presuppose
the objectivity of the Augustinian order and the justice of the law
against celebrating pagan holidays. A killing resulting from a series of
events that spin out of control (a law suppressing public expression of
pagan faith, an attempted celebration in the face of it, a counter-attempt
to suppress the celebration, a belligerent response to this attempt, a
complaint filed by offended Christians, a spontaneous killing of a
Christian by an unknown minority of pagans) is defined to be the
responsibility of those against whom the initial law was addressed. If
they had not disobeyed a just law, these unexpected consequences
would not have occurred. Pagans are to be tolerated, in the significant
sense that they are not to be put to death, tortured, or punished corpo-
really for their beliefs. But Augustine consistently characterizes paganism, not as a rival response to perplexing mysteries of being or a worthy

counter to his own demand for salvation, but as an inferior, licentious faith to be regulated by his church to the degree it is powerful enough to do so.

Each Augustinian description of pagan life and gods inculcates the intrinsic superiority of his faith, even when he is culling insights from its Platonic version to be incorporated into his own faith. Paganism is a precondition of Augustinianism to be authoritatively defined and regulated so that the intrinsic moral order can shine forth in its specific universality.

Perhaps the most powerful tool, though, for specification of Augustinian faith is the delineation of heresies, those ambiguous doctrines that arise within the faith and that must be expelled from it. Within the circle of his faith, Augustine evinces a measure of appreciation for plurality. The fine points of faith are complex and surrounded by mystery. Reasonable people may diverge in their interpretations within this zone. But stringent lines are drawn around this zone of tolerance, beyond which diversity is intolerable. What is the basis of these lines?

Consider again the moment in *The Confessions* when Augustine uncovers the divided will. The problem, recall, is that one side of the will wills the good while the other side trumps this with a veto of the first will. "Therefore there are two wills, since one of them is not complete, and what is lacking in one of them is present in the other."[15] This sentence closes chapter 9 of book 8; it is followed immediately by these lines at the beginning of chapter 10:

> Let them perish from before your face, O God, even as vain talkers and seducers of men's minds perish who detect in the act of deliberation two wills at work, and then assert that in us there are two natures of two minds, one good, the other evil. They themselves are truly evil, when they think such evil things.[16]

Those who entertain such evil thoughts of "two natures . . . , one good, the other evil," are, of course, the Manicheans. They are Christians who project two contending forces into the cosmos, those of lightness and darkness. Manicheanism is the heresy Augustine himself confessed for nine years. It protects its god from responsibility for evil by positing an opposing force to be the source of evil. Why must *this* contending faith be defined as a heresy advanced by "vain talkers" and "seducers" who are "truly evil" and deserve to "perish"? The official reason is that it deviates from the fundaments of the true faith, detracting from the perfection of the true god by denying the attribute of omnipotence to it. But why is omnipotence so indispensable that any members who deny it must be defined as *heretical*? I suspect the imperative behind this imperative is the quest for eternal salvation. The hope for eternal salvation is placed in extreme peril if omnipotence is subtracted from the being of the lord. The promise of salvation by a god less than omnipotent might be overturned by any number of contingencies or opposing forces. The imperative of eternal salvation, then, becomes the key consideration to discriminate between differences that are tolerable within the true faith and those that are heinous acts of heresy. Salvation is, recall, "the essential aim in all religion."

Heresy is indispensable to the Augustinian system because it enables authoritative propagators of the faith to fix its specificity whenever a vertiginous slide into confusion or undecidability is otherwise threatened. The definition of a contending position as heresy stills debate within the community by expelling one of the disputants. The particular set of heresies Augustine defines are effects of the specific drive to unity, salvation, and universality governing his system. Augustine comes close to such a characterization himself while, of course, containing it within a confession of the superiority of his own faith to his own lord. "In fact the refutation of heresies causes what your Church thinks, and what sound doctrine holds, to stand out. 'For there must be heresies, so that those who are approved may become manifest among the weak.' "[17] Some of the strong must be expelled to protect the weak from their lies.

Augustine convicts a counter-interpretation of heresy when it pursues a dangerous line of reflection latent in the hegemonic doctrine and/or exposes deep tensions otherwise concealed in the hegemonic doctrine. An Augustinian heresy is a *temptation* within his own faith in that its declarations receive their impetus from uncertainties and ambiguities floating within the authoritative doctrine itself; it is a political *threat* in that its articulation disturbs the highest hope the authoritative doctrine is designed to sustain; it is politically *indispensable* in that its constitution as heresy stills the threat within the doctrine and the self through exclusion of those giving voice to it. By converting tempting, dangerous, threatening themes floating within his own faith into determinate heresies expelled from it, *authoritative fervor and decidability is be-*

stowed on Augustinianism itself. "There must be heresies" to give Augustinianism solidity, determinacy, and fervor.

Let us test these assertions against the confession of divided will (re)introduced above. After confessing himself to be riven by "two wills," Augustine immediately moves to forestall the contention that they are manifestations of two competing cosmic "natures," a reading he attributes to the Manicheans and one that his later opponents, the Pelagians, contend is implied by his own doctrine of two wills. He can assert, as he does shortly thereafter in *The Confessions*, that his inner experience convinces him that it was he himself who willed both sides rather than two forces contending within him for primacy. And he can claim that the idea of the responsible agent would be jeopardized by acceptance of the Manichean option. But once the theme of division within the self has been confessed, a new terrain of debate opens up unlikely to be resolved either by a simple comparison of intuitions at this level or sustained arguments over the question of responsibility. Augustine's own doctrine of responsibility, for instance, with its complex/mysterious interactions among original sin, habit, will, and grace, is susceptible to the sort of charge he makes against the Manicheans (and, again, the Pelagians issue this charge against him).

Augustine thereby stitches up the tear just created by introduction of the doctrine of two wills before things get out of hand—before he, for instance, is accused of wandering back toward the heresy he once endorsed. He stills debate and uncertainty within his faith by denouncing as a heresy one of the possibilities his own analysis has just reopened. He requires the doctrine of two wills to cope with the experience of dissonance in the self and to make grace indispensable to salvation. But he must stifle a danger opened up by this very formulation that would (a) threaten the goal of salvation from another direction by defining the salvational god as limited and (b) highlight grave difficulties confronting his doctrine in defending simultaneously the *omnipotence* of this god and its *innocence* of responsibility for evil. For Manicheanism protects the innocence of its god by subtracting omnipotence from it; it preserves the innocence of divinity by investing so much limitation in it that its capacity to enact its salvational intentions becomes more doubtful. "There must be heresies . . . " or the doctrine of "two wills" could slide into that of "two forces."

The denunciation of Manicheanism functions as a warning to the faithful to stay within now-specified limits in interpreting the mysteries of the divided will. To define Manicheanism as heretical is to sew up a sore in Augustinianism. The heresy of Manicheanism is thus a temptation, a threat, and a valuable counterpoint through which to fix a central point of Augustinian faith.

The relation between Augustinian doctrine and this heresy is generalizable to other cases. Donatists hold that a priest has not truly delivered the sacraments unless he himself is free of sin. Such a position might be argued within the confines of Augustine's general faith, but acceptance of it would place human hope for eternal salvation in extreme peril, as parishioners worry whether the priest who baptized them is a secret sinner in a world where no human escapes the perils of sinful temptation. Augustine insists that the tasks of priesthood are attached to the office rather than the man (a *man* is always attached to the office), thereby relieving parishioners of this fear. He endorses the church's definition of Donatism as a heresy.

Pelagians hold, in sympathy with some early formulations by Augustine, that the faithful earn heaven by their own merit and faith. They treat free will to be within the capacity of humanity itself. But Augustine finds this late-blooming opponent to be the most deadly heresy of all. In denying the essential role of divine grace to his lord, it threatens to minimize the role of divinity in salvation. Even more significantly, by underplaying the obdurate role of habit in human life, the Pelagians threaten to take the prospect of salvation away inadvertently as they try to bring it more securely under self-control. For if the force of sinful habit is as powerful as Augustine contends, then it is hard to imagine how any human being could successfully negotiate this nest of snakes without the assistance of grace. Anyone who gives highest priority to the wish for eternal salvation, doctrinal priority to a long laundry list of deadly sins, and doctrinal recognition of the grave difficulty in breaking sins that have become habitual (say, incontinence, smoking, perverse sexual desire, sinful eating habits, and self-absorption) will be sorely pressed to define the Pelagian concept of freedom as heresy.

Augustine constitutes the heresy of Manicheanism to stop a slide into a doctrine of two cosmic forces, the heresy of Donatism to stop a slide into a doctrine of priestly perfection, and the heresy of Pelagianism to stop a slide into a doctrine of self-control over one's own will. In each case, he stills a debate circulating within his faith through authoritative expulsion of one of the parties to it. The underlying rationale is to protect the possibility of eternal salvation from several sources of disruption: from a dualism that limits the power of god, a perfectionism that demands too much from priests, and a perfectionism that demands too much from autonomous human will. In each case, the expulsion of disturbing voices exports comparisons that would otherwise highlight instabilities and disturbances within. To expel difference is to organize identity; and to keep the expelled difference alive as an object of condemnation is to forestall its re-constitution inside. "There must be heresies" for Augustinianism to be. And for the idea of a fixed, true identity to be as well.

To note just one example of the way expulsion represses tensions within the faith, Augustinianism endorses both free will and grace, but it is problematic just what relation each bears to the other and how a doctrine can retain one while endorsing the other. If a credible historical alternative to this position is eliminated as heresy, these difficulties are converted from a comparison of weak points between competing parties into mysteries floating within the one true faith. And the resultant collapse of this debate between parties further reduces the probability that some maverick group will creatively modify established terms of contestation between them by showing how *both* doctrines give problematical priority to the goal of salvation.

What price have those constituted as pagans, infidels, heretics, and nihilists throughout the centuries paid for this demand to confess an intrinsic moral order? Is active contestation of the priority of eternal salvation—as well as its modern, functional cousin, certainty in the intrinsic truth of one's identity—a way to challenge the proliferation of heresies? Is the construction of heresy designed above all to ward off the anxiety of death? These questions do not pose themselves directly to many of Augustine's adversaries, for several of them pursue the imperative of salvation as well. A voice within Job might appreciate them, though. A series of such interrogations might also have opened up lines of escape for Alex/ina. And a "pagan" such as Epicurus pursues them actively, as in the following:

But the intellect, by making a rational calculation of the end and the limit which govern the flesh, and by dispelling the fears about eternity, brings about the complete life, so that we no longer need the infinite time. But neither does it shun pleasure, nor even when circumstances bring about our departure from life does it suppose, as it perishes, that it has in any way fallen short of the best life.[18]

Augustine may reveal something fundamental about the drive to consolidate his faith through the construction of paganism and heresy when, early in *The Confessions*, he confesses that he would have given himself over to Epicurus as a youth if only the latter believed that "after death there remain for the soul life and rewards and punishments . . . "[19] Epicurus might reply that it is above all this demand for universalization of one doctrine designed to secure eternity that intensifies the drive to punish difference on earth. Better, then, to acknowledge that "when it comes to death we human beings all live in the same unwalled city."[20] Or to treat those adversaries who affirm the oblivion of death in order to celebrate life with the highest (adversarial) honor. For this very admission may place *them* under less internal pressure to construct heresies. Epicurus contends that the best way to subdue that resentment of the cosmos from which the urge to constitute heresies emerges is to affirm life, and that the most promising way to affirm life is to accept the oblivion of death. His very defect in the eyes of Augustine is a strength from the perspective I endorse.

Perhaps, then, the narcissistic insistence that a doctrine must deliver the highest prospects for life, rewards, and punishments "after death" fuels the drive to construct paganism and heresy as offenses before death. Augustine's double insistence on the priority of life after death and the delineation of an intrinsic moral order that confirms it is an issue to be posed immediately to him. But the Augustinian Imperative assumes a larger variety of forms in modern doctrines that relax the demand for eternal life but relocate the spirit of eternity in the cultural identities they endorse and the conceptions of intrinsic moral order they represent. These are the modern Augustinians. It is not so much what faiths they enunciate but how their adversaries are constituted in order to specify and secure these faiths.

Augustine generally favors restraints on punishment of heretics, though he endorsed coercive ordainment into Catholic priesthood of a

Donatist priest who appealed to him to reverse the act. He supports expulsion of Manicheans from the church. He becomes most single-minded, however, in pursuit of the Pelagians, the final group of heretics he combats. Some others in his church are prepared to let Pelagians debate their beliefs within its confines. But Augustine campaigns, first, to have Pelagianism defined as a heresy and, second, to tighten the screws of punishment against those so convicted.

In a letter in 416 to John, the Bishop of Jerusalem, Augustine urges him to expel Pelagius in accord with the finding of the Council of Carthage against him. "For he asserts and urgently argues that through free-will alone human nature can be sufficient to do the works of righteousness and keep all God's commandments."[21] These are not debatable or mistaken assertions to Augustine, but "perverted and sacrilegious arguments." He urges the bishop, who he knows to be fond of Pelagius, to express this love by correcting these foul thoughts. "Open his eyes then by teaching and exhorting him and praying for the salvation he ought to have in Christ, so that he may confess that grace of God the saints are proved to have confessed, when . . . He commanded them . . . ; for those things would not have been commanded unless to the end that our will be revealed, nor would they be asked for, unless to the end that the weakness of our will should have the help of Him who commanded them."[22] With respect to the key question of grace, Augustine is "anxious to know what [Pelagius] believes and holds, what he definitely confesses and preaches. In other points . . . , even if he be proved to be in error, none the less until he accepts correction it is more tolerable to bear with him."[23]

The hunt is on. It is pursued from an unquestioned presumption of doctrinal superiority. Certainly, there is no hint in this letter of corollary difficulties Augustine encounters in specifying the exact relation grace bears to free will and both bear to original sin in the quest for salvation. Such a concession might convert the case for expulsion into an occasion for sustained debate within the frame of the church. In another letter to followers whose doubts have been aroused by the Pelagian challenge, Augustine alludes to this issue obliquely, saying, "Put your faith for the present in the inspired statements that in man there is both free will and divine grace, without the aid of which free will can neither be turned to God nor make any advance towards God;

and pray that what you submissively put your faith in, you may wisely come to understand."[24]

Appeals to inspiration, submission, and prayer sew up itchy sores within the doctrine "for the present"; demands for immediate interrogation, exact specification of belief, and expulsion expose festering sores in the doctrine of the adversary. The sewing needle for those who accept authority and the surgical knife for those who don't: These are among the weapons Augustine wields to wage wars of identity\difference.

Authoritative measures are pushed another step when Augustine writes to Sixtus, Bishop of Rome, to celebrate his recent conversion to condemnation of Pelagianism. Augustine now calls on Sixtus not only to punish "with wholesome severity" those who "rave about that error" but also to employ all the "vigilance of a pastor against those who, though in a stealthier and more covert manner, still do not cease to whisper it."[25] The vigilant ear of the pastor must now listen to voices reduced to a whisper; it must even detect the hidden sores in those reduced to silence.

> Some . . . have suddenly become silent, so that it is impossible to ascertain whether they have been cured of it unless they not only refrain from uttering those false doctrines, but actually take up the defense of contrary doctrines with the same fervour they showed in propounding error. These, however, call for milder treatment: what need is there to terrify them, when their very silence shows that they are terrified enough? At the same time they are not to be spared remedial attention . . . because their sore is hidden. For . . . they yet ought to be taught, and, in my opinion, this process is easier while the fear they have of severe measures assists him who teaches them the truth.[26]

Because the specific doctrine Augustine confesses is not stabilizable by argument alone and because he earnestly seeks its stability and universality, he moves in this case to support coercive confession. He is moved, that is, to teach truth through fear and to verify acceptance of his teaching by requiring silenced adversaries to "take up the defense" of the truth "with the same fervour they showed in propounding error." What anxiety propels this imperative to coercive confession? Perhaps these reforming heretics must be compelled to recapitulate Augustine's path because its unanimous confession is the most reassuring validation Augustinian faith can receive on earth. Perhaps this amplification of coercion reveals the role confession itself plays in constituting the object of confession. For does the imperative to confess ever dispense altogether with force and fear? Is confession not inherently ambiguous?

> The morality of confession/confession
>   as a device of coercive moralization;
> empowerment through confession/confession
>   as an apparatus of doctrinal power;
> the anxiety of confession/confession
>   as a machine of anxiety formation.

The Ambiguity of Confession

Augustine's relations to the feuding sisters, Ecdicia, pagans who mock him, Nectarius, Manicheans, Donatists, and Pelagians convey multiple signs of an anxiety to consolidate, stabilize, and generalize his faith through confession, an anxiety to produce the truth through the confessional imperative. Through a variety of tactics he presses others to confirm his faith by speaking the words he needs to hear.

Augustine is *moved* by words strained through the soul and confessed to a god before other humans. So are his followers, his readers, and his opponents. Words as weapons against forces of perversion; words as vehicles of conversion; words as articulations of moral order; words as performances of divinization; words as enactments of condemnation. This Christian, trained in the arts of pagan rhetoric, knows how to do things with words; he knows how to arouse anxiety, to insinuate moral order into life, and to relieve distress through linguistic performances. Above all, he knows how to use words as instruments of conversion. As we experience through him the power of words to move, inflame, comfort, console, clarify, blame, convert, pervert, arouse guilt, and condemn, we become better able to appreciate the intimate relations between a discursive code and the formation of identity.

None of us escapes the confessional imperative entirely; each of us experiences it as productive and destructive to varying degrees in varying contexts. A writer, for instance, puts words on paper to warn, define, or inspire oneself and others. No writer is free from the drive to convert. Note how carefully a writer puts words together. If a particular cluster of words is not grouped together in the right way in the right context, something both fugitive and crucial might be lost. Some possibility for conversion might be forfeited. To write or speak with care is to disclose something about the power of confession. That, at any rate, is the faith implicitly inscribed in a large variety of linguistic enactments. This dense traffic in words reveals and conceals, organizes and disturbs, constitutes and defers, converts and perverts; even more, it helps to constitute what counts as revealing, disturbing, converting, perverting.

If there is a trace of the confessional in every sentence uttered or scrawled on paper or projected onto a computer screen, this may help to explain the anxiety with which a writer forms, revises, reforms, withholds, and releases sentences flowing through one. A residue of "the sentence" as juridical judgment clings persistently to "the sentence" as grammatical form. The relief of sentencing. The anxiety of sentencing. The sentencing of anxiety. We will never escape the influence of confession, nor would it simply be desirable if we did. That is precisely why dangers attached to the confessional imperative must be explored.

Augustine brings out the power of confession more richly and profoundly than anyone before or after. But he then fails (or refuses?) to explore dangers built in to an authoritative confessional practice bound to an imperative of intrinsic moral order. He fails to consider the ambiguity of confession as he confesses his conversion to the author of an intrinsic moral order. Better, he always converts anxiety aroused through attention to the ambiguity of confession into energy for a renewal of confession.

The Augustinian confessional complex is an incredibly powerful mechanism through which to nurture an authoritative identity and foster the experience of intrinsic moral order. Through the confessional imperative Augustine's god is constituted authoritatively, his own will is filled with a new order, members of his church are drawn closer to his faith, and opponents of his doctrine are brought into line. But this authoritative demand to confess must be invoked stringently, for the confessional mode is also inadvertently well devised to arouse the deepest doubts about the dark and dubious object to whom one confesses.

This anxiety to confess and this implicit confession of anxiety culminates in Augustine's demand to coerce confession from Pelagian heretics already reduced to silence. Faith consolidated through confession of its truth. Silence experienced as a threat to faith. Coercive confession as an antidote to dangerous silence. Augustine does not endorse torture or murder of his opponents. Coercive confession, rarely invoked by him, is one of the most severe intrusions he endorses. But its active commendation on this occasion may signify something pervasive about the relations among anxiety, confession, faith, and identity. What does this surge of anxiety reveal in the presence of silence? Perhaps it discloses the fragility of identity in a world where the ground upon which it seeks to stand is perpetually moved by articulations of it. Perhaps it reveals an incorrigible ambiguity in discourse as the element of *performance* in it repeatedly destabilizes the drive to *discover* a stable anchor. Augustine teaches explicitly about the power of confession and implicitly about the confessional imperative as a cultural mechanism of power. We need to ponder both dimensions together.

The Confession of Politics

It might be suggested that as Augustine ages an earlier idealism manifested in *The Confessions* gives way to that cranky authoritarianism often discernible in the later letters. Although such an interpretation is probably pertinent, it seems insufficient to me. The later letters evince numerous instances of the idealism apparent in the earlier text. Moreover, *The Confessions* also castigate pagans and introduce the theme of heresy. The fundamental dynamic seems to me to be this: The form created by the confessional imperative governs the shape assumed by the operational politics of identity and difference. Augustine would have to attenuate the universality, or morality, or certainty, or definiteness of the god he confesses to modify significantly the politics by which he seeks to fix, stabilize, and generalize things. Augustinian politics presupposes the confessional imperative and the confessional imperative constitutes the core of Augustinian politics.

Augustine probably did not perceive fully the operational politics implicit in the god he confessed at the time of *The Confessions*. And it is probably still possible to defend some version of intrinsic moral order while bypassing or blunting the effects we have discerned in the Augustinian version. But some who review the trail Augustine has traversed will find it preferable to rethink this moral/confessional ideal more radically in relation to the politics it spawns.

Perhaps that is why Zarathustra, a competing carrier of the spirit of "awakening," reconsiders the type of relation Augustine establishes with his adversaries. Z's adversaries, like Augustine's, are essential to him. They give him specificity. He needs them to be himself. And he says so. But he also appreciates the force of the paradox built in to the experience of conversion, and he ponders how contestable the "conjectures" guiding him are. He thus counsels a new *generosity* in social relations, one governed neither by the quest to uncover an intrinsic moral order nor by the ideal of maintaining cautious neutrality between alternative perspectives. The first ideal is doomed to spawn repression ("annihilation") of the other if it pursues its end relentlessly; the second can only avoid violence against others to the extent it empties itself of a capacity for action and specificity.

Zarathustra does try to "pass by" the "poisonous flies" of dogmatism whenever possible. For if you debate dogmatists and fundamentalists too long you too will be pulled into the swamp in which they live. But, wherever possible and above all, Zarathustra seeks to cultivate a new generosity among "noble" rivals. " 'Enemy' you shall say, but not 'villain'; 'sick' you shall say, but not 'scoundrel'; 'fool' you shall say, but not 'sinner.' "[27] To receive Zarathustra's message here one needs, first, to recall that he uses the word "sick" in this context before the 20th century medicalized a whole host of differences under the headings of *sickness* and *abnormality*. Second, one might add another pair to the list: " 'rival' you shall say, but not 'heretic.' "

Zarathustra's orientation thrives amidst a reciprocal recognition of cloudiness in the pool of "life" (or, from an alternative perspective, "divinity") from which rivals draw sustenance, amidst a reciprocal recognition of the way in which the very determinacy of your identity depends on the existence of my difference, and amidst reciprocal cultivation of appreciation for these ambiguous conditions of life. Z summarizes this ideal of agonistic reciprocity in a parable: "For many who are noble are needed, and noble men of many kinds, that there may be a nobility. Or as I once said in a parable: 'Precisely this is godlike, that there are gods, but no God.' "[28] The highest form of godliness is the type that does not demand capitalization, affirms self-limitation, divinizes contestation, and practices forbearance in its contestations. This type of godliness still remains uncommon.

Such a generosity of spirit amidst rivalry is difficult to sustain, to say the least. It presupposes a certain reciprocity of spirit that might be jeopardized by the closure or dogmatism of either party. This difficulty is amplified as each party strives to awaken others to its virtues and to its opponents' vices. As each practices the arts of conversion. My contestation of Augustinian politics represents one such effort to oppose a rival position actively while refusing to define it as heretical. The opposition must be lively and firm to make a political difference; but it must also evince the sense that the sources *it* draws on in pressing its case are *also* fugitive, ambiguous, and problematical. It exposes uncertainties, undecidabilities, and ambiguities in the opposition without pretending to do so from a ground that is solid, intrinsic, or incontestable. It affirms the element of paradox within which it works. It resists and counters its adversaries without striving to eliminate them.

In any event, the counsel of Zarathustra sets limits to the prerogatives of love and confession: It *restricts* the politics of alter-definition and conversion by attending to the paradoxical character of the enterprise within which soul-mates, allies, and adversaries are defined. And by pointing to the positive value served by a plurality of contending gods. Zarathustra may be a beacon to pursue after a durable history of experience with several varieties of Augustinianism. If the faith of Z is not likely to be universalized, its active introduction into the established terms of cultural debate might still engender productive effects on the way contending parties struggle with differences they are implicated in and threatened by.

Notes

1. Augustine, *The Confessions of St. Augustine*, trans. John K. Ryan (New York: Image Books, 1960), Bk. 9, chap. 1, 205.

2. *Confessions*, Bk. 10, chap. 2, 229.

3. *St. Augustine: Select Letters*, trans. James H. Baxter (Cambridge, MA: Harvard University Press, 1930), Epistle 211, 377.

4. *Select Letters*, Epistle 211, 381.

5. *Select Letters*, Epistle 211, 381.

6. *Select Letters*, Epistle 211. Fragments quoted appear between pages 383 and 390.

7. *Select Letters*, Epistle 211, 389.

8. *Select Letters*, Epistle 211, 391.

9. *Select Letters*, Epistle 211, 394-95.

10. *Select Letters*, Epistle 242, 501.

11. *Select Letters*, Epistle 242, 519.

12. *Select Letters*, Epistle 232, 471.

13. *Select Letters*, Epistle 232, 473.

14. *Select Letters*, Epistle 41, 163.

15. *Confessions*, Bk. 8, chap. 9, 107.

16. *Confessions*, Bk. 8, chap. 10, 197.

17. *Confessions*, Bk. 7, chap. 19, 178.

18. A. A. Long and D. N. Sedley, eds. and trans., *The Hellenistic Philosophers*, Vol. 1 (Cambridge, UK: Cambridge University Press, 1987), 150. I am not, of course, endorsing the entire doctrine of Epicurus (or whatever fragments of it we have) in supporting the spirit of this quotation. I do think that the orientation one adopts to the fact of mortality is significant in itself and a metaphor for the possible orientations one develops toward the contingent, incomplete, and relational character of one's own identity. See my *Identity\Difference: Democratic Negotiations of Political Paradox* (Ithaca, NY: Cornell University Press, 1991), especially chap. 6.

19. *Confessions*, Bk. 6, chap. 16, 154.

20. Epicurus in Long and Sedley, eds., *Hellenistic Philosophers*, 150.

21. *Select Letters*, Epistle 179, 309.

22. *Select Letters*, Epistle 179, 313.

23. *Select Letters*, Epistle 179, 315.

24. *Select Letters*, Epistle 214, 413.

25. *Select Letters*, Epistle 191, 339.

26. *Select Letters*, Epistle 191, 339.

27. Friedrich Nietzsche, *Thus Spoke Zarathustra*, trans. Walter Kaufmann (New York: Penguin, 1978), 38. Even with the qualification surrounding "sick" installed in the text, I am still less enamored with it than with the others in the sentence by Zarathustra. To call someone sick is hardly to invite him to reply vigorously; the condemnation seems total and devoid of an invitation to reciprocal rivalry. And yet there is something like "sickness" in a totalitarian drive to uniformity redeemed through an imperative of intrinsic moral order. I resist the word but can't refrain from the thought. More about this issue later.

28. *Thus Spoke Zarathustra*, 203.

4

The Genesis of Being

The Mythic

No culture dispenses with myth. To think you have done so is to shut your eyes while pouring the terms of a dominant myth into contemporary stories and philosophies, sciences and novels, dreams and nightmares, institutions of punishment and reward. Whenever a journalist greets a new invention of science such as gene splicing or space travel or amniocentesis by invoking the fear of a Brave New World, she unconsciously contemporalizes the mythic image of a natural, harmonious state of human being threatened by an imminent fall into alienation, exile, or punishment because of hubristic tampering.[1] Traces from the Promethean and Edenic myths infiltrate into such journalism. Indeed, in this extremely common version, the automatic pilot governing the story line draws attention to dangers in the new invention while diverting it from those attached to the current condition. For the unconscious structure of the narrative treats what we are (or are thought to have been in the discernible past) as "natural" and "given" by contrast to the introduction of artificial, constructed, alienated elements into life. Such a story line conceals the constructed character of the present in the way it laments new constructions. It pleads for a return to wholeness without asking whether there is something whole to return to, thereby loading the terms of comparison between the new and the old without recognizing it has done so. It recapitulates an old myth by avoiding scrutiny of the paradigmatic form the mythic assumes in this culture.

Donna Haraway, in *Primate Visions*, draws attention to how the *National Geographic* repeatedly prints photographs of a young woman naturalist touching an ape in the wilds of Africa.[2] The scene recapitulates the Edenic wish to return to a harmonious, natural state that precedes culture. It draws the tension of attraction and prohibition in the early myth into its recapitulation without drawing attention overtly to cultural issues posed by this recapitulation. It reinstates an old "nature/culture" divide while invoking the corollary experience of strange energies that flow across it. It unconsciously tells the old story in a new setting. Something of this electricity ("fire") was captured in news stories in the early 1980s about the Tassaday, a "stone age" people residing deep in the jungle of the Philippines, untouched by the alienation of modern culture/technology/desire until a couple of anthropologists introduced knives and mirrors to them. We gave them a touch of complexity and alienation; they gave us the memory of harmony and simplicity. Did "they" possess a myth of departure from wholeness before "we" arrived? We will never know, for the initial claims of pristine purity were soon liquidated, as "we" found out that their history of transactions with cultures outside themselves was far more extensive than initially imagined.

A myth, says Nietzsche,

> is a concentrated image of the world that, as a condensation of phenomena, cannot dispense with miracles. It is probable, however, that almost everyone, upon close examination, finds that the critical-historical spirit of our culture has so affected him that he can only make the former existence of myth credible to himself by means of scholarship, through intermediary abstractions. But without myth, every culture loses the healthy natural power of its creativity. . . . Myth alone saves all the powers of the imagination and of the Apollonian dream from their aimless wanderings.[3]

Nietzsche, at least in this early text, seems to think it possible to experience mythic truths without the mediation of interpretation. He thinks that folk music provides the vehicle. Something fundamental has been lost by modern intellectuals who can "only make the former existence . . . credible . . . by means of scholarship." This drive for immediate experience of the mythic disappears in his later work, but here it recapitulates the myth of a fall from wholeness while discussing the mythic. The wholeness lost is not that of a harmony within and without, but the direct experience of the tragic character of existence. I would say, against this, that interpretation is intrinsic to the mythic, that whenever you are in the territory of myth you are in a place where interpretation is both indispensable and problematical.

After this amendment, most of what Nietzsche says about the mythic seems salutary. A myth, in speaking to a culture, condenses and concentrates its experience of being. Mythic miracle, magic, and divinity make these abbreviations possible. They make it possible to glimpse the cultural unconscious through the mirror of myth. Without the abbreviations provided by miracles, and the like, no mirror would be small enough to reflect a cultural profile back to us. Pondering mythic abbreviations is thus a way to rethink elements in the cultural unconscious. And the points of ambiguity and mystery within a myth invite the most extensive reflection and interpretation. A myth invites us to project meanings and messages into it. And the projections reveal something fundamental about us, even though this moment of reflexivity is itself open to further interpretation. Attention to the mythic encourages us to attend both to the indispensability and problematicality of interpretation in life.

Myth is to theory/philosophy as faith is to argument. Every philosophical argument resides within a nest of cultural understandings not themselves up for consideration in that analysis. Thus, myth is more crucial to reflexivity in interpretation than a massive accumulation of detailed arguments is. Myth fuels the interpretive imagination and gives you new possibilities to argue about. Those who give primacy to arguments are the least likely to ponder the cultural unconscious that drives their thinking. They are the most likely to be thoughtless. A philosophical culture, for example, governed by the theme of the sufficiency of reason, could never establish the truth of this thesis by the only means it accepts for doing so.

A powerful myth registers things that must somehow be taken into account in life. Yet, each attempt to reduce it to a single formula of interpretation is almost certain to fail. Perhaps the enigmatic character of the mythic registers darkly a plenitude of being that exceeds the grasp of any single interpretation. Perhaps this is part of the wisdom that emerges out of the mythic.

The myth of Genesis is fundamental to Euro-American culture. It infiltrates into contemporary practices of identity, production, responsibility, guilt, punishment, confession, and faith. Its abbreviations enter into the cultural unconscious and the shifting terms of emphasis in the cultural unconscious flow into revised readings of it. The Augustinian reading of the Edenic myth remains authoritative. It exercises so much cultural power that it is difficult to read those old words without *immediately* projecting Augustine's meanings into them. Both those who celebrate the myth and those who condemn its punitive character tend to treat the Augustinian version as dispositive. Let us, then, introduce an element of creative estrangement into this context before moving to the Augustinian reading. Let us consider the version of Eden presented by "J" in *The Book of J*, translated by David Rosenberg and including a valuable interpretation by Harold Bloom.

Biblical scholars have long thought that the lines gathered together as Genesis (and other books as well) were written by several different authors at different times. "Normative priests," as Harold Bloom calls those exercising religious authority in early Judaic culture, gathered these disparate versions together and combined them to form the early books of the Bible as we know them today. This explains how several canonical events in Genesis, for instance, appear two or three times in awkward repetition. Anyway, those writings thought to be authored by J have recently been isolated and presented independently in *The Book of J*.

J presents the garden in Eden in the second paragraph, after Yahweh had spilled rain on the earth and shaped an earthling "from clay of this earth." "[T]he tree of life was there in the garden and the tree of knowing good and bad."[4] Yahweh warns the man not to eat of the tree of good and bad, or on that day death will touch him. Then Yahweh shapes creatures of the field and birds of the air out of the soil and fashions a woman out of the man's rib. "And look: they are naked, man and woman, untouched by shame, not knowing it."[5] The key action occurs when the snake, the woman and the man interact for the first time.

> Now the snake was smoother-tongued than any wild creature that Yahweh made. "Did the God really mean," he said to the woman, "you can't eat from any tree of the garden?"
>
> "But the fruit of the trees we may," said the woman to the snake. "Just the tree in the middle of the garden, the God said. You can't eat it, you can't touch—without death touching you." "Death will not touch you," said the snake to the woman. "The God knows on the day you eat from it your eyes will fall open like gods, knowing good and bad."
>
> Now the woman sees how good the tree looks, to eat from, how lovely to the eyes, lively to the mind. To its fruit she reached; ate, gave to her man, there with her, and he ate.
>
> And the eyes of both fall open, grasp knowledge of their naked skin. They wound together fig leaves, made coverings for themselves.[6]

When Yahweh returns to find the man hiding with shame in his nakedness, the man tells him that the woman gave him the fruit of the tree. And when the woman, also hiding, is asked, she tells him the smooth-tongued snake gave the fruit to her. The snake is not interrogated by the god. Yahweh then comes down heavily on all three, making the snake taste dirt as it crawls and live in eternal animosity to the seed of woman; giving woman pains of labor in birth and desire for the body of the eager man who makes her pregnant; and condemning man to labor each day in the field. Eventually man and woman will return to the earth from which they sprang, from dust to dust. In the meantime, "Yahweh made clothes from the skins of the wild animals for the man and woman, dressed them."[7]

That's it. The brevity of this fundamental text creates a wonderful, compelling site for interpretation.

Note how the initial rift in the order of being is pried open through a question posed by a snake, the first creature to speak after Yahweh. "Did the God really mean . . . ?" it asks the woman.[8] A question opening uncertainty into the web of being. A question, indeed, is the first non-divine act, and, as such, it may reveal something intrinsic to action.

This very first act calls the presumption of a seamless order of being into question. Is being thereby shown to contain uncertainty, contingency, freedom, possibility, and the capacity for creativity *in* its very structure? Or does the question suggest that the world would not have any rifts *if* the snake had not posed this fateful question?

As these two questions indicate, once the first question is posed, an endless series of others follows in its train. Questioning indicates something about being. Augustine, one might suggest, fills this rift by translating the steady flow of questions into an endless stream of confessions. The confessional mode provides his response to the question of whether the first question revealed or produced a rift in being. As others ponder how the first words spoken by a creature take the form of a question, they might be moved to conclude that a rift is intrinsic to the constitution of being. To them, it may seem that Augustine is terrorized by the rift in being. Everything else changes if you respond in this way to the experience of questioning.

Take the issue of responsibility. Responsibility for eating from the tree of good and bad is susceptible to several readings. If the culture of the West were not already saturated with the Augustinian Eden, it would be plausible to conclude that all four figures in this relationship share responsibility: Yahweh because he engendered the trio with their respective dispositions; the three engendered beings because each made an indispensable contribution to the act in question. No omnipotent, omniscient god on this reading. An energetic, active, impatient god who has things to learn about the effects of its interventions.

But this disposition raises the question why "responsibility" is the most fundamental issue to pose here. Maybe that is a childish demand to impose on a text about the cloudy deeds of children. Maybe the text presents an accidental nexus of divine inventions, unexpected events, newly crystallized desires, fateful interactions, and divine responses, an accidental conjunction of beings, events and deeds in which human beings end up getting kicked around. Only those who have other reasons to do so would be required to read this story as a primordial lesson in responsibility. Otherwise, they might find the god to be a cruel bungler. First he warns against an act; next he brings three beings into contact whose interactions engender it; then he comes down extremely hard on them for the effect he opposes. Perhaps this is a god to be dealt with strategically: learning not to expect too much beneficence from it because of its limitations and arbitrariness, but learning as well to be wary of saying too much about these characteristics because of its demonstrated power and will-ingness to do you in. It may be possible to respect such a being, to welcome it as an unruly force to contend with and against. But it would not be reasonable to worship it with abject humility or to expect it to perform huge miracles in the future. Unless it terrifies you . . . ; and you unconsciously respond to this terror with a discreet strategy to convert it to the being you wish it to be.

It is not so clear that this 'origin story' presents a blissful, harmonious state from which humanity "falls." There is ambiguity, uncertainty, and tension in the garden "from the beginning." The smooth-tongued snake is a part of the "original condition," and its actions recoil back on the divinity who engendered it. Yahweh appears on this reading as an unsteady character who has a slippery grip on the effects of its own power. Moreover, the knowledge of "good and bad" that emerges is an advance in some respects even if it is experienced as a setback in others. Perhaps the original condition could neither sustain itself without the introduction of this knowledge nor stabilize itself with it. In that event, a tragic conception of life is implicit in the narrative of the garden. And certainly not all of the effects of this knowledge are simply setbacks. What would life be without death, anyway? What about life without reflection on good and bad?

These suggestions and queries can't proceed very far, however, unless they are set in a more specific context of presentation. The key point is that Augustine does as much as anyone in Western history to set future contexts of discussion. Every interpretive point I have suggested so far responds somehow to the authoritative reading Augustine offers.

We shall keep these points in mind as we turn to a review of Harold Bloom's reading of J's Genesis. For Bloom has Augustine in mind, I think, almost as much as he does J. He thus affirms and denies possibilities that might never have occurred to J, since she lacked access to Augustine's work on her story, as well as to Paul's work before him. Crucial elements in the context through which *we* come to terms with this story were unavailable to "her," as Bloom would have it. We will never escape the presence of Augustine. But the sparse, vibrant prose of J may help us to respond to it more reflectively. She seems less terrified to me than he does, even though she, too, registers a rift in being.

Bloom, first, doubts that "woman" in this story is presented as subordinate to man. She is engendered second, out of man, but the description of her production is more detailed, and she is made out of flesh rather than dust. There is more subtlety in this being (which can be used for or against her). And, Bloom's J suggests, Yahweh learned how to do a better job "the second time around."

Second, the snake in its smoothness epitomizes unashamed naked-ness (the man and the woman are "smooth" too). Although the snake is sly and the two humans lack slyness, Bloom wonders, "How did the charming serpent of J ever become Satan?" Sure, satan is charming, but what makes charm satanic? The snake would have to know in advance what effects its persuasion would have, but nothing in the presentation requires the assumption that it does. And the fact that it too suffers the blows of Yahweh after the event seems to speak against this (though Bloom does not explicitly make this point). Bloom does suggest: "The serpent is in Eden because it belongs there; its presence, speech and discernment do not astonish the woman, and so we are not to think of it as magical or mythological. It is Yahweh's creature, his subtlest, and perhaps we can say now it is Yahweh's most ironical creature."[9] I think Bloom finds the snake to be Yahweh's most ironical creature because its intervention is indispensable to the first human act, while its very presence points back dramatically to its creator as the (inadvertent?) source of the very action the creator condemns and punishes.

Third, Bloom notes that the first act of violence in this story occurs as Yahweh clothes the two humans in the skins of animals. These animals had to be killed before their skins could be used for clothing. But J is too alert to the volatile sensitivity of this god to call attention to this implication explicitly. This divine act of violence and J's subtle indication of it leads Bloom to his next point: The punishment by Yahweh of his creatures is "incommensurate" with the deed punished. The punishment presents a god whose arbitrariness and cruelty become factors to be reckoned with from that moment on.

I will consider a feature that seems to follow from Bloom's reading, but is not addressed there. Perhaps all four of the parties learn some-thing from this series of events, even while the punishment for the events fell disproportionately on the snake, the man, and the woman. They learn that the knowledge of good and bad is essential to human action. A certain innocence is shed when one learns this; one can no longer experience life in the same way. Yahweh had not quite realized that the tree of knowledge had to be picked for human life to proceed. Learning this lesson through an embarrassing experience of disobedience to his will, he punishes those who inadvertently teach it to him. Bloom, as I say, emphasizes the importance of this knowledge, without calling it *new knowledge* learned by Yahweh as an effect of actions he had forbidden others to take. Bloom says, "Good and bad is no less than everything, freedom and the limits of freedom, self-knowledge, angelic, almost godlike. When you know yourself, you know your own nakedness. . . . To open your eyes is to see everything, all at once, and so to see oneself as others might see one, as an object."[10]

To see yourself as an object is to realize that you can be used, exploited, abused, dominated, killed by other humans, and that you can be harmed, damaged, hurt, and destroyed by nature or its god(s). It is also to realize that you can be helped, loved, nurtured, and befriended by others and blessed by nature/god. Your sense of vulnerability and possibility expand together when you experience the mirror effect of yourself as object. The two humans begin to acquire that knowledge when they eat from the tree. They hide themselves on experiencing their objectivity. The lesson that they are objects is underlined dramatically by Yahweh's punishment of them. You acquire new fears, slyness, toughness, and yearnings when you eat from the tree of knowledge. So, perhaps, does Yahweh.

These reflections encourage me to add another dimension to Bloom's reading. Perhaps the snake should be understood as the concealed hero of this drama. The form (eventually) bestowed on the snake by Yahweh belies the crucial role it plays. For it exposes a rift in the order of being by posing a question. And it comes the closest to anticipating the necessity of eating from the tree of knowledge. Its intervention is fundamental and timely. "The God," it says, "knows on the day you eat from it your eyes will fall open like gods, knowing good and bad."

The god, while knowing that the eyes of humans will fall open like gods, does not anticipate the *necessity* of the snake's intervention; it only anticipates how insulting the effect of eating from the tree of knowledge would be to its sense of godliness, to its sense of supreme superiority. It seems to think, at least in its early, adolescent phase, that human life could flourish without the division and suffering attendant on knowledge. It wants humans to be, without their eyes falling open "like gods." Unless your interpretation of this story begins with the *prior* assumption that the god must be omnipotent and omniscient, the text may encourage you to see the god as limited in wisdom and the snake as an embodiment of it. Neither the god nor the snake possess "omniscience." But the snake exposes necessity by prodding humans into action. Because its intervention reveals a divine mistake and because it insults the god's supremacy in doing so, the snake is punished, along with the two children it prods into action. Because the two humans are still very much like children, they may accept the divine act of punitive power as a mysterious sign of their moral desert. It is unlikely that the snake goes along with them on this score, but it is not allowed to say. This acceptance of justice in divine punishment, signaled by the shame of the two humans, propels the idea of an intrinsic moral order into being. Or do "they" accept it? At any rate, most readers of this story project this fateful acceptance into it.

Power and wisdom are not concentrated in the same figure in this story. They are distributed between Yahweh and the snake, between divinity and nature. To seal the gap just revealed between its awesome power and its deficiency in wisdom, Yahweh converts the snake into a figure of contempt and fear rather than wisdom and beauty, even though a subordinate tradition in the West has persistently treated the snake to be a symbol of wisdom. Yahweh exercises his power of punishment to cover up his limitations in wisdom.

The snake—once you peer through its miserable appearance after Yahweh's punishment—bears a closer resemblance to a hero in Greek tragedy than does any other figure in this absorbing tale. It is punished for revelation of a hard truth it anticipates darkly and helps to nudge into being. Why is it punished? Because a drive circulates in this garden to look for someone to hold responsible when utopian hopes are shattered by hard realities? Such a drive is deeply bound up with the problem of evil in Western culture. We tend to look for a responsible agent whenever suffering occurs, and dominant readings of the Edenic myth encourage and exacerbate this disposition. If we were to read the snake as the first scapegoat required to protect the perfection of Yahweh, we might be in a better position to subject this tendency to critical reflection. The very first attribution of responsibility would be subjected to interrogation. We might come to think of responsibility as an indispensable social practice that typically contains elements of injustice in it, as a necessary activity inherently susceptible to inflation by those who impose utopian dreams of unity, salvation, freedom, or agency onto life.[11] We might come to terms in this way with a tragic dimension in modern practices of responsibility. If we were to treat the snake as a figure of respect because of the assistance it gives in pondering this issue, we might reflect on the tragic character of Eden more productively. But the myth of an omnipotent god would evaporate as we proceeded. And we would have to subdue the terror that seems to accompany initial experience of a tear or rift in the very fabric of being.

The Methodism of Augustine

Augustine delivers a lengthy reading of the Edenic myth designed to render credible an omnipotent, omniscient, and benevolent god who is also innocent of responsibility for evil and who, therefore, possesses both the capacity to provide eternal salvation for human beings and an interest in doing so. It is not an easy agenda to fill, but Augustine brings an impressive set of skills to it.

To approach Genesis with the proper spirit and interpretive sensibility Augustine devises a method for reading Scripture correctly. The essentials of this method are developed in *On Christian Doctrine*. These rules are attached to a spirituality that makes them function effectively, for "we do not come to Him who is everywhere present by moving from place to place, but by good endeavour and good habits."[12] The first and most fundamental rule to follow, then, in making sense of Scripture is a rule of faith.

This faith maintains, and it must be believed: neither the soul nor the human body may suffer complete annihilation, but the impious shall rise again into everlasting punishment, and the just into life everlasting.[13]

The importance of the rule of faith comes out as Augustine reviews difficulties in interpreting statements in which the text might be read either "literally" or "figuratively." How to decide between these two alternatives in specific instances?

> When investigation reveals an uncertainty as to how a locution should be pointed or construed, the rule of faith should be consulted as it is found in the more open places of the Scriptures and in the authority of the Church. But if both meanings, or all of them, in the event that there are several, remain ambiguous after the faith has been consulted, then it is necessary to examine the context of the preceding and following parts surrounding the ambiguous place, so that we may determine which of the meanings which suggest themselves it would allow to be consistent.[14]

Note how faith helps to determine the sense of context and how the context then helps to set the terms of faith. There is no such thing as context *simpliciter*; reference to it alone is never sufficient to guide the reading of a text. For a "context" results from a problematical conjunction of the assumptions, hopes, anxieties, and demands you bring to a text and the setting in which the text was written. These first rules (faith, context, consistency) are crucial for distinguishing between literal statements and figurative ones on Augustinian terms. But a supplementary guideline helps to solidify these three, "that whatever appears in the divine Word that does not literally pertain to virtuous behavior or to the truth of faith you must take to be figurative."[15] This is important, because sometimes a passage will appear to justify vice or crime, until the rule governing its proper placement between the figurative and the literal is introduced.

Still, sometimes, while following the rules of faith, context, consistency, and conviction of intrinsic moral order, a difficulty may persist. Here Augustine introduces an appreciation of mystery.

> But just as it is a servile infirmity to follow the letter and to take signs for the things that they signify, in the same way it is an evil of wandering error to interpret signs in a useless way. However, he who does not know what a sign means but does know that it is a sign, is not in servitude. Thus it is better to be burdened by unknown but useful signs than to interpret signs in a useless way so that one is led from the yoke of servitude only to thrust his neck into the snares of error.[16]

We have already learned how dangerous the snares of error can be to heretics.

It would be a mistake to think either that the primacy of method awaited the emergence of Descartes in the 17th century or that Augustine's introduction of a "rule of faith" is alien to later forms of method. The construction of methods precedes Descartes by several centuries, and certain rules of faith persist in every method introduced before, by, and after Descartes, including the methods of rationalism and empiricism in the modern age. Augustine's method has the virtue of being open about the particular faith that sustains it, while modern methods more often conceal the particular patterns of insistence that give them credibility.

Augustine introduces a method of textual reading because it is needed to tame and organize the protean Scripture that serves as the textual source of his faith. He could not have his faith without sacred Scripture, but also, a universalization of the reading of Scripture consonant with his faith is not assured until he devises an authoritative method for reading it. What, then, is the basis of this method? It does not seem to be grounded simply in Scripture, because it is a method for reading Scripture. But it cannot stand outside Scripture, for the word the lord relayed through Scripture is the ultimate ground of everything. Augustine introduces a circular process of vindication here, thought to transcend the trap of a vicious circle in which the claims to be defended are presupposed by the means through which they are defended. The key is to begin with a preliminary faith and then to have that faith validated, deepened, and improved as you apply it to the fundamental text; then you draw this amplified faith into guidelines that govern later textual readings. A productive spiral is thereby generated. The Augustinian method is thus a recipe rooted in a prior experience of faith and reading, not an abstract set of criteria mechanically applied to alien materials.

Still, for those who resist key presumptions governing the method, the dogmatism with which it is delineated seems disproportionate to the fundamentally controversial professions of faith that serve as its basis. This, too, is a common characteristic of modern doctrines that pretend to give primacy to a method while they actually bestow primacy on the articles of faith that undergird it. The principal difference between them and Augustine is that Augustine confidently and openly specifies the role that faith plays in the method he prescribes. Because Augustine fixes the terms through which Scripture must be read even as he claims that these terms flow from a reverential reading of Scripture, some of his critics may detect traces of the paradox of conversion circulating within this recipe for textual interpretation. Whatever one thinks of the status of the method, though, it is fair enough to say that it summarizes the sensibility through which Augustine appropriates the Edenic myth.

The Augustinian Genesis

The things you project into the porous text of Eden tell as much about your own hopes, fears, anxieties, and animosities as they do about necessities installed in the story. But the vantage point from which the projections of another are assessed is similarly informative. Where is the transcendental place from which these projections and counter-projections might be assessed? What if there is no such place? These questions may be borne in mind as we consider Augustine's brief on Eden and my de-briefing of it.

Augustine must not allow a limited or blundering or amoral god to enter Eden. He recognizes an allegorical dimension in the myth, but he also insists that these events actually occurred in history. "There is no prohibition against such [allegorical] exegesis, provided we also believe in the truth of the story as a faithful record of historical fact."[17] He must be alert to control the interpretation of key metaphors in this creation story so that no trace of the limitation in them sticks to the creator. Thus, though man is fashioned out of the "dust of the earth," this does not mean that the god worked as an artist works, with limited materials at his disposal. "He" worked as an omnipotent god works, achieving "visible results by invisible means."[18]

In Augustine's Eden, the god created Adam with free will. Adam acted through free will to disobey the single command issued by this god. And the god then delivered a punishment proportionate to the crime. The will of Adam is thus the window through which evil enters the world. This act makes Adam responsible for evil and deserving of punishment. The original sin of Adam created the divided will that humans experience thereafter through inheritance of the first sin. This inheritance makes the grace of the god indispensable to a healing of the will and the possibility of salvation. The woman named Eve is a subordinate figure in Augustine's presentation, more like a transmission belt than an active agent.

If you read Augustine as a sovereign politician of Scripture who constructs a sovereign, beneficent, salvational god out of scriptural materials, it is not too difficult to ascertain the imperatives governing his construction. He must drive a firm wedge between the god and the introduction of evil to preserve omnipotence and innocence together in the same divinity. Indeed, as we shall see, he must drive two wedges, one separating the will of Adam from god's responsibility, the other separating the will of the snake from god's responsibility. The gap between the god and evil is produced by the free will he attributes to the first two actors. The human will is *invented* to protect a will-ful god above all, but it is *presented* as an intrinsic property of human being that lifts it to the highest position among god's creatures because its composition reflects the image of the god's will. The attribution of *evil* to these first acts flows from the way they deviate from the intrinsic moral order Augustine identifies in Eden. Let's examine these strategic moments.

Our first parents, says Augustine, disobeyed the god's commandments and for the first time "felt a novel disturbance in their disobedient flesh, as a punishment which answered to their own disobedience." The disobedience of the god's command is an act of will attributed solely to them.

> The soul, in fact, rejoiced in its own freedom to act perversely and disdained to be God's servant; and so it was deprived of obedient service which its body had first rendered. At its own pleasure the soul deserted its superior and master; and so it no longer retained its inferior and servant obedient to its will. It did not keep its own flesh subject to it in all respects, as it could have kept it forever if it had itself continued in subjection to God.[19]

Augustine needs and asserts the absolute freedom of Adam. For if God "created man aright," as Augustine insists, the rift in being for which humans are "justly and rightly condemned" must come from "defects" for which Adam is responsible.[20] Adam "could have kept" this state of bliss forever, but acted freely not to. And inheritance of this "first sin" by all succeeding humans, who "*were* that one man who fell into sin through the woman who was made from him before the first sin," enables

Augustine to explain the human experience of a divided will thereafter.[21] The first, pristine act of will separates the god from evil by devolving evil on "man"; the resultant punishment of death, labor, and a divided will explains the common condition of humanity afterward.

The inheritance of original sin can be seen to be essential to Augustine's doctrine of Eden, once one begins to appreciate the profundity in his understanding of the role obdurate habit plays in shaping human conduct (after the fall). Original sin, as I read it, is a softening agent in the Augustinian narrative. It offers a weak excuse for the repetition of sin through recourse to the inheritance of a divided will; and it provides a miserable explanation for the human experience of dissonance within life that this god must not be held responsible for. But a poor excuse and a miserable explanation may be better than none, when the stakes are infinitely high. The inheritance of original sin is functionally indispensable to the protection of Augustine's conception of divinity; and it also provides humans living under the gaze of this omnipotent being with the hope that the baleful effects of obdurate and sinful habits might be redeemed by its abundant grace. Omnipotence, original sin, divided will, obduracy of habit, and grace go together in this system. If you drop one of the elements all of the others will have to be modified significantly. Within this complex, the inheritance of obdurate tendencies to sinfulness suggests the need for grace; grace is the hope of hopes for those who blame themselves for the rift, fear eternal damnation, and hold salvation to be beyond the capacity of their own wills alone. It would be psychologically intolerable to retain the other elements of the doctrine while dropping original sin and grace, for the experience of habit, sin, and divided will would then defeat every hope for salvation. This is the moment of truth in Augustine's repudiation of Pelagianism, though the critique is not presented as necessary to retain the psychological plausibility of his own doctrine. The doctrine of original sin is often presented as the one element in Augustinianism most in need of revision because of the sense of injustice that attaches to it. But, again, *within* the hard compound into which it is mixed, it is a softening agent.

But, granting that these elements (a pristine act of pure will, human guilt for the rift in being, the inheritance of original sin, the pure separation of good from evil, the desert of divine punishment, the role of grace) are *functionally indispensable* to Augustine's concept of omnipotent divinity, how *could* the very first human act have been an act of "will"? For something can be functionally indispensable to a faith or practice and nonetheless highly problematic in its credibility. Augustine is acutely aware of this issue, and we will return to it.

Augustine insists not only that Adam's act is the only pure act before the introduction of the divided will, but that the punishment meted out by the god for this pure act of disobedience is proportionate to the crime. The crime is willful rebellion, willful disobedience to the will of the god. The penalties are severe: a slimy life for the snake, labor in childbirth for women, toilsome work for men, a divided will for humans in general, a first death for the twosome followed by a "second death" that takes the form of damnation.[22] The punishment may seem a little excessive to some. But Augustine finds it appropriate because the pristine act of will generates such a fundamental rift in being and because the rift would have been so easy to avoid.

> The injunction . . . was so easy to observe, so brief to remember; above all, it was given at a time when desire was not yet in opposition to the will. . . . Therefore the unrighteousness of violating the prohibition was so much the greater, in proportion to the ease with which it could have been observed and fulfilled.[23]

An omnipotent, benevolent, salvational god; an unnecessary rift in being created through the pristine will of the first human; an original fall into sinfulness inherited by every human to follow; severe and deserved punishment for the act; obedience to the god as the sign of a healed will; the grace of the god as crucial to healing of the divided will; salvation as the hope attached to grace. This is the logic governing the Augustinian reading of Eden. Suffering is explained by making human beings primordially responsible for it. Human responsibility is explained through the doctrine of pristine will. The god is protected from responsibility for evil through the introduction of human will into the order of being. All these effects ensue, that is, as long as this slender "will" can bear the load Augustine imposes on it.

What role does the snake play here? Do *its* actions not recoil back on the divinity that created it?

Augustine's reading of the snake provides the second wedge between his god and responsibility for evil. The snake is a mask worn by Lucifer.

Lucifer, an angel who fell from this god through a previous, proud act of willful disobedience, enters Eden in a fallen state. The snake form is particularly appropriate to Lucifer because of its "slippery body, moving along in tortuous twists and turns."[24] Lucifer, crawling along in Eden, envies the unfallen state of the first two humans. It knows it cannot fool Adam directly—the superior human in this twosome of Adam and Eve because his will is given the purest form—so it practices its powers of seduction on the woman, the subordinate, seducible creature. This snake is very sly, "supposing that man would not be trapped by a false move on his own part, but only if he yielded to another's mistake."[25] Eve is successfully deceived. Adam, in his turn, "yields" to her "suggestion," not because he too is deceived, but because he does not want to forfeit the pleasure promised. It is clear why this highest human in the intrinsic order of things (Adam) must not be deceived by the snake, for otherwise he would not be blameworthy enough and the god would not be pushed far enough away from implication in responsibility for evil. So Adam, the third creature drawn into this series of sinful suggestions—unless you, reasonably enough, count Yahweh's command as the first suggestion—"sinned knowingly and deliberately."[26] But it is still not clear to me why Eve, the one being in this foursome (the god, the snake, Adam, Eve) *not* said by Augustine to act with full and deliberate will, deserves the harsh punishment visited upon her—unless her subordination in the intrinsic order of things makes the sins of males automatically recoil on the females dependent on them.

Now the structure of the story is set. The god is protected by two pristine acts of will creating a gap between it and the inception of evil, suffering, divided will, labor in childbirth, and imposition of a double death. Humanity is guilty. Its future salvation is preserved as a possibility. Good is separated cleanly from evil in the intrinsic order of things. Augustine knows how to construct a reading producing the effect he demands. This creative theologization of Eden, prepared to some degree by Paul's writings before Augustine, delivers rich dividends for the faith that energizes it.

Two sores, however, begin to "fester" within the bowels of this story. First, if an omnipotent god created these beings and an omniscient, moral god possesses foreknowledge of these events, how can it avoid moral implication in the acts for which it holds them responsible?

Second, how can the *first acts* of evil by Lucifer and Adam, respectively, be attributed to their wills without any responsibility flowing back to the god who created these willful beings? These questions do not stare out as directly as others would have had Augustine confessed his god without intervening in the story of Eden. They displace a blunt question: How could or would an omnipotent, omniscient, moral god ever allow suffering and punishment to enter the world? The more subtle questions generated by Augustine's rewriting of Eden are posed above all by those who wish to remain within the folds of this faith but find themselves troubled by nagging doubts as they study its details. The faithful can be counselled to renew their faith as they ponder these puzzles, and to treat insistent reiteration of them as possible signs of a lack of piety that impedes the very understanding sought. These displaced questions are thus politically less disruptive. The Augustinian theologization of Eden depoliticizes difficulties that might otherwise destabilize its faith; but this strategy of deferral and displacement is susceptible to destabilization in its turn. That's politics.

I state the two questions in the terms appropriate to Augustine's conception of an intrinsic order commanded/designed by an omnipotent god. If you were to drop the Augustinian Imperative, the form of the questions would change significantly. In examining these two issues, we will remain close to the Augustinian formulation of them, reserving the right, however, to ask as well how they appear from a place outside this particular pattern of insistence.

Augustine's god must have foreknowledge of everything that will occur, or else it would not be omniscient. But foreknowledge of these fateful events in Eden so close to the creative moment seems to implicate it in them, and his combination of benevolence and omnipotence would seem to require that he act to circumvent these effects if their implications were clear to him in advance. "God was well aware that man would sin," and he was equally aware of the effects of this sin. But he also knew that through them a process would be set in motion in which the good would eventually "enter into fellowship with the holy angels in eternal peace, when the 'last enemy,' death, had been destroyed."[27] Here Augustine invokes a "Hegelian conception before Hegel" of historical progress through the providential effects of suffering. But Augustine also evinces awareness that the treatment of evil as a vehicle of future perfection cannot be satisfying to those who take god's omnipotence seriously. They will ask: "Why could your perfect god not come up with a better way that did not involve so much suffering and punishment?" So this theme of the providential effects of evil, often introduced as a palliative, is superseded by a more fundamental assertion. The god foresees and foreknows everything in all time without being responsible for the evil events foreknown.

How? The question forms part of a more general issue as to how the god could know the future if the future does not take the form of a return of the past. The cyclical theory of return had been introduced by Stoics to answer the question skeptics posed to them: What was god doing *before* it invented the world? This question is an embarrassment to both Augustine and the Stoics. Its embarrassment to Augustine resides, first, in the suggestion that there was a time before his god invented time and, second, in the judgment that his god created this world because of some deficit in itself before the creation. Perhaps it was bored or lazy or needy or incomplete before it created the world, and the creation was designed to fill one or more of those lacks. The Stoic answer to such charges: There was no time before the world because the world is governed by long cycles that eternally recur. The god knows each cycle because it has lived through the preceding ones. But this resolves the problem of the god/time relation (was there a time before a god in time invented time?) by introducing a world in which the god is now limited by the eternal return of the same cycle of events. The notion of eternal return, Augustine insists, is thus "blasphemous." Augustine rejects the Stoic solution while retaining god's omnipotence, timelessness, benevolence, and foreknowledge of all events. He says,

> Who are we mere men to presume to set limits to his knowledge, by saying that if temporal things and events are not repeated in periodic cycles, God cannot foreknow all things which he makes. . . . In fact his wisdom is multiple in its simplicity, and multiform in uniformity. It comprehends all incomprehensible things with such incomprehensible comprehension that if he wished always to create new things of every possible kind, each of them unlike its predecessor, none of them could be for him undesigned and unforeseen. . . . God's wisdom would contain each and all of them in his eternal prescience.[28]

I take Augustine to say that his god, through its infinitely superior powers of action and comprehension, (somehow) knows the future even though it (somehow) is not morally responsible for evil in the future. This foreknowledge is (somehow) the knowledge of a god who does not preside over a world governed by eternally recurring cycles but over one that it invented. Even though Augustine considered further arguments in other places on behalf of this thesis,[29] the general thrust of them is well enough capsulized in the above formulation of faith.

It is reasonable enough to point to the incomprehensible comprehension of an incomprehensible god—that is, to mystery—in presenting a god who is by definition mysterious to finite humanity.[30] But Augustine reverts to mystery only after evincing authoritative certainty about so many things: the omnipotence, omniscience, and benevolence of a salvational god, an intrinsic moral order against which sin is defined, a free will that makes humans responsible for the fault in the intrinsic order, the snake as Lucifer, the justice of the god's penalties, and so on, and so on. A series of absolute injunctions followed by the strategic deployment of mystery to protect them. Why not invoke the incomprehensibility of this god earlier, with respect to some of the above formulations? Why first insist so fervently on these basic elements of faith and then invoke mystery authoritatively wherever it is required to save them? Put another way, if there is mystery at this point, nothing but the earthly power of supporters of the doctrine in conjunction with the hopes of those implicated in it stops that mystery from leaking into the other areas of the doctrine as well, opening them up to robust contestation. The flow of mystery into one section of the doctrine leaks through the prophylactic wrapped around the core themes. The celebration of "the incomprehensible comprehension of incomprehensible things" might, then, become an occasion to acknowledge the uncertainty and contestability of all aspects of the doctrine; it might become a moment to welcome contestation over these issues. But Augustine is a politician of mystery.

Augustine's vaunted celebrations of mystery are deployed to depoliticize theological issues: The selective presentations of authoritative faith at some junctions, mystery at others, and heresy at still others function to conceal, control, and occlude the corrosive effects of mystery on the certainty and authoritativeness of the primary doctrine. The

strategic introduction of blasphemy in his critique of the Stoic conception of eternal return parallels strategic invocations of heresy in other
delicate places. "If men can say this, it only remains for them to plunge
into the depths of blasphemy by daring to allege that God does not know
all the numbers."[31] Is Augustine's deployment of mystery as a political
resource of theology driven by an urge to universalize a moral, salvational god who rewards and punishes after life as well as during it? Are
the putative risks of questioning the presumption of an omnipotent,
salvational god too severe to encourage appreciation of agonistic
diversity on these matters? Are these stakes and responses echoed in
contemporary doctrines that insist on the certainty and universality of
those claims to self-identity they cherish the most? Would only a snake
pose such questions?

The point here is not a rationalist one in which Augustine is to be
criticized for invoking mystery because everything important must be
assumed to fall within the scope of possible knowledge. Augustine has
excellent replies to the sufficiency of this sort of rationalism. The point,
rather, is that he deploys mystery as a dogmatic instrument of power,
refusing to qualify denunciations of alternative doctrines through reference to deep mysteries in his own. His method for reading Scripture,
as we saw earlier, presents such a demand as a criterion of good
exegesis. One might prefer "J," who spins out the myth of Eden with a
few ironic suggestions, leaving space for people to fill it in alternative
ways. Or Job, who demands time and space to contest the idea of
intrinsic moral order governing his community amidst the injuries he
suffers. Or Harold Bloom, who presents his reading of Eden as a
contestable projection into a protean text.

Augustine contributes significantly to future reflection through his
confessions of the persistence of mystery. The persistence of mystery may
show faith (of some sort) to be an incorrigible precondition of human
action. This is a fundamental and durable insight. But an affirmative
appreciation of the incorrigibility of mystery might also spawn a more
generous appreciation of the virtue of regular contestation over fundamental questions. The very first question posed at the inception of human life
may indicate that there are numerous mysteries, including a persistent
mystery over a fundamental rift in being. Augustine's selective invocations of mystery are balanced by a refusal to celebrate the creativity of

this very first question about the mystery of being. Today, though, it may be timely to take the monopoly of mystery away from mono-tonists and mono-theists.

I bypass here the familiar question as to why all those succeeding the first two humans deserve punishment for this first act of will. Let us, though, return to the will of the first two major actors in the drama of being. Augustine insists that Adam "fell" from unity and bliss through a pure act of "will" and that this willful fall makes us responsible for evil. Through Adam we are all guilty, and through Lucifer's prior fall from grace we learn something about the character of Adam's will. How could Adam and Lucifer perform acts of will separating them from the will of the creator if they themselves are at different "times," pristine products of its creation?

Augustine avoids detailed discussion of this issue in the case of Adam, who appears, remember, more as a child in Eden than a mature adult in the world. I take this avoidance to be tactical. It shifts the issue to a setting before Eden in which Lucifer falls from grace as an angel and to a chapter in *The City of God* before the crucial chapter on Eden. It shifts it to a place where its potential volatility is more manageable. The will of Lucifer is already formed when it makes its contribution to the drama of Eden through the mask of a snake. If human will is crucial to Augustine's conception of human agency, responsibility, and guilt, then certain features of Lucifer's will serve as a model for the will of Adam.

The question pressing against the Augustinian doctrine is this. How can that act by which a created being first falls away from god be an act of will for which it is responsible? If it possessed sufficient density of character before the act to act willfully (such as language, intelligence, experience, maturity of judgment, knowledge of good and bad, the capacity to coordinate its intentions with its actions, etc.), the elements installed in its character during creation would recoil back on the god who created it. But if it lacked such a density of character, it would seem that its action could not be an act of will, but either an arbitrary deed or a determined event: If arbitrary, only the omnipotent god could be responsible for it; if determined, only the omnipotent god could be responsible for it. With respect to either alternative, then—density or its absence prior to the act—the assertion of willful responsibility becomes highly problematic. But Augustine needs the wedge of pure

will to drive the crucial gap between this god and responsibility for evil.
He takes up the issue by considering the fall of the bad angels from the
grace of his god.

> When we ask the cause of the evil angels' misery, we find that it is the
> just result of their turning away from him who supremely is, and their
> turning toward themselves who do not exist in that supreme degree. What
> other name is there for this fault than pride?[32]

The angels are not responsible for the bliss they receive. That is the
gift of a god who is responsible for everything good. Angels and humans
can only act independently of the god to produce evil, to turn away from
its grace; everything good they do is a result of the grace of a god who
is responsible for all good. Okay. But what makes this fall away from
the god an evil act of will?

> If you try to find the efficient cause of this evil choice, there is none to be
> found. For nothing causes an evil will, since it is the evil will itself which
> causes the evil act . . . ; if anything exists, it either has, or has not, a will.
> If it has, that will is either good or bad; and if it is good, will anyone be
> fool enough to say that a good will causes an evil will?[33]

This rules out the god as an efficient cause of the evil choice, and it
rules out any cause exterior to the will itself. Still, the key question
remains, What makes this fateful fall an act of pure will and not
something else? Here Augustine turns to an argument by elimination,
an argument that supports the desired answer, not by showing affirmatively how the will works in its pure state, but by eliminating all other
alternatives as incredible. Although the case before us is now Lucifer—
the paradigm case of a fallen angel—Augustine clarifies this case
through a hypothetical example of two men who are exactly alike in
their physical and mental makeup. They are both tempted by an attractive woman. One of them follows by acting on an "unlawful" desire,
while the other remains steadfast in his chastity. What is the source of
difference between them? It could not be the flesh of the first, for they
have the same physical composition; it could not be the mind of the
first, for they are alike in mind. And a temptation presented to one by
a "malignant spirit" is not enough either, for that would imply that his
deed was determined by an external influence.

> Now if both experienced the same temptation, and one succumbed and consented to it, while the other remained unmoved, the only way to solve the difficulty is evidently to say that one refused and the other agreed to lose his chastity. What other reason could there be than this personal decision, given that their dispositions were precisely the same, in body and mind?[34]

The very first act of perversity is not *clarified* here; it is *named* an act of consent or will and presented as a necessary assumption. Augustine concedes that he cannot resolve the mystery residing within the Augustinian Imperative of a pure will (exercised only once by each of two paradigm agents) by the argument through which he asserts its necessity. The doctrine of will is necessary to save this god's omnipotence and innocence. So, "What other reason could there be . . . ?" In conceding the will to be filled with mystery while asserting its necessity through an argument by elimination, Augustine implicitly builds upon an edifice of authority already established by political means. For this conclusion through elimination gains its necessity only because a series of other possible answers have been ruled out by prior acts of authority.

There would be numerous other possibilities to consider at this point if only they had not been eliminated by charges of heresy, paganism, or blasphemy against the omnipotent, salvational god. Manicheans could introduce a war of two cosmic forces; tragedians might speak metaphorically of demons in the self that move it mysteriously and variably at passionate moments; those who revere a limited god might speak of rifts in the initial design of the world to which the passions respond in unpredictable ways; those who express godless wonder for the wonder of being might construe the moment to be an index of mystery in the problematical constitution of agency; those who discern tragedy in the very inception of being might compare the social indispensability of responsibility to the problematical desert of those to whom it is applied; those who appreciate the beauty of sensuality in a world without an intrinsic moral order might celebrate the act while confessing wonder at the forces drawing the parties together; those impressed by the volatile energy of sexuality but worried about a potential for violence residing in it might look for ways to manage its dangers without destroying its beauty; and so on. Augustine's argument by elimination does its work only because he has already set up the situation to be one in which the *rift* in being must be a *fault* in the agents who have fallen from an omnipotent, innocent god. Take that imperative away and a lot of other mysterious alternatives appear. "What else could it be?" Many things, all of them containing their portions of mystery too.

Augustine's reading of Eden postulates two originary acts of pure will as mysterious in operation as they are indispensable to the reading. The fact that the act of Adam had only to occur once, and that it is followed thereafter by a more familiar, cloudy mode of willfulness, helps to divert attention from its profoundly problematical character. As in the case of his god's necessary foreknowledge of suffering, Augustine defines the place of mystery through authoritative stratagems that subdue its disruptive effects on core dimensions of his faith.

Exposure of some of the sores in this reading of Eden does not refute the reading. That would require an alternative that had no sores of its own. And it would presuppose that the first reading presented itself in the first place as a "proof." It merely opens a gate to exploration of alternative possibilities. Those stepping through this gate might reflect on an implication flowing from this de-briefing of Augustine: If you demand preservation of an omnipotent, innocent, salvational god you may be pressed eventually to become very punitive in your orientation to human life. Epicurus predicted this effect and Nietzsche retrodicted it. Why, then, pose such a demand? Are Augustinians terrified by a rift in being exposed by a snake?

A Rift in Being

A question posed by a snake to the first woman, a feeling of shame by two humans who view their nudity for the first time, a whirlwind from which a divine voice speaks, a cultural slash in the gender of a young teenager, the experience of a divided will—all of these seem to register a gap or rift or fault or rent in being that must somehow be engaged. Readings of the myth of Eden most typically present this gap as a "fault," as Augustine does. The idea of a fault is suggestive because it contains several dimensions contending with and against one another. It can be located on a moral register, an existential register, a theological register, a geological register, or several of them together. A fault might exist in the will of human being or in the order in which it is set; it might invoke a failing that warrants punishment or an incompleteness that engenders effects; it might indicate a break that injures life or an opening that releases possibilities. Or it might combine these possibilities in a variety of ways. For example, a fault in being might both foster suffering and the possibility of creativity. It might join them together in a fateful combination in which the possibility of the latter is never neatly separable from the probability of the former.

Augustine links the experience of fault to the imperative of confession; he draws fault into human will, emphasizes the role of human responsibility in it, justifies divine punishment for it, and encourages hope for divine redemption from it. Augustine's presentation of faultfulness has become so definitive—both for those who oppose it and those who endorse it—that explorations wishing to go beyond him might do well to introduce a different term. I will use the term *rift*. The point is not to erase the enigma of the fault/rift, but to recast the Augustinian distribution of emphasis through which it is engaged. For those who would repudiate Augustinianism by simply denying that there is a fault or rift to be explored, seem to me doomed to be drawn back into the orbit of the Augustinian problematic. We return, then, to the territory upon which the snake crawls.

Paul Ricoeur, a Christian philosopher appalled by the Augustinian reading of Eden, introduces a couple of possibilities here. In the *Symbolism of Evil*, his opposition to Augustine revolves around the doctrine of original sin. "The harm that has been done to souls, during the centuries of Christianity, first by the literal interpretation of the story of Adam, and then by the confusion of this myth, treated as history, with later speculations, principally Augustinian about original sin, will never be adequately told."[35] Ricoeur suggests that human consciousness of responsibility for a "fault" in being precedes historical consolidation of the theme of human will. Such a primordial sense of mysterious responsibility seems to circulate in Genesis. It sets the stage upon which Augustine constructs his plot of original sin and finds people ready enough to believe it.

Ricoeur compares the Edenic myth to Greek tragic myths and concludes that the former can profitably draw from the latter. The Edenic myth already contains traces of the tragic within it, but these are insufficient. And to the extent they are present they have been too thoroughly subdued by the hegemony of Pauline/Augustinian readings. The key elements in a tragic conception of being, Ricoeur suggests, are, first, the understanding that a fault is traceable back to the order of being itself; second, that the hero through hubristic action brings out this rift while also exacerbating it; third, that human responsibility for existential grief is still present though reduced in scope and magnitude; and, fourth, that an awakening to morally contradictory situations of choice in life through the unfortunate actions of a hero can make a positive difference to how people behave in the future. A tragic conception of being is not a dismal reading of life; it provides a sober reading of human prospects for redemption from alienation and suffering, and a sympathetic presentation of their periodic implication in contradictory imperatives of action. The first two humans, for instance, seemed to find themselves in precisely such a situation.

Ricoeur's valuable emendations of the myth of Eden are compromised for me by a corollary insistence on giving priority to the role of Christ in redeeming the tragic element of existence. It is not perfectly clear whether Ricoeur speaks for himself in the following passage or whether he means to delineate generous elements in the tradition of discourse under examination, but the continuation of exactly this uncertainty throughout the book leads me to construe the passage as the center of gravity around which *The Symbolism of Evil* revolves.

> Salvation evolves a history; in symbolic terms: the second Adam [Christ] is *greater than* the first Adam; the first Adam is *with a view to* the second Adam. We must go this far in order to understand that the Bible never speaks of sin except in the perspective of salvation that delivers from sin. This . . . makes the pessimism of the fall abound in order that the optimism of salvation may superabound.[36]

This "Christology" of "optimism," although implicitly subtracting omnipotence from its god (for it is compelled to intervene a second time) and explicitly introducing a larger measure of generosity into relations with traditions it contests, seems to me to build too much *human resignation* into its recognition of the tragic character of life and, as a corollary, too much *hope for outside redemption* from the existential condition it delineates. If one encountered, though, only adversaries as generous as Ricoeur in their rivalry with opposing traditions of interpretation, the Nietzschean utopian ideal of rivalry between competitors who reciprocally recognize their difference and indebtedness would be well on its way to actualization.

Let us, then, consider *a* Nietzschean response to Genesis. In note #1019 of *The Will to Power*, Nietzsche offers an alternative condensation of the tragic vision. Evil, he says, is grounded in the experience of chance, the uncertain, the sudden. "Primitive man," conceives of it as an intentional power and tries to make a treaty with it; others try to discern a deeper meaning and redemptive purpose in it; and others justify evil as deserved punishment. But the "whole religio-moral interpretation is only a form of submission to evil. The faith that a good meaning lies in evil means to abandon the struggle against it."[37] I take Nietzsche to mean that the tragic is something to affirm as fundamental to life; you do so by struggling against the coils in which it traps you in specific instances without allowing yourself to become resentful in general against a mode of existence that has this fundamental character. You affirm the rich ambiguity of life, along with the rifts it reveals in the smooth order of being you anticipated. To treat an evil human will to be the source of an otherwise unnecessary rift in being, and to plead for redemption from the effects of this primordial fault for which you are primordially at fault, is to express resentment against the human condition. And unless this resentment is fought off, you will eventually make yourself into its target (the divided will, the sinful self, the prideful being) while simultaneously pursuing redemption through punishment of other human beings (blasphemers, heretics, Jews, infidels, pagans). For existential resentment requires the cultural construction of responsible agents to take aim against; otherwise it could not sustain itself as resentment rather than, say, a feeling of misfortune or affirmation of the fateful ambiguity of human action. So human beings eventually turn out to be the paradigmatic types on which existential revenge is exercised. That is the lesson of Job as well as Nietzsche, who is, of course, a modern Jobian.

Generosity of spirit comes out of "a pessimism of strength" that affirms the joy of life in the midst of its tragic character. It is ethically laudatory, then, to cultivate this affirmation, to cultivate it while dispensing with the existential demand that the world be designed with an intrinsic moral order. The Nietzschean response treats a world without intrinsic moral order to be "the actually achieved highest possible ideal." It stops yearning for a way of being without rifts and fundamental discordances and without the suffering that comes with the loss of loved ones and the prospect of death for oneself. It suffers; it feels the urge to take revenge against specific assaults; and it grieves specific instances of loss. But it dispenses with the demand for a doctrine that promises eventual redemption from the rift in being.

This squares with Nietzsche's immodest claim to have grasped the character of the tragic better even than Greeks such as Sophocles and, especially, Aristotle (and Christians such as Ricoeur). "I have been the first to discover the tragic. The Greeks, thanks to their moralistic superficiality, misunderstood it. Even resignation is not a lesson of tragedy, but a misunderstanding of it. Yearning for nothingness is a denial of tragic wisdom, its opposite."[38] Experience of the tragic character of existence encourages some to plumb more deeply the affirmation of life already flowing through them, as they actively affirm the rift in the center of existence, as they experience the creative energies flowing through this gateway as well as the suffering that necessarily accompanies them.

Nietzsche draws this stance closer to the garden of Eden in *Thus Spoke Zarathustra*, which can be read as a construction of a counter-myth/bible to compete with the dominant myths/bibles of Western culture. It is a text of ethical awakening comparable to and competitive with Augustine's *Confessions*. In a section entitled "On The Vision and The Riddle," Zarathustra responds to the "spirit of gravity" he feels around him and within him. That spirit is represented by a dwarf who had been accompanying him until the moment he fell into a reverie. The reverie, indeed, has a moment in common with the reverie recorded by Augustine when he and Monica briefly touched the edge of eternity. As he emerges out of the reverie, Zarathustra encounters a grotesque sight.

> And verily, what I saw—I had never seen the like. A young shepherd I saw, writhing, gagging, in spasms, his face distorted, and a heavy black snake hung out of his mouth. . . . . He seemed to have been asleep when the snake crawled into his throat, and there bit itself fast. My hand tore at the snake and tore in vain. . . . Then it cried out of me: "Bite! Bite! Bite its head off! Bite!" Thus it cried out of me—my dread, my hatred, my nausea, my pity, all that is good and wicked in me cried out of me with a single cry.[39]

Zarathustra challenges his readers to decipher this "riddle," admitting much later that he himself was this "shepherd." Does he here pose a challenge to both the Augustinian and Ricoeurian readings of Eden? Augustine orders humanity to swallow the snake. They obey if they swallow the doctrine of an omnipotent god, intrinsic moral order, pristine will, and primordial human responsibility for the rift in being. By letting the snake crawl all the way down their throats they internalize unilateral responsibility for evil. Ricoeur would have humanity let the snake crawl into its mouth, trying to stop it halfway down the throat canal, letting its heavy black tail hang out of their mouths when they speak. He counsels them not to accept full responsibility for the rift through original sin, but to see themselves as the site of a "fault" that hopes to be redeemed by a power larger than themselves.

Zarathustra opposes both of these images. He reminds us that a snake can be a symbol of evil, or a penis with a mind of its own, or earthly wisdom, or natural forces, or one of the gods of a defeated culture. It can be different things at different times, and several things at one time. Zarathustra, for instance, draws on the mythic wisdom of the snake while pursuing the question of eternal return. I take this latter serpent to parallel the smooth-tongued snake in Eden, the one that exposed a rift in the order of things by putting a question to a woman who then experienced something of the wonder of chance, contingency, openness, slipperiness, possibility, alienation from wholeness, and danger in being. This is the snake before it has been demonized by Augustinians living before, during, and after the life of Augustine. Zarathustra cries out to the shepherd in himself, not to bite off the head of the smooth snake of wisdom, but to bite off the head of the heavy black snake. For this heavy snake has been loaded down with the thematic of sin; it has been fashioned into the snake that would tempt you to internalize blame for the rift in being by crawling into your soul. The temptation to swallow it takes the form of a hope for redemption from the rift. Bite! Bite off the head of *that* snake!

Zarathustra has affinities to that voice in Job we encountered earlier. He also has eerie affinities to Augustine in the way he invokes themes of rift, awakening, temptation, and redemption while contesting the forms imposed on them by this competitor.

It is terribly frightening to bite off the head of a heavy black snake that attached itself to your throat while your mind was slumbering and your mouth hung open; it is difficult to do anything at all at such a terrifying moment. If you don't act it will remain attached, muffling every word you speak in the future. But to recognize this effect from a distance is not to guarantee that you will succeed in overcoming paralysis at the strategic moment. There are no guarantees anywhere, anytime, in a Nietzschean universe. That is part of the contingency of things. If you remain passive, though, paralyzed by fear and uncertainty, the Augustinian Imperative will triumph. The culture is so saturated with this imperative that to do nothing is to allow its directives to crawl down your throat.

But what could be the effect of biting off the head of that snake, anyway? It certainly would not *heal* the rift in being. Zarathustra is not presenting a new myth of redemption from alienation through salvation. The very first question posed in Eden exposes hollowness in that aspiration, to anyone whose ears are not already packed with the cotton of a transcendental imperative. The smooth snake, as a symbol of earthy wisdom in Zarathustra, embodies the understanding that there is a tragic rift in being that cannot be eliminated. To bite off the head of this heavy snake, then, must mean to affirm the rift in being without assuming unilateral blame for it or whining for transcendental redemption from it. Does it also mean to bite off "the head" of a masculinism that insists that there is an essential moral order (given by a god or reason), that men are superior in it, that sovereign rulers are in touch with the intrinsic order, that singular authority is intrinsic to it, and that strict order is imperative to it? Probably. For to bite off the head of the heavy snake is to allow a rift in being to be. Zarathustra's "overman," it seems to me, is neither "masculine" nor "feminine," but an aspiration that strives to rise *over* "man."

Zarathustra brings out the character of this rift in a passage that invites comparison in its power and economy to the poetics of J. He is talking to his dwarf in the section "On The Vision and The Riddle," just as they pause in front of a gateway.

> "Behold this gateway, dwarf!" I continued. "It has two faces. Two paths meet here; no one has yet followed either to its end. This long lane stretches back for an eternity. And the long lane out there, is another eternity. They contradict each other, these paths; they offend each other

face to face; and it is here at this gateway that they come together. The name of the gateway is inscribed above: 'Moment.' "[40]

A rift recurs in *each* moment. It resides within the i/n from the inception of being. It is a temporal rift built permanently into the structure of the moment (as long as moments last). The snake in Eden exposed a small breach in the apparent seamlessness of being. "Did the God really mean . . . ?" The rift in the moment is a gateway; the gateway contains possibilities that point in different directions; each contains an element of irreversibility once it is taken; and no one has the capacity to peer far enough down either path to see exactly where it heads. Chance and fate come together in the disjunctive structure of the moment. *Chance* in that when you throw the dice you neither know what will come up nor exactly what the stakes are. *Fate* in that as the dice come down the implications of your selection are sealed until the next moment. Or, on another register, *chance* in that you throw the dice, but *fate* in that the throw is not made by an abstract person, but by a particular self with a specific identity in an established setting. This disjunctive conjunction of chance and fate is the rift in being. It recurs i/n every moment, and no new moment allows you to return to the one that just passed. The rift is a gap, a break, a rupture, a fault that cannot be closed. It recurs eternally.

Each gateway you face, while containing this uncanny characteristic, is also crucially and specifically yours. "Behold *this* gateway, dwarf. . . . Two paths meet *here*. . . . " You are born of a pagan father and Christian mother during a time when the contest between these faiths just happened to be intense; you bump into Epicureanism almost by chance; your mother makes life a campaign to secure your conversion to Christianity; the faith you develop collides with your desire to live with the mother of your child; a theologian called Pelagius challenges the doctrine of grace you have refined, and so on. Each of these moments is a gateway, and each gateway is opened by the intersection between new events and what went before; the way you pass through each gateway enters *somehow* into the contingent and conflicted density of your identity. This identity opens up new gateways to you and closes others, but it does so in discordant conjunction with events and happenings that your particular past had no hand in shaping (being born as the son of a pagan father and Christian mother, the conversion of an emperor to Christianity, an invasion by Vandals) and with those you have some influence over (cultivation of classroom skill in pagan rhetoric, hearing the voice of a child during exactly the moment you were prepared to undergo conversion, a gathering of faithful looking to draft a priest when you come to town). New gateways emerge out of these discordant concordances, and fate, as unfathomable mixture of deed and contingency, conditions your very next encounter with the rift in being.

You can't re-turn to fateful moments in order to re-write them. You gnash your teeth over the "it was." And this resentment of the open, irreversible structure of the moment, this resentment of temporality, along with the mortality it signifies, tempts you to project a mode of redemption into the rift, to devise an onto-theo-philo-sophy that enables you to hope for erasure of the most dispiriting moments in your past or redemption from the rift that keeps the unending flow of contingency coming. This response forms the essence of existential resentment. A Nietzschean response is to try to fashion fateful moments that condition your fate/identity into features you can affirm because you have recrafted them into preconditions of new actions you admire.[41] Zarathustra's hunchback might fashion the fateful disadvantage of its crooked back into a distinctive insight into the sources of existential resentment and a consolidation of energies to ward it off. The hunchback's distinctive condition, and the resentment of being it encourages, enables it to discern how a more general and pervasive spirit of resentment against temporality arises; it is then in better position to struggle against this temptation in itself. But it will face this issue again and again in different forms, and there are no guarantees that it will continue to meet with success in responding to it. Perhaps it is later stricken down by epilepsy, and this combination becomes too much to take. Or it finds itself blessed with an eloquence that helps it to elevate itself through the very success it has in convincing others. The idea is to affirm the rift with its chancy combinations of chance and fate, deeds and events, without demanding the guiding hand of a providential god or an intrinsic purpose or a sufficient reason or a free will. For each of those latter demands eventually recoils back onto you as the self-loathing of a faulty self, a guilty agent, a deviant, or a sinner. And typically those who are filled with self-loathing look for others against whom to unload this heavy burden.

It is not as if you live a seamless life now, preparing for the big moment that will someday arrive in a timely fashion. Rather, every moment has the same structure and any moment might be fundamentally determinative. There is a fundamental contingency and "oblivion of difference" in being ineliminable by any god. The Greek gods had a better sense of this than any monotheism evinces, for the competitive plurality they built into the experience of being drew attention to rifts opening up between and within them. They were somewhat less disposed to reduce the rift to existential human fault.

Eve experienced the fatefulness of the moment when a question posed to her opened up a possibility. Which way to turn? She turned one way rather than the other. And fate came crashing down. Some of the elements in this fate might not have seemed quite so terrible had she not been tempted to project, first, transcendental meaning into the event and, second, existential fault for it and its effects onto herself. The second temptation follows the first, for without the acceptance of existential blame the god who serves as the source of the meaning sought would be compromised with limitation from the start. Did she succumb to both temptations? She tried not to at first, though the god within pressed hard for her to do so. She doesn't speak later. So, you can't tell for sure by reading the story. The persistent temptation, though, is simultaneously to accept existential fault for the rift and to plead for its repair by a god or god substitute powerful and providential enough to do the job. The various god substitutes constitute the afterlife of traditional monotheism. What do these gods and their substitutes indicate? Perhaps that people remain terrified by experience of the rift? Perhaps that this terror in turn tempts them to transcendental terrorism of one sort or another? A lot of people have suffered immensely under the weight of this spirit of gravity.

You might mark the uncanniness of the rift by filling it with a "free will," but if you do so you might also acknowledge this to be a complex, muddy construction imposed on a problematical experience that has never been proven to correspond to it intrinsically. Even Augustine admits that pure free will was exercised only once by a human, and lurking inside that admission is a second acknowledgment that it remains inherently mysterious just how this single pure act could have occurred. The "divided will" through which he thereafter encounters the rift consists in a putative falling away from a problematical standard of a "healed will"; it defines the rift as a mysterious human fault through a prayer of redemption, rather than an intrinsically clear faculty of human being or an unavoidable assumption presupposed by a necessary concept of rationality. At this historical juncture, the idea of *free will* remains highly ambiguous; it seems indispensable to judgments of merit, worth, and responsibility that we can never wholly avoid making with respect to one another and it remains highly problematical as a representation of how conduct proceeds. It is probably wise today to treat every judgment enunciated in its terms as problematical and revisable, not simply because "we" are not sure how free the will of an actor might have been in this or that case, but because we lack both a credible conception of the will and a credible alternative through which to replace its function in discursive relations. It is a problematical, mysterious category/ideal/plea/standard of judgment designed to cover the abyss opened by a rift in being, one that has been taken too literally and too punitively by too many for too long. For the assertion of free will continues to take the form of a communal prayer backed by the sovereign power of punishment. Whenever someone says, "She acted freely," he is about to say "And she deserves what we are about to do to her."

Nietzsche affirms a rift that fills each moment with abundance, contingency, creative possibility, and danger. A rift that fills life with ambiguity. For to affirm the creative possibilities within it is to affirm its dangers too: they are knotted together. That is the adventure and the rub. The affirmation of life and the earth is the affirmation of the coming together of chance and fate in a recurring series of contradictory conjunctions. An affirmation of one throw of the dice followed by others in the eternal return of the same structure. The moments keep coming, until you die; and the issue keeps returning. The Nietzschean *faith* is that cultivation of this affirmative stance fosters both a richer experience of life and a greater generosity to others who make different selections in their moments. These are big articles of faith. About as big as the ones they contest.

This generosity does not solicit consensus and harmony among all members of a fictive community, nor does it flow from concord with an intrinsic harmony in being. These aspirations for transcendental redemption constitute the danger of dangers for Nietzsche. Countless charges of heresy and blasphemy are needed to sustain them. It is an effect of the Nietzschean "vision and riddle" that he cannot guarantee either success in the pursuit he commends or the consequences his faith bestows on it for those who live within its terms. The myth of Zarathustra contains enigmas and articles of faith, too, even though it avoids the charge of heresy against its opponents in presenting them.

Action is impossible without faith. But the premises of a particular faith are never assured of realization in action. How could they be in a world in which a rift appears i/n every moment. Nietzsche and Augustine move close together for a moment in this set of acknowledgments. But then each fills a rift registered by the other with a different vision/riddle. Nietzsche's vision relinquishes insistence on an intrinsic moral order; it therefore relinquishes the moral god who commands a code or realizes a design we can intuit. That is why his ethic does not take the form of obedience to a command or correspondence to a seamless design, the two major forms morality has assumed in the West. It solicits generosity from those who experience a *gateway* in the rift and refuse to seek a god or god substitute to heal it.

"This is my vision and my riddle," Nietzsche seems to say, "if you don't like it, work out your own; but please don't try to govern *others* by an imperative of rift-redemption insinuated into vengeful practices of identity, responsibility, and punishment." The first two clauses in this message ask merely to be left alone; the third suggests this to be impossible, since any operative moral ideal enters into the currency of social life. This disjunction creates a distinctive break (a rift) in the heart of Nietzsche's idealism. It drives Nietzsche toward a social ethic when Zarathustra seeks to cultivate an individual ideal. Perhaps it opens up a gap between the idealism of Zarathustra and the vision of Nietzsche. If Nietzsche's riddle of the rift implicates him (very reluctantly) in an agonistic politics comparable to the way in which Augustine's confession of the wounded will implicates him in a confessional politics, it becomes imperative to think and rethink what can be said on behalf of one path over the other. For these two paradigmatic thinkers of the West offend and challenge each other. Two paths meet here; no one has yet followed either to its end. They contradict each other, these paths; they offend each other face to face; and it is here at this gateway, at this rift in being, that they meet.

Notes

1. My example is taken from a fascinating paper by Valerie Hartouni, "Brave New World," presented at Johns Hopkins University in the fall of 1990. It is published in Jane Bennett and William Chaloupka, eds., *In the Nature of Things: Language, Politics and the Environment* (Minneapolis: University of Minnesota Press, 1993).

2. Donna Haraway, *Primate Visions* (New York: Routledge, 1989), chap. 7.

3. Friedrich Nietzsche, *The Birth of Tragedy*, trans. Walter Kaufmann (New York: Vintage Books, 1967), 135.

4. *The Book of J*, translated by David Rosenberg and interpreted by Harold Bloom (New York: Grove Weidenfeld, 1990), 62.

5. *Book of J*, 62.

6. *Book of J*, 63. Rosenberg and Bloom prefer the translation "snake" to "serpent," though the latter may underline the probable extent to which the presence of this animal draws "pagan" myth into this story that is so central to both Judaism and Christianity. If the serpent was associated with the fertility worship of Baal in Canaanite religion, then the introduction of the "snake" here, as a figure of temptation through the fateful invitation to fertilize, could form part of that recurrent process by which old gods are demonized to create space for the primacy of new ones.

7. *Book of J*, 63. Is the Rosenberg translation of the "J text" reliable and has he successfully isolated the parts "J" wrote? I am not qualified to say. The attractive thing about Rosenberg's attempt is that it opens up for imaginative rethinking a text that has been fundamental to "the West" and has almost always been read through translations by those to whom it has been fundamental. Robert Alter, in *The World of Biblical Literature* (New York: Basic Books, 1991, 153-169), argues that Rosenberg's translation is defective and that its attribution of some sections to J is questionable. I am sure he is right about the second point and I am unqualified to judge the first. But Alter's own presentation of the issues often seems to presuppose the availability of a neutral translation that is itself not deeply invested with an interpretive orientation. And his critique of Bloom's explicit projection of "J" as a woman with an ironic sensibility seems to me to forget how this projection functions in Bloom. Bloom is more prepared to acknowledge and respond overtly to the inevitable role of fictions and projections in translation/interpretation than Alter. Or better, Alter voices such a willingness at the abstract level, but retreats to a literalism in his specific critiques of Rosenberg/Bloom. His essay typifies the neoconservative academic who loves adventurism in general but always repudiates it in particular. If I were to criticize Bloom, my focus would be on his tendency to replace the fundamentalism of a literal translation/interpretation with the fundamentalism of a "genius" who is not profoundly shaped by the oral/discursive traditions in which the story he/she writes is already set. But Bloom is not the primary issue here. The way "we" receive this story is.

8. This feature of the text was pointed out by Patrick Lee in a seminar at Johns Hopkins, "Augustine and Nietzsche," spring, 1991. I am grateful to him for it. Once it is called to one's attention, protean possibilities residing in this text become more audible.

9. *Book of J*, 182.

10. *Book of J*, 183.

11. I have examined the inflationary pressures in the logic of responsibility in *Identity\Difference: Democratic Negotiations of Political Paradox* (Ithaca, NY: Cornell University Press, 1991), chap. 5, "Responsibility for Evil."

12. Augustine, *On Christian Doctrine*, trans. D. W. Robertson (New York: Macmillan, 1958), 13.

13. *On Christian Doctrine*, 30.

14. *On Christian Doctrine*, 79.

15. *On Christian Doctrine*, 87-88.

16. *On Christian Doctrine*, 87.

17. Augustine, *Concerning the City of God: Against the Pagans*, trans. Henry Bettenson (Middlesex, UK: Penguin, 1984), Bk. 13, chap. 22, 535.

18. *City of God*, Bk. 12, chap. 24, 504.

19. *City of God*, Bk. 13, chap. 15, 522-23.

20. *City of God*, Bk. 13, chap. 14, 523.

21. *City of God*, Bk. 13, chap. 14, 523.

22. *City of God*, Bk. 13, chap. 13, 522. "Thus when God spoke about the forbidden food . . . , the threat embraced not only the first part of the first death, when the soul is bereft of God, not only the second part, in which the body is bereft of the soul; it comprised every kind of death, down to the last or second death, which has no other death to follow it."

23. *City of God*, Bk. 14, chap. 13, 571.

24. *City of God*, Bk. 14, chap. 11, 570.

25. *City of God*, Bk. 14, chap. 11, 571.

26. *City of God*, Bk. 14, chap. 13, 570.

27. *City of God*, Bk. 12, chap. 23, 503.

28. *City of God*, Bk. 12, chap. 20, 497. A more subtle invocation of mystery is more directly connected to the relation between foreknowledge and absence of divine responsibility in the following question. The context is the god's foreknowledge of the painful death of the martyrs and the necessity of these deaths to produce divinely desired earthly effects: "How is it that the martyrs, who were slain for the faith . . . , have the power to work such marvels? For God may himself perform them by himself, through that wonderful operation of his power, whereby, being eternal, he is active in temporal events; or he may effect them through the agency of his servants . . . , [for example] through the spirits of the martyrs . . . ; or he may affect all those wonders through the service of angels. . . . Or it may be that some miracles . . . are affected by different methods which are quite beyond mortal comprehension. Be that as it may, they all testify to the faith in which the resurrection to eternal life is proclaimed." (*City of God*, Bk. 22, chap. 11, 1049) The first question is never answered, but transformed into a pious wonder enclosed inside a more fundamental faith through "that wonderful operation of his power," "all those wonders," "it may be," "be that as it may," "testify to the faith," and through this laundry list of alternative methods of influence on temporality available to the eternal god in which only he knows why or how one type is selected over others at specific times. In typical Augustinian style, the next sentence starting the next section asserts, "At this point we shall probably be told that the pagan gods have performed some miracles."

29. This question is examined carefully and in detail in Christopher Kirwan, *Augustine* (New York: Routledge, 1989). See particularly Chapters 7-9.

30. In *The Christian Philosophy of Saint Augustine*, trans. L.E.M. Lynch (New York: Random House, 1960), Etienne Gilson summarizes Augustine on mystery in this area in a way that is highly sympathetic to his general faith. "Augustine's last word on this obscure problem is, therefore, an admission of ignorance. Man bows before a mystery he cannot probe . . . ; [but], according to St. Augustine, the secret which escapes us only

conceals a perfect justice. Moreover, it is clear that in such a doctrine the precise foreknowledge God has of human acts in no way alters their freedom." (156) This summarizes the issue from a perspective more sympathetic to the Augustinian deployment of mystery than mine. And this is the best study of Augustinianism by one who follows its general geography of faith of which I am aware. Is the best response to mystery to bow before it within the terms of fixed doctrine, or to respond to its emergence by considering identifications and readings of mystery in alternative doctrines?

31. *City of God*, Bk. 12, chap. 20, 496.

32. *City of God*, Bk. 12, chap. 6, 477.

33. *City of God*, Bk. 12, chap. 6, 477.

34. *City of God*, Bk. 12, chap. 7, 479.

35. Paul Ricoeur, *The Symbolism of Evil*, trans. Emerson Buchanan (Boston: Beacon Press, 1967), 239.

36. *Symbolism of Evil*, 274.

37. Friedrich Nietzsche, *The Will to Power*, trans. Walter Kaufmann (New York: Vintage, 1968), #1019, 527.

38. *Will to Power*, #1029, 531-32.

39. Friedrich Nietzsche, *Thus Spoke Zarathustra*, trans. Walter Kaufmann (New York: Penguin, 1978), 159.

40. *Thus Spoke Zarathustra*, 157-158.

41. I am aware, of course, that the vision and the riddle can be read as a kind of fatedness in which nothing in the past can be worked on so that its effects on the future are modified. "And are not all things so knotted together so firmly that this moment draws after it *all* that is to come?" (158) But I interpret the rift in each moment as the opening through which chance and contingency enter life, even while the effects of each previous moment establish future thresholds of action and events. If Nietzsche and I break on this shoal, so much the worse for one of us. I will go with the reading supported later in "On Old and New Tablets," when Zarathustra refers back to his riddle and the relation it bears to creativity.

> I taught them all *my* creating and striving, to create and carry together into One what in man is fragment and riddle and dreadful accident; a creator, guesser of riddles, and redeemer of accidents, I taught them to *work on the future* and *redeem with their creation* all that *has been*. To redeem what is past in man and to re-create all "it was" until the will says, "Thus I willed it! Thus I shall will it."—this I call redemption and this alone I taught them to call redemption. (*Thus Spoke Zarathustra*, 198; some of the emphases are mine.)

This reading of the vision and the riddle squares it with the message of treating the self as a work of art presented in Nietzsche's *The Gay Science*, trans. Walter Kaufmann (New York: Vintage, 1974). I offer a reading of the self as work of art in *Political Theory and Modernity* (Oxford: Basil Blackwell, 1988), chap. 5. It is taken up more briefly here in Chapter 5.

5

Beyond the Moral Imperative

The Uncanny and the Moral

Nietzsche, in *Beyond Good and Evil*, says that to "be ashamed of one's immorality—that is a step on the staircase at whose end one is also ashamed of one's morality."[1] This sounds strange. How could one become ashamed of one's morality without stepping outside the very practice that renders shame possible? Nietzsche is suggesting that the morality of good and evil itself forgets or covers over injustices in the process of protecting its experience of a smooth moral economy. It suppresses the surpluses, uncertainties, and paradoxes in its own economy of judgment. Nietzsche wants to make us ashamed of the established logic of moral equivalences so that we might become amenable to a more subtle and ambiguous ethical sensibility. He seeks to anchor this shame of morality in a source on the edge of the moral tradition as we receive it.

Nietzsche contends, along with Hannah Arendt, Michel Foucault, Tzvetan Todorov, and others, that there is arbitrary cruelty installed in the morality of good and evil, a cruelty installed in those moral economies that take themselves to embody the will of god, a Law of laws, an Intrinsic Purpose in Being, or a fictive Contract. To reach "beyond" good and evil—to reach beyond these righteous divisions between the true faith and the heresy it spawns, or the intrinsic identity and those differences that threaten its self-security, or the normal and its self-protective constitution of the abnormal—is not to become immoral. It is not to execute a release from self-restraint so that "anything goes." Rather, it is to become ashamed of the smooth, closed economies within which moral judgment all too readily becomes encased. It is to nurture a new sense of restraint and a revised orientation to the very differences through which an individual and a culture achieve self-definition. It is to reach "beyond" the Augustinian Imperative, while cautiously drawing sustenance from selective strands within the thought of Augustine.

A moral economy, you might say, constitutes a set of equivalences between thought, words, action, freedom, responsibility, desert, and punishment. Moral economies, so understood, are indispensable to life. But every moral economy also involves a certain forgetting, a forgetting of arbitrary impositions in the very pattern of equivalences it places under the star of morality. This logic of forgetting built into the equivalences of morality needs to be engaged if we are to subject morality to critical ethical scrutiny.

We might approach the double relation between memory and forgetting along one dimension and between morality and denial along another through an engagement with the uncanny. For a moral economy is exactly one that tends either to divest the experience of the uncanny or to invest it in an authoritative point above the economy of moral judgment (e.g., in a God, a Law of laws, a Design) in a way that reinforces the imperatives governing the economy.

According to Sigmund Freud, the shock of the uncanny—of the *Unheimlich* or the "unhomely"—is the shock of recognition in the experience of something that is otherwise strange, surprising, and disturbing. It is the experience of unhomeliness in that which usually seems familiar and close to home. The experience of the uncanny fosters anxiety. And anxiety readily becomes translated into those pangs of guilt through which a moral economy reinstates the equivalences that had just been disturbed. So the experience of the uncanny is fragile, deniable, and fugitive. And yet it is important.

If you experience the uncanny, what you thought was "in place" now seems to be filled with that which displaces or disturbs it. So you lose secure bearings. You become unhinged, momentarily at least, from a familiar pattern of judgment even while you continue to be inhabited by it. Freud appropriates the uncanny to psychoanalysis when he asserts that "an uncanny experience occurs either when infantile complexes which have been repressed are once more revived by some impression, or when primitive beliefs which have been surmounted seem once more to be confirmed."[2] The first experience might occur when you encounter an authority who invokes feelings you projected onto an authoritative adult when you were young, perhaps your father or mother. The second experience emerges from a coincidence so compelling that only magic or a miracle seems sufficient to explain it, encouraging you to activate the magical sense of causality clinging to you as a residue from childhood. Such experiences are relevant to the uncanny. I want to suggest, though, that the uncanny is not exhausted by them.

Let us return to the J version of Genesis. The power the J-Genesis exercises over those who encounter it is probably bound up with its ability to evoke repressed memories about the power, apparent arbitrariness, and possible wisdom of the Father, as experienced from the perspective of children such as Adam and Hava (Eve). For Yahweh resembles an arbitrary father. He issues statements that are fuzzy and uncertain in meaning to the child-like beings who receive them. And his rapid, severe, implacable response to the murky chain of deeds that follow these words appears awesome, frightening, and incomprehensible from the vantage point of children who do not yet know what they have done. So the chain of events in Genesis recalls childhood experiences of our own actions and adult authority in an uncanny way. It recalls earlier enactments by us that were murky and insignificant during enactment and then retroactively defined to be sharp and significant. The children know not what they do when they "act," but the patriarchal response that follows leads them to interpret those same events retroactively as willful acts deserving of the punishment inflicted on them. The act in its clarity is taken to precede the response while its clarity as an act only follows the response. And the punishment, preceding and defining the "crime," is taken retroactively to follow from it. This unformulated shock of recognition by adults of the retroactive character of their own judgments, and the pressures to repress this experience in the interests of treating themselves as moral agents, contributes to the magnetic power of Genesis. Adults have an uncanny recollection of how the story goes even before Augustine tells them how to read it. Augustine provides the adult reading of a childlike experience that precedes and resists this reading, amidst the deniable sense that this resistance itself must somehow be forgotten again. Genesis and Augustine together recapitulate the deniable experience of how morality is invested with obligatory forgetfulness.

This sort of reflection, although very pertinent, stops just before the most uncanny element in this story is allowed to surface. So consider. A series of deeds at the inception of being: a fuzzy warning ("death will touch you") that the recipient cannot really understand; two simple, naked beings; a snake who poses a question and opens a possibility; a woman who eats from the tree and gives to the man; a man who partakes; sharp interrogation from a godlike being; and a set of penalties imposed on the snake, the man, and the woman. The gaps and disjunctions *between* the deeds combine with dissonances *within* the descriptions applied to each deed ("command," "warning," "willful act," "shame," "just punishment") to register slippages and uncertainties in the moral economy through which they are equilibrated. Above all, the gaps exacerbate a strangely familiar experience of dissonance between the social imperative to bring the disparate elements of act, desert, reward, and punishment into just equilibrium and a subterranean sense of persistent injustice haunting every claim to have fulfilled that imperative.

The myth of Genesis, then, points to a recurrent, fugitive experience of arbitrariness and surplus in the very experience of the moral, a disturbing experience installed in the porosity within words and the gaps between them. A disruptive experience of arbitrariness within the indispensable practice of morality, a disruption always on the verge of being buried by powerful counterpressures to forget it in the interests of precise thinking, clean distinctions, and just responses. These gaps "in between" the "acts," these absences that separate words drawn together into a narrative, constitute the most fundamental experience of the uncanny in the genesis of morality. Authority, responsibility, and justice, indispensable to social life in some way or other, are also more cruel and blunt than morality recognizes them to be. Morality is too crude, ruthless, and blind to do the job we pretend it accomplishes. It covers up its own ineptitude in the interests of accomplishing the social task we call on it to carry out. Morality, then, is, in tendency, immoral. And this tendency is installed in the function it is called on to play, in the task we give it of deciding what penalty fits this infraction, which assumptions of will are appropriate to this action, and so forth. This is the uncanny experience fostered by Genesis before moralists return to cancel it by saying (something like), "Hey, you cannot even have an experience of 'immorality' unless you presuppose the rectitude of morality." But let us resist for a while longer this predictable (moral) imperative to cancel the experience of the uncanny within the moral.

The very simplicity and starkness of the J prose renders possible the deniable, uncanny experience of violence within morality. This text is thereby more illuminating than the most refined texts of moral philosophy. For the J text places dissonant, interdependent elements into problematical juxtaposition without developing an elaborate strategy to iron out discrepancies or close up disjunctions between them. It jumps from event to act and from act to retroactive judgment without filling the space created by these leaps with reassuring, justificatory words. The moralist insistently forgets or represses this disturbing experience, filling in the gaps as quickly and quietly as possible. But the disturbance keeps returning through one vehicle or another. Is it, perhaps, unethical to cover up these disturbances within the territory of the moral?

What, exactly, is the proportionate response to the simple deeds of these child-like beings? Are they worthy of punishment? Does the will to punish here reflect a certain drive to revenge against a world that comes pre-equipped neither with an affirmative answer to the quest to escape death nor with the common measure we expect it to have? Or, perhaps, is punishment in some sense necessary to the fabric of social order but underdeserved by its recipients? Similarly, does the sense of proportionality between act and response arise as we encounter each step in the series or is it installed retroactively after we learn how the Big Father actually responds? Could this "first" economy of moral equivalences suggest a lack of full commensurability among basic elements in every moral economy? What is the common measure, anyway, through which an "act" is brought into coordination with the punishment (or merit) appropriate to it? To what extent does the invention of "the will"—a discursive construction designed above all to protect the innocence of an omnipotent god and never proven to conform to the beings to whom it is applied—work to manufacture forgetfulness in this territory? Is the moralization of this series of deeds in Genesis itself the act to be most ashamed of? Augustine, in his (dominant) role as moralist, resolves these questions in one direction: "The *injunction* . . . was so *easy* to observe, so *brief* to remember; above all, it was given at a time when *desire was not yet in opposition to the will* . . ."[3] In these ways he effaces gaps, blurs dissonances, and conceals incommensurabilities otherwise rendered palpable by J.

Augustine subdues the uncanny *within* morality by investing it in an omnipotent, benevolent god who commands morality and exceeds its dictates. J exposes the uncanny within morality by refusing to moralize so thoroughly the god who authorizes this set of equivalences. Perhaps J is the more ethical of the two. The Augustinian transcendentalization of the uncanny represses the uncanny *within morality*, because now any identification of it there constitutes impiety against the mysterious god who commands it. Piety is the key Augustinian weapon on behalf of morality. Piety is thus the self-protective tactic that must not be allowed to go unchallenged by those who pursue the uncanny in morality for ethical reasons. Is it possible to develop an ethical sensibility that endorses action while striving to attend to these gaps within morality? To develop an ethical sensibility without reducing oneself to a moral economist?

The most productive and dangerous effect of the uncanny is the feeling of anxiety it foments. Anxiety is a fluid mood of estrangement from an uncertain object. Such a feeling *cries* for interpretation. But how to interpret it? It might, first, be taken to signify disturbance of a belief or identity to which one is deeply attached, as Augustine was disturbed by the Epicurean quest to still the impulse to immortality in the interests of reducing existential resentment, as the friends of Job were disturbed by his charge that their god is not moral, as I was disturbed, on reading *Herculine Barbin*, by the emergence of a new sense of contingency and cruelty within my insistent experience of gender duality. The danger, then, is this: If a surge of anxiety disturbs or dislodges a conviction that had fostered security, self-confidence, or moral rectitude, it can all too easily become translated into energy to reinstate those same convictions with a vengeance. Anxiety is all too easily colonizable by a moral interpretation that takes deniable revenge against the very figure or presentation that occasions it. The moralist produces anxiety in order to dissolve it into a moral formula. This logic is abundantly apparent, for example, in Augustine's letter to the feuding sisters in a convent.

Perhaps the logic of conversion works something like this. Anxiety is interpreted as a "lack" or "fault" somewhere in one's identity. When attached to a powerful moral interpretation, this fault readily becomes an experience of guilt for failure to live up to what one already is intrinsically. The feeling of guilt becomes interpreted in turn as a sign of one's failure to live up to a Law (command, principle, categorical imperative, design, identity) one is obligated to obey. One now falls under a powerful obligation to heal the identity or faith just disturbed, to reinstate more intensely the conviction of identity or morality or gender duality, or the like, just disrupted. These are the deniable linkages Freud explores among (a) ambivalent identification with a power figure, (b) guilt over the (imagined or actual) killing of this figure, (c) production of a law of faith or identity through *retroactive* interpretation of this guilt as if it followed from disobedience to the Law rather than providing the existential source from which the Law is manufactured, (d) suppression of the uncanny experience that propelled these very translations into being through punishment of those, including oneself, who foster this disconcerting experience.[4]

But these moralizing effects do not exhaust the possibilities tied to the uncanny. The anxiety of the uncanny can also provide a basis from which to ponder the ethical implications of surplus and incorrigible elements of arbitrariness in established moral economies. It might even become a prod through which to reconsider the demand to have an intrinsic identity or to represent an intrinsic moral order, reconsidering this demand in the interests of resisting those deniable violences that accompany its institutionalization. That is the ethical promise inside the experience of the uncanny, the promise worthy of cultivation in the interests of ethical decency.

How, though, can this productive possibility be pursued without becoming overwhelmed by the counterpressures for concealment that accompany it? The "Nietzschean" faith is that four activities in combination hold some promise here. First, you pursue genealogies of established conceptions of gender, identity, nature, the will, truth, the Law, and so forth, to loosen the hold they exert over moral judgment when they are treated as given, necessary, or intrinsic; second, you cultivate fugitive excesses or surpluses in the experience of life to fold greater generosity into the ethical sensibility governing you; third, you apply subtle tactics to the self to render it more amenable to the experience of the uncanny and less compelled to convert the experience of the uncanny into energy to intensify established moral economies; fourth, though Nietzsche himself may dissent here, you develop *political* strategies to fold agonistic generosity more deeply into the cultural ethos of a democratic society.

If one considers a genealogy to be, in the broadest sense, any investigation of established truths that loosens the sense of necessity, lawfulness, unity, or intrinsic purpose attached to them, then the examples of Job and Alex/ina presented earlier in this study can exemplify some of the ways and means through which genealogy is practiced. In what follows we shall concentrate on the last three dimensions, then, considering a variety of charges that might be brought against these efforts as we develop them. Nietzsche and Foucault, sometimes separately, often in combination, will provide us with guideposts in cultivating a sensibility ashamed of some components in morality. Since both of these thinkers will be drawn on, the combination that emerges will be reducible to neither. I will assume responsibility for that.

From Morality to Ethics

Nietzsche resists the grand words of morality: Conscience, Law, God, Sin, Good/Evil, the Categorical Imperative. They easily become conduits for the transcendentalization of selfishness. The most important thing is to check the force of these blind imperatives by reflecting on the ways they come into being and maintain themselves. "Your understanding of the *manner in which moral judgments have originated* would spoil these grand words for you, just as other grand words, like "sin" and "salvation of the soul" and "redemption" have been spoiled for you. —And don't cite the categorical imperative, my friend! This term tickles my ear and makes me laugh."[5] Laughter sometimes registers the effects of the uncanny; Nietzsche thus distrusts any morality that is never accompanied by laughter of this sort. Nietzsche wants to disrupt the drive that demands that everyone respond as the blind Law within you judges. "For it is selfish to experience one's own judgment as a universal law, and this selfishness is blind, petty and frugal . . . "[6] The Nietzschean agenda is first to disturb the presumptive transcendentalization of what you have become by accident, then to translate the anxiety accompanying this disturbance of what you are into energy through which to refigure the basis of your identity, and then to explore alternative ways through which to relate to the strangeness within and without produced by this collision.

But moralists typically find such a strategy to be self-defeating. Every neo-Kantian and teleo-communitarian in North America, for instance, has issued this charge against Nietzsche and Foucault (and those lumped with them today as "post-modernists") at some point during the decade of the 1980s. Those who pursue genealogy for ethical reasons, it seems, are caught in a pragmatic contradiction or trapped in a (unique) pit of incoherences; as a result, they emerge either as nihilists who refuse ethical restraint or as parasites who are killing the moral host they suck sustenance from. How can you have a morality without grounding it in the Law or the Good, or, at the very least, in the Contract, the Rational Consensus, the Normal, or the Useful?

From my perspective, these responses embody a transcendental egoism in need of contestation. Each is egoistic because it silently takes its own fundamental identity to be the source that must guide moral life in general; it is transcendental because it insists that its identity is anchored in an intrinsic purpose or law or potential consensus that can be known to be true. In Nietzsche's language, such moralists insist, "I am morality itself and nothing besides is morality." They veil egoism behind the pious demand to universalize what they are by presenting it as what they are commanded to be by the Law or elevated to by experience of the Good. They present themselves as disinterested *servants*

of the Law or the Good, and they respond to each challenge to their
ego-idealism through a ritual of reiteration, restating the external,
necessary, intrinsic character of the fundament they serve.[7]

But so what? How does such a rejoinder speak to the fundamental
question posed to the genealogist? That is, "How can a *genealogist*
cultivate an ethical sensibility? And what makes such a sensibility
ethical?"

One line of reply might be to challenge theories of intrinsic moral
order with a competing ethical sensibility. To create a little space
between morality and ethics—with appropriate apologies to Hegel.

A moralist often (but not always) thinks that a moral code can be
separated from other elements in social and political practice and
presented more or less systematically, whereas a post-Nietzschean
thinks that at best an ethical sensibility can be cultivated that informs
the quality of future interpretations, actions, and relationships. More
definitively, a moralist explicitly or implicitly gives priority to the idea
of a fundamental order of identity, gender, sexuality, and the like
governing cultural formations. One type accentuates the verb form *to
order*, construing morality to be obedience to a god or nature or the
dictates of reason or a transcendental argument or a categorical imperative. Another accentuates the noun form *order*, construing "moral
order" now as an inherent, harmonious design of being. Both types often
anchor moral order in a god, either as a commander of last resort, a
postulate required to give virtue its just reward in the last instance, or
an ultimate source of the harmonious design discernible in being. Those
who eschew a theological story present narratives in which the fundamental nature of things is supposed to be highly compatible with strong
conceptions of identity, agency, rationality, autonomy, responsibility,
and punishment. The moralist, to put it briefly, finds some way or other
to flatten out Nietzschean conceptions of "life," "will to power,"
"*différance*," and such in the name of a smooth moral economy of
equivalences, either by projecting an intrinsic purpose, a law, or the
plasticity of nature/bodies into the order of things.[8]

Moral order as inherent command or harmonious purpose, or as
(inter)subjective imposition by humans whose subjectivity acts on plastic
bodies and nature. Often these are united in some unstable combination.
Sometimes such perspectives are explicitly articulated, but more often

today they are implicitly installed in narratives of nature, identity, gender, sexuality, agency, normality, responsibility, freedom, and goodness.

A post-Nietzschean ethical sensibility might, first, claim that most contemporary moralists are implicated in one or several of these moral economies, and, second, contest the sense that they exhaust the range of admirable alternatives. As the contestation proceeds, instructive points of convergence unfold between one traditional type of moral order delineated above—the design/teleological conception—and a post-Nietzschean sensibility.

Consider a few intersections between a teleological morality and an anti-teleological ethic. First, both challenge authoritarian temptations residing within the command tradition. Second, both construe the self to be a complex micro-social structure, replete with foreign relations, rather than a "disengaged" unit solid or universal enough to anchor morality in itself. Third, both oppose, though differently, plastic conceptions of nature and bodies often presupposed by command theories, paying attention to how human powers of agency and mastery are inflated by these presumptions of plasticity and "disembodiment." Fourth, both pursue a morality/ethics of cultivation in place of one of command or rational demonstration: Neither attempts to isolate a systematic "moral theory"; each cultivates a *sensibility* that enters into the interpretations and actions it endorses.[9]

It is this last intersection I will pursue. Both the genealogist and the teleologist, then, advance ethics of cultivation. What is cultivated? Not a Law or a categorical imperative, but possibilities of being imperfectly installed in established institutional practices. Where are these possibilities located? How are they cultivated? These are the difficult questions for both perspectives.[10]

Charles Taylor, to my mind the most thoughtful and flexible among contemporary defenders of a teleo-communitarian morality, speaks of "moral sources" ambiguously lodged between established practices and a higher, fugitive experience of intrinsic purpose floating above them. Taylor's "moral sources" are neither simple objects to be represented nor transcendental laws to be deduced. A "source" changes as it is drawn into discursive practice; but it also provides indispensable sustenance from which moral articulation draws. "Moral sources empower. To come closer to them, to have a clearer view of them, to come to grasp

what they involve, is for those who recognize them to be moved to love
or respect them, and through this love/respect to be better enabled to
live up to them. And articulation can bring them closer. That is why
words can empower; why words can at times have tremendous moral
force."[11]

If you substitute "genealogy" for "articulation," "affirm" for "recognize," "ethical sensibility" for "moral force," and (reading between the
lines) "the abundance of life" for "a purposive god," you will have at
once marked momentary points of convergence and fundamental lines
of divergence between a teleo-communitarian morality and an agono-
pluralistic ethic. These two orientations produce each other as competitors; they manufacture competition in which neither is in a good
position to write its adversary off as inconceivable, incoherent, or
unthinkable because the elements of strength and weakness in each are
too close for comfort to those in the other. These two sensibilities are
well suited—to use terms to be redeemed later—to enter into competitive relations of agonistic respect.

Taylor almost recognizes this moment of affinity within difference
with respect to Nietzsche, but he fails to do so with respect to Foucault
and Derrida. Nonetheless, the line of demarcation he draws between a
viable moral sensibility and the moral incoherence of "post-modernism"
cannot be sustained once Nietzsche has been admitted into the charmed
circle of ethics. Taylor anchors his highest morality in an ambiguous
relation between two dimensions—(a) an identity deepening itself
through progressive attunement to (b) a higher purpose in being. A
post-Nietzschean might draw corollary sustenance from (a) a contingent identity affirming (b) the rich abundance of "life" exceeding every
particular organization of it. In the Nietzschean tradition, such fugitive
sources as "life," "bodies," "earth," "will to power," "the oblivion of
difference," "différance," "resistances," an "untamed exteriority," and
"untruth" play a structural role remarkably close to the roles that "a
god," "intrinsic purpose," "a higher direction," and "the essentially
embodied self" play in the teleological tradition Taylor invokes. Several of the anarchistic sources on the first list serve, in Nietzsche's texts,
as contestable "conjectures" or projections informing the ethical sensibility he cultivates. Genealogy takes you to the edge of the abyss of
difference, even though it can never re-present this surplus within and

around the organization of things.[12] Taylor's sources also embody this ambiguous, fugitive character, since the higher direction cultivated is never fully articulable by finite beings, and since human articulation always changes the inchoate source it draws into the (revised) linguistic web. Nietzsche, Foucault, and Taylor (almost) converge in grasping the productive role of excess in ethico-political interpretation, separating themselves from a host of realists and rationalists who either have yet to plumb this dimension of their own practices or (as Taylor may do) are driven to treat the experience of excess as a "lack" or "fault" in a divided self always yet to be remedied.

In Nietzsche's work, as I read it, *life,* and other terms of its type, functions as an indispensable, non-fixable marker, challenging every attempt to treat a concept, settlement, or principle as complete, without surplus or resistance. This projection challenges alternatives that project a commanding god, a designing god, an intrinsic identity, or the sufficiency of reason. The case for it is closely linked to recurrent demonstrations of the operational failure of the other contenders to achieve the presence their representatives (sometimes) promise.[13] The excess of life over identity provides the fugitive source from which one comes to appreciate, and perhaps to love, the an-archy of being amidst the organ-ization of identity\difference.

Genealogy, by itself, might lead either to repression of the experience of contingency it enables or to passive nihilism. Genealogy must thus be combined with tactics applied by the self to itself to fend off resentment against the very an-archy of being it begins to expose. Only when genealogy and cultivation of resistance to existential resentment are pursued together does one develop a more generous or "noble" sensibility. That is why Nietzsche and Foucault alike are involved serially with the genealogy of fixed experience and the application of tactics by the self to itself. Both are crucial to sensibilities endorsed by each; neither alone nor both in conjunction can guarantee the effects it seeks. This latter acknowledgment is a defining mark of the post-Nietzschean sensibility, since the demand for guarantees in this area is precisely what fosters the most authoritarian versions of the moralities of Law and Purpose.

A post-Nietzschean ethical sensibility, then, strives, first, to expose artifice in hegemonic identities and the definitions of otherness (evil) through which they propel their self-certainty; second, to destabilize codes of moral order within which prevailing identities are set, when doing so crystallizes the element of resentment in these constructions of difference; third, to cultivate generosity—that is, a "pathos of distance"—in those indispensable rivalries between alternative moral/ethical perspectives by emphasizing the contestable character of each perspective, including one's own, and the inevitability of these contestations in life; and, fourth—as Foucault eventually endorsed—to contest moral visions that suppress the constructed, contingent, relational character of identity with a positive alternative that goes some distance in specifying the ideal of political life inspiring it.[14] I draw these themes from Foucault and Nietzsche, respectively: The ethical importance of the struggle against existential resentment is emphasized by Nietzsche and the politicization of an ethical sensibility is emphasized by Foucault. Before pursuing Foucault on the second register, let me quote from the divine source (or madman) himself concerning the basis of an admirable ethical sensibility.

> Thus I deny morality as I deny alchemy, that is, I deny their premises: but I do *not* deny that there have been alchemists who believed in these premises and acted in accordance with them. —I also deny immorality: *not* that countless people *feel* themselves to be immoral, but that there is any *true* reason so to feel. It goes without saying that I do not deny—unless I am a fool—that many actions called immoral ought to be avoided and resisted, or that many called moral ought to be done and encouraged—but I think the one should be encouraged and the other avoided *for other reasons than hitherto*. We have to *learn to think differently*—in order at last, perhaps very late on, to attain even more: *to feel differently.*[15]

The "we" is a solicitation rather than a command. A new sensibility is *rendered possible* through genealogies. Then a set of experiments is enacted by the self on its self to revise vengeful sensibilities that have become fixed. Nietzsche, like Foucault after him, commends a set of artful techniques to modify these contingent installations, these "feelings." The sensibility these techniques install functions as a corollary to the cultivation of "virtues" in teleological theories. Thus, to cite one example of such a practice, Nietzsche in *Daybreak* marks the importance of "little deviant acts" in a life where accumulated conventions are always becoming naturalized and moralized. "For nothing *matters* more," Nietzsche asserts, "than that an already mighty, anciently established and irrationally recognized custom should be once more confirmed by a person recognized as rational. . . . All respect to your opinions! But *little deviant acts are worth more*."[16] Ethical generosity becomes effective when it is installed in the feelings, and this involves a series of tactics patiently applied by a self to itself: "All the virtues and efficiency of body and soul are acquired laboriously and little by little, through much industry, self-constraint, limitation, through much obstinate, faithful repetition of the same labors, the same renunciations."[17] Echoes from the Augustinian tradition can be heard here as elsewhere in Nietzsche, but these techniques of the self are designed to foster affirmation of a contingent, incomplete, relational identity interdependent with differences it contests rather than to discover a transcendental identity waiting to be released or to acknowledge obedience to a commanding/designing god.

When Nietzsche, and later Foucault, commend the self as a work of art acting modestly and artfully on its own entrenched contingencies, the aim is not self-narcissism, as neo-Kantians love to insist. *The point is to ward off the violence of transcendental narcissism.* To modify sensibilities of the self through delicate techniques, to do so to reach "beyond good and evil," so that you no longer require the constitution of difference as evil to protect a precarious faith in an intrinsic identity or order. The goal is to modify an already contingent self—working within the narrow terms of craftsmanship available to an adult—so that you are better able to ward off the Augustinian temptation to transcendentalize what you are by constructing difference as heresy or evil.[18] In Foucault's terms, "care of the self" is the operative practice. In Nietzsche's terms, "one thing is needful: that a human being should *attain* satisfaction with himself, whether it be by means of this or that poetry and art; only then is a human being at all tolerable to behold. Whoever is dissatisfied with himself is continually ready for revenge; and we others will be his victims, if only by having to endure his ugly sight."[19] The "ugliness" Nietzsche opposes, then, reflects the demand to ratify a contingent identity by transcendental means. Look around at the next faculty meeting, if you need empirical verification of this ratification process.

But so far we have merely outlined some of the aspirations within this ethical sensibility. We have only glimpsed the dangers, paradoxes, and limits within which it operates.

The Ontalogical Problematic

Foucault resists the language of "life" Nietzsche invokes.[20] He does so, I think, to fend off the suggestion such a term conveys to some (though not to the mature Nietzsche) either of an elemental energy directly accessible to experience by nonlinguistic means or of a vital, purposive force that must be allowed expression regardless of the implications it carries for anyone or anything else. But if Foucault denies a law or purpose in being, while also resisting the language of life (and "will to power"), does this mean that the ethical sensibility he endorses is free of ontological (or "essentialist") dimensions?[21] Does this sensibility liquidate every semblance of "the universal"?

In a recent essay on Foucault's "cultivation of the self," Pierre Hadot asserts that Foucault misreads the Stoics and the Epicureans in a way that vitiates his own ethic. To these Greeks, "the point was not to forge a spiritual identity by writing but to free oneself from one's individuality, to raise oneself to universality."[22] Foucault's reduction of the universal back into the individual, Hadot fears, results in a solipsistic self: "By defining his ethical model as an ethic of existence, Foucault might have been advancing a cultivation of the self which was too purely aesthetic—that is to say, I fear a new form of dandyism, a late-twentieth century version."[23] I fear that Hadot, in the company of others, collapses the space in which the distinctive Foucauldian sensibility is formed, doing so by the way he deploys "the universal" in relation to "the self," "the aesthetic," and "dandyism."

Foucault, I want to say, affirms a hypothetical universal that does not conform to any possibility Hadot recognizes. He affirms a hypothetical, ontalogical universal, one designed to disturb the closure and narcissism of dogmatic identities, one affirmed to be a contestable projection, and one treated as an alternative to ontologies of Law and Purpose. Foucault struggles, against the grain of the language he uses and is used by, not to project a "logic" or moral order into the fundamental character of being. He invokes what might be called an ontalogy, a "reading" of Jobian vitality that exceeds every stabilization of things, a reading that resists imputing either a logic or plasticity to that which precedes culture. It is this fugitive, deniable, and contestable experience, always

resistant to articulation, that is approached through the arts of genealogy and affirmed through techniques of the self. And it is this critical
task that must be renewed perpetually because of pressures installed in
language and other elements of communal life to reinstate the fundamental "logic" of good and evil into the experience of being.

Consider again a quotation presented earlier. Foucault says, "We
have to dig *deeply* to show how things are historically *contingent* . . . ,
intelligible but not *necessary* . . . ," making the "intelligible appear
against a *background of emptiness.*" A deep contingency, a lack of
necessity in things, a background of emptiness. These themes, inserted
into the agenda of genealogy, gesture toward the ont-*a*logical universal
Foucault would endorse. The "emptiness" of things suggests the absence of a Law or Purpose governing existence. In a similar way,
numerous expressions of "plenitude," "doubles," and an "untamed
exterior" gesture toward an abundance that exceeds any particular set
of conventions without assuming the form of a Law, Identity, or Purpose governing things. An emptiness with respect to an intrinsic order;
an abundance with respect to any actual organ-ization of actuality.
These are fugitive experiences to cultivate through genealogy, doing so
to enhance generosity in rivalries between identity and alter-identity
that provide each with its ambiguous conditions of existence.[24]

In one essay Foucault strives to express this ont*a*logical problematic
most actively. Here he makes it clear that the ont-*a*logy installed in his
researches is not one that is or is likely to become known to be true. It
takes the form of a "happy posit-ivism" (dash added) or "critical principle"
through which questions are posed and critical comparisons with other
positions are explored. It shares this paradoxical character with all other
fundaments presumed or posited to date in ethico-political interpretation,
even though many of the latter strive so hard to conceal this status of their
own faith. Allow me to condense a few pages from "The Order of Discourse" into a few lines, doing so to underline how Foucault both elabo-
rates his stance and exposes tactics by which alternative stances of its
type conceal their posit-ivistic and comparative character.

"*It seems to me,*" Foucault says, "that beneath this apparent venera-
tion of discourse, under this apparent logophilia, a certain fear is
hidden. *It is just as if* prohibitions, thresholds and limits have been set

up in order to master, at least partly, the great proliferation of discourse in order to remove from its richness its most dangerous part." Next, marching orders are presented to those who endorse such semblances. "And *if* we want to" analyze the terms of this fear, *then* "we must call into question our will to truth . . . ; we must not imagine there is a great unsaid or a great unthought . . . which we would have to articulate or think at last . . . ; we must not imagine that the world turns towards us a legible face which we would have only to decipher." This stack of negative imperatives, stretched out after a small "if", finally culminates in an affirmative whose standing at the end of a long chain of hypotheticals has (almost) been forgotten: "We must conceive discourse as a violence which we do to things, or in any case as a practice which we impose on them; and it is in this practice that the events of discourse find the principle of their regularity."[25]

Two things. First, Foucault's conception of discourse, containing its own uncertainties and proliferations, is initially presented as a critical principle "we" pursue in our researches. But as the imperatives that operationalize this practice pile up, it shortly begins to be heard as an imperative of being as such. The posit-ivism on which it is founded is all too easy to forget. This contrived forgetfulness, condensed into the space of a couple of pages, mimics and exposes the ontological forgetfulness of moralist-political discourse. The hypothetical character of the fundamental presumptions becomes buried beneath the weight of discursive practice, and because it is impossible to proceed without implicitly invoking some set of fundaments, this set as well all too readily becomes received as a set of absolute imperatives installed in the order of things. Genealogy breaks up this inertia of presumption, which constantly reinstates itself as Nature, God, Law, or Purpose; it scrambles the sense of ontological necessity implicit in contingent consolidations.[26]

Second, Foucault contests implicit and explicit ontologies of intrinsic order or plasticity, not simply by showing how each conceals the hypothetical character and multiple sites of undecidability in its own imperatives, but also by projecting in competition with them an (always underdeveloped) ontology of that which is "violent, pugnacious, disorderly . . . , perilous, incessant . . . , and buzzing" within and below discursive practice.

If this anti-logical logos is hypothetical, comparative, and problematical, why struggle to operationalize it through critical comparison to other familiar alternatives? There is unlikely to be a final answer to this question, just as there is none forthcoming with respect to the alternatives against which it contends. But one response resides in the fact that every interpretation presupposes or invokes some such problematical stance with respect to the fundamental character of being; to try to eliminate such a stance altogether from interpretation is either to repress crucial dimensions of one's own perspective or to lapse into a passive nihilism of resolute silence. Passive nihilism cedes the activity of interpretation to dogmatic perspectives; it secretly concedes too much to fundamentalists by treating the problematical standing of its own projections as a sufficient reason to withdraw from the field of interpretation. It still presumes that this condition of discourse is a "fault" or "lack" that "ought not to be," rather than a productive source of creativity that makes life possible and keeps things moving.

The Foucauldian problematic elicits fugitive, subterranean elements in contemporary experience, where old verities have fallen onto hard times and where the sense of violence in them may be more palpable to more people. Foucault's *ontological* projection speaks to a problematical experience increasingly available, while contending against insistences and resentments that press us to deny, evade, avoid, or defer its fugitive power. Its thematization alters the terms of contestation in political discourse. Familiar debates between the advocates of Law, Purpose, Plasticity, and Normality no longer seem to exhaust the available terms of debate. The sense of necessity governing the old debate is broken; and a set of complementary assumptions not subjected to debate by these debating partners now becomes open to interrogation. Each alternative, including the one Foucault advances, is now more likely to be received as a "problematic" than a "position" or "theory": It is construed as a particular, tension-ridden gathering of impulses, insistences, presumptions, and questions through which interpretation proceeds rather than a coherent set of imperatives upon which it "rests."[27] Such a modification in the terms of self-presentation can have salutary effects on the character of ethical discourse.

Foucault identifies, though more lightly and obliquely than the mentor who inspires him, *ressentiment* as a source from which the problematics of moral order are constructed. Some of us now begin to hear each of these orientations as point and counterpoint in the same melody of deniable revenge; more of us refuse to treat them as The Set that exhausts the possible terms of ethical debate. Foucault:

> Nothing is fundamental. That is what is interesting in the analysis of society. That is why nothing irritates me as much as these inquiries— which are by definition metaphysical—on the foundations of power in a society or the self-institution of a society, etc. These are not fundamental phenomena. There are only reciprocal relations, and the perpetual gaps between intentions in relation to one another.[28]

It assists my interpretation if you read the first sentence along two registers. "Nothing is *fundamental*" in the sense that no fundamental Law or Purpose or Contract governs things. "*Nothing* is fundamental" in the sense that energies and forces exceeding the social construction of subjects and things circulate through "gaps" in these institutionalizations.

So there is a politics of forgetfulness built in to social discourse, the imperatives of social coordination, the drives to revenge against the contingency of things, and the insecurities of identity. Genealogy disturbs this forgetfulness, in the interests of drawing us closer to the experience that nothing is fundamental. The results of genealogy are then to be translated into noble effects, as you reach toward a sensibility beyond good and evil. But how can this combination of genealogical disturbance and noble sensibility ever establish itself securely in a self or a culture at any particular time? It cannot. The Nietzsche/Foucault sensibility (taking various forms such as passing by, generosity, agonistic respect, a pathos of distance, the spiritualization of enmity) consists of a set of elements that cannot be combined together perfectly at any single time. They lack "compossibility" not because of "weakness of will" or "the crooked timber of humanity," where the primordial "fault" resides within the self, but because the accentuation of one element in this combination at any moment necessarily impedes the other at that time. The (post) Nietzschean ideals of nobility, a pathos of distance, agonistic care, and passing by never arrive; they are at best always coming to be. One element is always incompletely articulated with the other to which it must be united. Here we encounter a rift or dissonance not within but between human capacity and the temporality in which it is set.

More and more it seems to me that the philosopher, being of *necessity* a man of tomorrow and the day after tomorrow, has always found himself, and *had* to find himself, in contradiction to his today."[29]

This means, I take it, not only that the cultivator of such a sensibility regularly encounters conflict with a culture inscribed by the logic of good and evil, but that the pursuer, given the continuing power of forgetfulness amidst the quest to incorporate generosity into one's corporeal sensibilities, always has more to do to arrive beyond the logic of good and evil. To celebrate such a philosophy is always to offer "A Prelude to a Philosophy of the Future," and that paradoxical condition too must be affirmed by those who struggle against *ressentiment*. Foucault places this Nietzschean theme on a political register when he says, perhaps in response to a question posed by Charles Taylor during a collective interview, "the farthest I would go is to say that perhaps one must not be for consensuality, but one must be against non-consensuality."[30] This is Foucault's condensed formulation of the principle of "critical pluralism" introduced in chapter 1 of this study. In a Nietzschean-Foucauldian world, something is always out of joint ethically because it is impossible to combine all the elements of nobility perfectly in one site at one time. The struggle to reach beyond good and evil is salutary, but the claim to have arrived there is always a falsification that reiterates the dogmatism of the duality you resist. That is why, I think, Foucault celebrates the ambiguity of politics and finds politics, in one register or another, always to be appropriate.

An Ethico-Political Spirituality

An ethical sensibility, *anchored* in an ontological problematic, *rendered* through genealogies of the possible, *cultivated* through tactics applied by the self to itself, *embodied* as care for an enlarged diversity of life in which plural constituencies co-exist in more creative ways than sustained by a communitarian idea of harmony or a liberal idea of tolerance, *politicized* through a series of critical engagements with established dualities of good/evil, normal/abnormal, guilt/innocence, rationality/irrationality, autonomy/dependence, security/insecurity. Several of these dimensions can be heard in the following celebration of "curiosity":

> I like the word [curiosity]. It evokes "care"; it evokes the care of what exists and might exist; a sharpened sense of reality, but one that is never immobilized before it; a readiness to find what surrounds us strange and odd; a certain determination to throw off familiar ways of thought and to look at the same things in a different way . . . ; a lack of respect for the traditional hierarchies of what is important and fundamental.[31]

Let me locate this sensibility more actively on a political register, doing so, first, by modifying the received democratic imaginary to correspond more closely to a timely politics of care for the strife and interdependence of contingent identity\difference relations; second, by considering what relationships such a sensibility might strive to establish with the fundamentalisms circulating through contemporary life; and, third, by engaging tensions that persist between an ethic of cultivation and persistent circumstances of political engagement.

The idea is that the ethical sensibility will be strengthened by its ability to amplify important themes already operative in the culture of democracy and that established conceptions of democracy can be improved by testing them against the terms of such a sensibility.

Foucault does not articulate a vision of democracy. His early objection against political ideals as prisons militates against it; and his later, cautious affirmation of a positive political imagination never takes this form. But numerous comments in the context of his participation in public protests and demonstrations are suggestive on this score. It seems to me that a series of correspondences can be delineated between the ethical sensibility cultivated by Foucault and a more general ethos of democracy. Consider three dimensions of democratic practice in this light.[32]

1. Democracy within the territorial state. A viable democratic ethos embodies a productive ambiguity at its very core. Its role as an instrument of rule and governance is balanced and countered by its logic as a medium for the periodic disturbance and denaturalization of settled identities and sedimented conventions. Both dimensions are crucial. But the second functions politically to extend the cultural effects of genealogy, to open up the play of possibility by subtracting the sense of necessity, completeness, and smugness from established organ-izations of life. If the democratic task of governance ever buries the democratic ethos of disturbance and politicization under the weight of national consensus, historical necessity, and state security, state mechanisms of electoral accountability will be reduced to conduits for the production of internal/ external others against whom to wage moral wars of all too familiar sorts.

2. *The limits of the state.* We live during a time when an asymmetry between the globalization of relations and the confinement of electoral institutions to the territorial state functions too often to intensify state chauvinism and violence. The nostalgia in political theory (and many other sites too) for a "politics of place," in which territoriality, sovereignty, electoral accountability, nationality, and public belonging must all map the same space, depoliticizes global issues and fosters democratic state chauvinism. During the late-modern time, productive possibilities of thought and practice might be opened up by a creative disaggregation of elements in the modern democratic imagination, paying attention, for instance, to how a democratic ethos might exceed the boundaries of the state, even when electoral institutions of democratic accountability are confined to the state. During a time when corporate structures, financial institutions, intelligence networks, communication media, and criminal rings are increasingly global in character, democratic energies, active below and through the state, might also reach beyond these parameters to cross-national, extra-statist social movements. A new and timely pluralization of attachments, identifications, and spaces of political action beyond the boundaries of the state, already unfolding before us in the late-modern era, might eventually compromise the state's ability to colonize the terms of collective identity at key historical moments. Foucault's 1981 declaration at a press conference on behalf of the "boat people" is suggestive on this score, in its protest against treatment of the stateless by states, in its insistence on extending political identifications beyond the state, and in its identification of that which diverse constituencies within states

share that might serve as a contingent basis for extra-statist, cross-national mobilization:

> There exists an international citizenry that has its rights, that has its duties, and that is committed to rise up against every abuse of power, no matter who the author, no matter who the victims. After all, we are all ruled, and as such, we are in solidarity. . . . The will of individuals must be inscribed in a reality that the governments wanted to monopolize. This monopoly must be wrested from them bit by bit, each and every day.[33]

3. The politicization of non-statist global movements. Boundary-crossing political movements—with respect to, say, gay/lesbian rights, disturbance of international patterns of state secrecy and surveillance, contestation of the state's monopoly over potent symbols of danger and practices of security, and the renegotiation of first-world patterns of consumption that impinge on the future of the earth—can both contribute to the democratic drive to participate in events that define our lives and ventilate dead pockets of air within contemporary states. As a variety of cross-national, extra-statist movements already in motion accelerate, they might extend the democratic ethos beyond the state through a pluralization of democratic spaces of action. They might compromise the state as the ultimate source of collective identity whenever a crisis arises and contest its monopoly over the rules of boundary crossing. If and as such cross-national, non-statist movements become consolidated, they will not extinguish the state as *a* site of democratic action and accountability; rather, they will pluralize the sites of democratic action and allegiance, creating spaces of action below, at, and above the level of the state.

These, then, are some of the elements in the ethico-political sensibility under scrutiny: genealogies that dissolve apparent necessities into contingent formations; cultivation of care for possibilities of life that challenge claims to an intrinsic moral order; democratic disturbances of sedimented identities that conceal violence in their terms of closure; practices that enable multifarious styles of life to co-exist on the same territory; a plurality of political identifications extending through and beyond the state to break up the monopolies of state-centered politics.

But surely, politicization of this sensibility will continue to meet with opposition and outrage from the various fundamentalisms circulating through contemporary life. Nietzsche and Foucault both teach us how the more optimistic hopes of the Enlightenment on this score are unlikely to succeed. Theistic and secular priests persist as voices in and around us: the inertia of shared practices, the forces of *ressentiment*, the pressures of guilt arising from ambivalent identifications, the effects of social coordination on the reification of selves and institutions—all these forces press against the effective generalization of generous sensibilities. They make genealogies and politicizations of dogmatic identities into perpetual tasks. They render the move "beyond good and evil" always a movement and never a secure achievement. What, then, can be the terms of engagement between an ethical sensibility affirming care for the contingency of things and those moral fundamentalisms that oppose it as nihilistic, relativistic, or parasitic? (As if everyone, everything, and every institution were not parasitical, in some way!)

One salutary possibility installed within this perspective, I think, is the drive to convert some relations of antagonism between fundamentalists into those (as I call them) of *agonistic respect* among contenders who, first, have become a little more skeptical respectively about the basis of what they are and, second, may therefore recognize possibilities of alliance on some future issues with some of the same parties they now oppose most actively. The effective possibilities here are limited, but they are nonetheless real. Agonistic respect constitutes an element in an impossible utopia, worth pursuit even amidst the impossibility of its full or final realization. An ethos of agonistic respect among interdependent and contending constituencies forms one of the cultural conditions of that critical pluralism considered in Chapter 1.

Agonistic respect, as I construe it, is a social relation of respect for the opponent against whom you define yourself even while you resist its imperatives and strive to delimit its spaces of hegemony. Care for the strife and interdependence of contingent identities and the differences through which they define themselves, for instance, means that "we" (the we is an invitation) cannot pursue the ethic that inspires us without contesting claims to the universality and sufficiency of the moral fundamentalisms we disturb. Hence genealogy and deconstruction. But this antagonism can be translated into something closer to agonistic respect in some cases, as each party comes to appreciate the extent to which its self-definition is bound up with the other and the degree to which the comparative projections of both are contestable. We opponents can become bonded together, partially and contingently, through an enhanced experience of the contestability of the problematic each pursues most fervently and through the anticipation that some of us may well be allies on other occasions for other purposes in the future. This is approximately what Nietzsche meant by the "spiritualization of enmity,"[34] though he thought the capacity to operationalize such a relationship was limited.

Agonistic respect differs from its sibling, liberal tolerance, in affirming a more ambiguous relation of interdependence and strife between identities over a passive letting the other be. The latter may be desirable on occasion, but it is less available in late-modern life than some liberals presume. To an idealist of agonistic respect, it is not sufficient to shed "prejudice," because our identities are bound up with each other in a world where pressures to enact general policies always remain active. Agonistic respect "cuts" deeper than tolerance because it folds contestation into the foundations of the identity from which liberal tolerance is often derived and delimited. But, still, this perspective remains close enough to liberal tolerance to invite comparison and critical negotiation, pressing its debating partner to fold the spirit of genealogy more actively into its characterization of "the individual" and arguing against the spirit of complacency too often lodged in liberal bifurcations between the private and the public.

There is considerable irony and foolishness in a call to agonistic reciprocity, since it invites the fundamentalist to incorporate an element we endorse into its own identity. The invitation may be refused. The very invitation might be repudiated through the charge of heresy, nihilism, relativism, or anarchism. But the call is made in the context of acknowledging the contestability of our fundaments, by showing the fundamentalist some ways in which his fundaments too are contestable and by revealing the unneccessary violence done to the other through efforts to secure the self-certainty of a hegemonic cultural identity. And we do not demand that the fundamentalist incorporate the sensibility of its opponent as a condition of respect; we merely call on the fundamentalist to acknowledge the contestability of its claim to intrinsic moral order and to affirm self-restrictions in the way it advances *its* agenda in the light of this admission. In this way, space for politics can be opened through a degree of reciprocity amidst contestation; new possibilities for the negotiation of difference are created by identifying traces in the other of the sensibility one identifies in oneself and locating in the self elements of the sensibility attributed to the other. An element of care is built in to contestation and of contestation in to care.

But the difficulties continue. For there are, in addition, numerous times and places where the terms of opposition are likely to remain implacable even after the initial positions have been opened up by reciprocal acknowledgment of the contestability of each stance. Debates over the di(per)versity of sexuality, over abortion, and, perhaps, over the right to take one's own life when one decides the time is right, might have this character to varying degrees. Some fundamentalists who treat homosexuality as per-verse, for instance, might be moved to cultivate either a studied indifference or agonistic respect in relation to those who celebrate sexual di-versity. But they will be less likely to do so with respect to the issue of gay parents. Those of us who celebrate diversity here will have to try to disrupt their operational presumptions concerning what is "natural," maintaining confidence in the possible efficacy of genealogy and struggle in this domain.[35] So, introduction of a Foucauldian sensibility into the terms of political contestation is likely, first, to be resisted belligerently by many constituencies, and, second, to encounter obdurate instances of nonnegotiability even between constituencies willing to engage it.

The Foucauldian faith, if I may put it this way, is that more extensive cultivation of a political ethos of agonistic care makes a real difference in private and public life, even if it remains a minority stance within that life. For it is a political problematic of interrogation, engagement, and negotiation, not a political doctrine of intrinsic identity, consensus, and resolution. Its impossible utopia is agonistic respect among differences irreducible to a rational consensus in settings where it is often necessary to establish general policies. It locates freedom in the gaps and spaces fostered by these collisions and negotiations rather than in a pattern of harmonious unity or private sanctuary it hopes to realize. It counsels recurrent disturbance and negotiation of the numerous paradoxes of political life over attempts to conceal, resolve, or repress them.

These last reflections, linking an ethical sensibility to an ethos of politics, reveal another tension between these two registers amidst the durable connection between them. An *ethic of cultivation* requires attention to the nuances of life; it applies tactics patiently and experimentally to the self; it affirms ambiguity and uncertainty in the categories through which ethical judgment is made. But a *politics of engagement and insurgency* often generalizes conflicts so that one set of concerns becomes overwhelmed by others; it opens up the probability of more definite, totalistic definitions of one side by its opponents; it sometimes foments rapid transformations exceeding the temporal and spatial rhythms of ethical cultivation. Cultivation of agonistic care for the contingency of things and engagement in political contestation, then, are locked into a relation of strife amidst their mutual implication.[36]

There is no way to eliminate these tensions. The pretense to do so always presupposes either an intrinsic harmony that is highly contestable or a fictive model of unified political agency that has never been displayed anywhere. The tension between genealogy and ethical sensibility identified earlier, then, now catapults into the medium of politics. Particularly politics infused by a democratic ethos in a contingent world. The struggle against resentment of a world in which "nothing is fundamental" involves a willingness to act in highly ambiguous circumstances where the ethical sensibility requires a critical ethos as one of its conditions of existence while the ethos disables the sensibility from full or complete attainment.[37] The aspiration is to draw agonistic respect from the effects of politics and to fold agonistic respect into the art of politics. The danger of dangers flows from suppression of such tensions and ambiguities in the name of some higher intrinsic order.

Perhaps Foucault can be allowed to have the last word (for the moment) here:

> There's an optimism that consists in saying that things couldn't be better. My optimism would consist rather in saying that so many things can be changed, fragile as they are, bound up more with circumstances than necessities, more arbitrary than self-evident, more a matter of complex, but temporary, historical circumstances than of inevitable anthropological constants. . . . You know, to say that we are much more recent than we think, is to place at the disposal of the work that we can do on ourselves the greatest possible share of what is presented to us as inaccessible.[38]

Notes

1. Friedrich Nietzsche, *Beyond Good and Evil: Prelude to a Philosophy of the Future*, trans. Walter Kaufmann (New York: Vintage, 1966), 83.

2. Sigmund Freud, "The 'Uncanny' " in *The Standard Edition of the Complete Works of Sigmund Freud*, Vol. 6, trans. James Strachey (London: Hogarth Press, 1953-54), 243. I am indebted to Jane Bennett for calling my attention to this essay and for suggesting how exploration of the uncanny is intimately involved with an exploration of closure in a moral economy of equivalences.

3. Augustine, *Concerning the City of God: Against the Pagans*, trans. Henry Bettenson (Middlesex, UK: Penguin, 1984), Bk. 14, chap. 13, 571. My emphases.

4. This theme is most fully developed in Sigmund Freud, *Moses and Monotheism*, trans. Katherine Jones (New York: Vintage, 1939).

5. Friedrich Nietzsche, *The Gay Science*, trans. Walter Kaufmann (New York: Vintage, 1974), #335, 264.

6. *Gay Science*, #335, 265.

7. I hope it becomes clear as we proceed that not all those who anchor their morality in the Law or the Good are locked into transcendental egoism. Only those who insist that the "other" cannot devise a morality *unless* s/he accepts these fundaments are so locked in. Thinkers such as Foucault, Derrida, and Nietzsche are excellent at bringing out the subterranean fundamentalism of many who otherwise deny it. To convict the Nietzschean of incoherence is one of the best signs of such a mentality. Those who emphasize the contestability of the Law or Good they represent have taken the first step away from the egoism of self-universalization. Those who acknowledge an ironic debt to the differences they contest have taken a second. When those two steps are combined, preconditions for *agonistic respect* with the doctrines you oppose, including the Foucauldian sensibility, have been opened up.

8. A world with no commanding or designing god is likely to be marked by contingency, discordances, accidents, and chance. This is exactly the sort of world in which Nietzsche and Foucault seek to cultivate an ethical sensibility. This world, in turn, is not a likely source of a teleological ethic. A world with an omnipotent god, as the nominalists tried to show the Thomists, is unlikely to be one limited by any prior design of the world. For an omnipotent god is most comfortable with a highly contingent world it can vary in any way at any time; its omni-potence is threatened by any design that restricts it. A teleological morality without a god is problematic, then, but it is also difficult to construct one with an omnipotent god. It is not that a god filling the bill is impossible to construct, but the care required to construct it to fit just this bill immediately raises the question as to whether the deity involved is discovered or invented to fill the exact purpose it is supposed to reveal. Once that question is posed, either debate sets in and ethical pluralism has a chance to flourish, or repression sets in. However, an omnipotent god seems most compatible with a morality grounded in a transcendental imperative, and neo-Kantians have had a difficult time demonstrating this imperative without recourse to such a deeply contestable faith. Hans Blumenberg pursues the theological issues extensively in his lengthy history of onto-theological paradox and debates that have marked the West since the inception of Augustinianism (*The Legitimacy of the Modern Age*, Cambridge, MA:

MIT Press, 1983). A last "theological" point. Although there are powerful pressures binding the command and design traditions to the authority of a god, it is not imperative that a "post-Nietzschean" ethic deny or oppose every conception of divinity. A god as "absence," for instance, could be compatible with what I will call the "ont-*a*logy of a post-Nietzschean sensibility." And some conceptions of poly-theism are supportive of a robust ethical pluralism. I endorse none of these theologies, but "nontheistic reverence for the ambiguity of being." Let us pray together to radically different gods.

9. In these comparisons I take Charles Taylor to represent the "teleological" model. His version of it, I think, brings out effectively assumptions implicit in the other formulations. He might resist the title I have bestowed on him, but the language through which his morality is couched is very teleological by comparison to the Nietzschean/Foucauldian sensibility defended here. Those are the only terms of comparison that interest me at the moment. See Charles Taylor, *Philosophical Papers*, Vols. 1 and 2 (New York: Cambridge University Press, 1985).

10. Notice how the favorite critique neo-Kantians pose against teleo-communitarians loses its bite against post-Nietzscheans. They contend that it is impossible to reach universal agreement on the nature of the good, commending instead the same quest with respect to rights or the procedures of justice. We concur that a grounded consensus on the good is unlikely, even though we emphasize much more than neo-Kantians how much established conventions are treated implicitly by neo-Kantians and teleo-communitarians as if they were grounded. For both parties tend to eschew genealogy. We, of course, are similarly dubious about the ability to locate a similar ground for rights and justice.

11. Charles Taylor, *Sources of the Self: The Making of the Modern Identity* (Cambridge, MA: Harvard University Press, 1989), 96. A powerful argument in Taylor's study is that advocates of "disengaged" morality are unable to account for the sources of their own moral inspirations. Bernard Williams, in an insightful review of this study, points to the strength of this argument, while claiming that Taylor's framework of analysis is not well suited to come to terms with Nietzschean thought. "I think that Taylor, in his search for the sources of value, seems not to have taken seriously enough Nietzsche's thought that if there is, not only no God, but no metaphysical order of any kind, then this imposes quite new demands on our self-understanding." (*New York Review of Books*, Nov. 4, 1990, 48.) I concur with this judgment. This chapter explores an ethical alternative that might emerge when one does take that possibility seriously.

12. In *Identity and Difference* (New York: Harper & Row, 1969), trans. Joan Stambaugh, Martin Heidegger speaks of "the oblivion of difference." "We speak of the *difference* between Being and beings. . . . That is the *oblivion of difference*. The oblivion here to be thought is the veiling of the difference as such." (50) The thought is very similar to Nietzsche's elusive presentations of life. You never lift the veil of difference as such, for difference is that which differs from the organ-ized, conceptualized, fixed, and determinate. But you might encounter the oblivion of difference through artful techniques; you might experience the way in which the organ-ization of experience draws from and on that which is itself not yet organ-ized.

13. Hence the indispensability of deconstruction and genealogy to the sensibility in question.

14. "But, in the end, I've become rather irritated by an attitude, which for a long time was mine, too, and which I no longer subscribe to, which consists in saying: our problem is to denounce and to criticize; let them get on with their legislation and their reforms.

That doesn't seem to me the right attitude." Lawrence D. Kritzman, ed., *Michel Foucault: Politics, Philosophy, Culture*, trans. Alan Sheridan (New York: Routledge, 1988), 209.

15. Friedrich Nietzsche, *Daybreak*, trans. R. J. Hollingdale (Cambridge, UK: Cambridge University Press, 1982), #103, 104. Alan White gives an excellent reading of this formulation, and other dimensions of Nietzsche's thought, too, in *Within Nietzsche's Labyrinth* (New York: Routledge, 1990).

16. *Daybreak*, #149, 97. In *The Will to Power* (trans. Walter Kaufmann and R. J. Hollingdale, New York: Random House, 1967), #1019, Nietzsche lists six practices that have been wrecked by the church's monopoly and misuse of them. They are asceticism, fasting, the monastery, feasts, the courage to endure one's nature, and death. In each of these cases Nietzsche would refigure the practice in question into one that fends off existential resentment and fosters a "nobility" that reaches beyond the ugly narcissism of good and evil. In general, the notes in *Will to Power* that focus on the body also focus on the priority of techniques of the self over rational argumentation or direct reform of "the will" in fostering the ethical sensibility commended. I explore some ingredients in a Nietzschean ethic and discuss "preparing to die at the right time" in *Identity\Difference: Democratic Negotiations of Political Paradox* (Ithaca, NY: Cornell University Press, 1991), Introduction and chap. 6.

17. *The Will to Power*, #995. Nietzsche's commendation of preparing oneself to die at the right time is another tactic of exactly this type. In so preparing yourself, you also affirm the contingency of life.

18. Narcissus loved not himself, but his image in the pond. The transcendental narcissist loves its own image projected into a transcendental command or direction.

19. *Gay Science*, #290, 233.

20. Nietzsche himself invokes the vocabulary of life in one way in his early work and in a modified way in his later work. He gives up the idea that one can have direct access to life through music in his later work, though the comparison between certain forms of music and the structure of language continues to be presented as one way to think about the moment of imposition in the translation of bodily pressures into a linguistic mode. I will not pursue that issue here. It is the later use of "life" that I am drawn to.

21. I generally try to avoid the language of "essentialism." It is invoked to mean, variously, (a) a philosophy that pretends a highest law, nature, or principle is, has, or can be brought to full presence, (b) the confidence that there is a fundamental law or purpose governing existence that can be more closely approximated in life through hermeneutic piety though it can never be made perfectly transparent, (c) the claim that every actor and every interpreter invokes a set of fundamental assumptions about the character of being each time he or she acts or interprets. Because it means any or all of these things, anyone can successfully accuse anyone else of "being an essentialist" in some way or other. Foucault, as I read him, is not an "essentialist" on the first two scores, but is on the third. He comes close to what you might call the "vague essentialism" advanced by Gilles Deleuze and Felix Guattari in *A Thousand Plateaus* (Minneapolis: University of Minnesota Press, 1970). "So how are we to define this matter-movement, this matter-energy, this matter flow, this matter in variation that enters assemblages and leaves them? It is a destratified, deterritorialized matter. It seems to us that Husserl brought thought a decisive step forward when he discovered a region of vague and material essences (in other words, essences that are vagabond, anexact and yet rigorous), distinguishing them from fixed, metric and formal essences." (407) Husserl, of course, did not pursue this insight far

enough for Deleuze and Guattari. Deleuze and Guattari do in plateau 6, "How Do You Make Yourself a Body Without Organs?" This plateau enacts the sort of strategies Foucault and Nietzsche endorse, though the examples it offers at the beginning are (predictably) far more extreme and dangerous than those it endorses on reflection. For American conceptions that move toward such a Lawless Essentialism see Jane Bennett, *Unthinking Faith and Enlightenment* (New York: New York University Press, 1986) and Donna Haraway, *Primate Visions* (New York: Routledge, 1989).

22. Pierre Hadot, "Reflections on the notion of 'the cultivation of the self,' " in Timothy J. Armstrong, ed. and trans., *Michel Foucault: Philosopher* (New York: Routledge, 1992), 229.

23. Hadot, "Reflections," 230. Hadot goes on to say, "For my part, I believe firmly . . . in the opportunity for modern man . . . to become aware of our situation as belonging to the universe. . . . This exercise in wisdom will therefore be an attempt to open ourselves up to the universal."

24. This ontological level is the one Habermasians, to date, have been hesitant to engage in Foucault. Although they do not postulate a Law or Design in being, the terms through which "communicative ethics" are delineated seem to me to presuppose a plasticity of things and a susceptibility to consensus in life challenged by Foucault. These two competing "communicative ethics" will enter into more reflective engagement with each other when both parties actively consider how differences in their most fundamental projections into nature and bodies affect their divergent readings of "discourse." Habermas evinces awareness of this dimension when he engages communitarians such as Taylor, Sandel, and MacIntyre. In one note, he indicates how Sandel would have to explicate the normative content of "community, embodied and shared self-understanding" more carefully to sustain his theory. "If he did, he would realize just how onerous the burden of proof is that neo-Aristotelian approaches must bear, as in the case of A. MacIntyre in *After Virtue*. . . . They must demonstrate how an objective moral order can be grounded without recourse to metaphysical premises." (*Moral Consciousness and Communicative Action* (Cambridge, MA: MIT Press, 1990), 183. Habermas, in turn, would have to show how the conception of nature presupposed in his discourse ethics is superior to the projection Foucault endorses in "The Order of Discourse" (see Note 25) and elsewhere. It only defers the engagement to reduce the options to a choice between a morally obnoxious "vitalism" or the model of communication Habermas himself invokes. I pursue this issue among Habermas, Foucault, and Taylor in "The Irony of Interpretation" in Daniel Conway and John Seery, eds., *Politics and Irony* (New York: St. Martin's Press, 1992).

25. Michel Foucault, "The Order of Discourse," in Michael Shapiro, ed., *Language and Politics* (Oxford: Basil Blackwell, 1984), 125-127, emphases added. This was originally presented as Foucault's inaugural address to the College de France in 1970. I prefer the clause "a practice which we impose on them" to "a violence which we do to things." The latter is too susceptible to the interpretation that nothing can or could be done to relieve that violence, therefore that nothing turns on the effort to overcome the Augustinian temptation to dogmatize your own faith. I presented an earlier analysis of this formulation in *Politics and Ambiguity* (Madison, WI: University of Wisconsin Press, 1987), chap. 10, "Where the Word Breaks Off."

26. The forgetfulness pursued here runs deeper than I have so far intimated. It is built into the very character of shared vocabularies, where the conditions of existence of a common language require an imposition of equivalences within the concepts deployed that "forget" those excesses that do not fit into these configurations. Nietzsche discusses this level of forgetting in *On the Genealogy of Morals*, trans. Walter Kaufmann (New

York: Random House, 1967). And in the very texts in which this logic of equivalences is discussed he also develops linguistic strategies that cut against the grain of them. I cannot pursue that issue further here, though it is very relevant to the thesis of this section.

27. See "Polemics, Politics, and Problematizations: An Interview with Michel Foucault," in *The Foucault Reader*, ed. Paul Rabinow (New York: Pantheon, 1984), 381-389.

28. Michel Foucault, "An Ethics of Pleasure," in *Foucault Live*, ed. Sylvere Lotringer and trans. John Johnston (New York: Semiotext(e), 1989), 267.

29. *Beyond Good and Evil*, #212, 137.

30. Michel Foucault, "Politics and Ethics: An Interview," in Paul Rabinow, ed., *The Foucault Reader* (New York: Pantheon Books, 1984), 379. Foucault refuses the language of "regulative ideal" in pointing out his relation to consensus, probably because he thinks such a concept inadequately expresses the complexity of his relation to his own ideal. It is not merely that it is unlikely to be realized because of historical limitations, it contains a series of elements existing in productive tension with each other.

31. Michel Foucault, "The Masked Philosopher," in Kritzman, ed., *Politics, Philosophy, Culture*, 328.

32. These dimensions are developed more fully in Connolly, *Identity\Difference*, especially the last two chapters; and in Connolly, "Democracy and Territoriality," *Millennium* (December, 1991), 463-484.

33. Quoted in Didier Eribon, *Michel Foucault*, trans. Betsy Wing (Cambridge, MA: Harvard University Press, 1991), 279. Thomas Keenan, in "The 'Paradox' of Knowledge and Power," *Political Theory* (February, 1987), discusses this statement thoughtfully and extensively.

34. "The Church has at all times desired the destruction of its enemies: we, we immoralists and anti-Christians, see that is to our advantage that the church exists. . . . In politics, too, enmity has become much more spiritual—much more prudent, much more thoughtful, much more *forbearing*. . . . We adopt the same attitude toward the 'enemy within': there too we have spiritualized enmity, there too we have grasped its *value*." Friedrich Nietzsche, *Twilight of the Idols*, trans. R. J. Hollingdale (New York: Penguin, 1968), under "Morality as Anti-Nature," 43-44.

35. This is about the juncture, I have found while giving papers, that someone interrupts, charging: "Murder is perverse! Torture is perverse! Your ethic of 'generosity' sanctions these perversities. Certainly it lacks the ability to oppose them." But of course it does not carry such implications. Its governing sensibility of care for the interdependence and strife of identity\difference clearly opposes such acts. Indeed, very often murder and torture express the very dogmatism of identity and abstract revenge against life the sensibility in question seeks to curtail. So why is such a charge so predictable at this juncture? I suspect that some who wrap themselves in a fictive Law they cannot demonstrate would like to silence those of us who keep pounding away, first, at the paradox of identity and, second, at cruelties installed in transcendental narcissism. The next time this charge is issued, examine the demeanor of the one who issues it. Does he look capable of killing you? Fortunately, there are still laws to restrain dogmatists from acting on these impulses.

36. These comments on tensions between an ethic of cultivation and a politics of critical engagement are inspired from one side by a critique delivered to me every other day by Dick Flathman and from another by a critique offered by Stephen White of a paper of mine at the 1991 meeting of the Southern Political Science Association, Tampa, Florida, entitled "Territoriality and Democracy." Flathman is tempted by an anti-politics that expects little of politics because of its ugly character. This sensibility is brought out

effectively in *Toward a Liberalism* (Ithaca, NY: Cornell University Press, 1990) and in a study of Hobbes soon to be published by Sage Publications in its *Modernity and Political Thought* series. White finds my "ethic of cultivation" to be in conflict with a "politics of radical hope." I find the terms in which he recognizes the tension to be too stark for my position. I do not have "radical hopes" for a political transformation; rather, I support radical critiques that might open up new spaces for life to be while supporting new possibilities of democratic change. Together these two put considerable pressure on the position I seek to inhabit. It is only after I compare the tensions in my stance with those in theirs, respectively, that my confidence begins to reassert itself.

37. How can resentment find expression against a world lacking the kind of agency capable of receiving this animus? It cannot. That is what makes existential resentment so dangerous. For it preserves itself by manufacturing viable substitutes on which to displace itself. You and I are good candidates for it. It (re)invents the logic of good and evil to locate evil agents to hold responsible for an apparent contingency of things that *should not be this way*. But whence, asks Nietzsche, comes this last "should not"? From the same pool of existential resentment that keeps refilling itself. We strive to move "beyond good and evil" but its logic keeps returning in one form or another. I doubt that Nietzsche thought that even an "overman" would actually get "beyond" it fully. It is time to laugh at the overman, too.

38. Michel Foucault, "Practicing Criticism," in Kritzman, ed., *Michel Foucault: Politics, Philosophy, Culture*, 156. Does Foucault underplay the power of "God," "the Law," "Nature," and "Intrinsic Purpose" to reinstate themselves offstage even as the contingencies within them are addressed on stage? Perhaps. But I prefer to say that he chooses to act *as if* these enactments can be challenged effectively through counter-en-actments. Girard, Freud, Lacan, and others are excellent at showing *how* final markers reinstate themselves even though they lack the transcendental basis their most earnest supporters yearn for. Thus, in Freud, guilt flows from ambivalent identification with a model one has just (perhaps in the imagination) killed; it precedes the God and the Law invented retroactively to explain it. Freud et al. effectively challenge moralisms that translate the experience of necessity into conviction of a transcendental source. But the next step is to develop strategies through which to challenge this recurrent conversion of contingency into necessity and to politicize violences accompanying the conversion process. This is where they are deficient and where Foucault's genius glimmers. It is also where the genius of Luce Irigaray shines. For she does to Lacan with respect to the masculine/feminine divide what Nietzsche does to Augustine with respect to the law of his god. See Luce Irigaray, *This Sex Which Is Not One*, trans. Catherine Porter (Ithaca, NY: Cornell University Press, 1977). This general area, involving the translation of Augustinian "why" questions into "how" questions and the resulting reinstatement of necessity on a new register, is the territory I would like to examine next. Foucault and Irigaray will be indispensable to the terms of contestation needed on this register.

Index

About the Author

William E. Connolly teaches political theory at Johns Hopkins University, where he is a professor of political science. He is the editor of *Contestations: Cornell Studies in Political Theory*. His books include *Political Theory and Modernity* and *Identity\Difference: Democratic Negotiations of Political Paradox.*